LETTERS WRITTEN IN FRANCE,
IN THE SUMMER 1790

Portrait of Helen Maria Williams, engraved by Joseph Singleton (1792)
© Copyright The British Museum

LETTERS WRITTEN IN FRANCE,

IN THE SUMMER 1790, TO A FRIEND IN ENGLAND; CONTAINING VARIOUS ANECDOTES RELATIVE TO THE FRENCH REVOLUTION

Helen Maria Williams

edited by
Neil Fraistat and Susan S. Lanser

Associate Editors
David Brookshire
Stephanie Burley
Stephanie Fitz
Elizabeth Geiman
Carie Jones-Barrow
Erin E. Kelly
David Payne
Robin V. Smiles

broadview literary texts

Canadian Cataloguing in Publication Data

Williams, Helen Maria, 1762-1827
    Letters written in France, in the summer 1790, to a friend in England

(Broadview literary texts)
ISBN 1-55111-255-8

1. Williams, Helen Maria, 1762-1827 — Correspondence.   2. France —
History — Revolution, 1789-1799.   3. Thomas du Fossé, Augustin François,
1750-1833.   4. Lettres de cachet.   5. Detention of persons — France —
History — 18th century.   I. Lanser, Susan Sniader, 1944- .   II. Fraistat, Neil,
1952- .   III. Title.   IV. Series.

DC146.W54A4 2001   944.04'092   C00-932869-6

Broadview Press Ltd. is an independent, international publishing house, incorporated in 1985

North America
Post Office Box 1243, Peterborough, Ontario, Canada K9J 7H5
3576 California Road, Orchard Park, NY 14127
Tel: (705) 743-8990; Fax: (705) 743-8353;
e-mail: customerservice@broadviewpress.com

United Kingdom:
Thomas Lyster, Ltd.,
Unit 9, Ormskirk Industrial Park, Old Boundary Way, Burscough Rd,
Ormskirk, Lancashire L39 2YW   Tel: (1695) 575112; Fax: (1695) 570120;
E-Mail: books@tlyster.co.uk

Australia:
St. Clair Press, P.O. Box 287, Rozelle, NSW 2039
Tel: (02) 818-1942; Fax: (02) 418-1923

www.broadviewpress.com

Broadview Press is grateful to Professor Eugene Benson for advice on editorial
matters for the Broadview Literary Texts series.

Broadview Press gratefully acknowledges the financial support of the Book
Publishing Industry Development Program, Ministry of Canadian Heritage,
Government of Canada.

Typesetting and assembly: True to Type Inc., Mississauga, Canada.
PRINTED IN CANADA

Contents

Acknowledgments

This classroom edition had its origin within a classroom of our own, a graduate seminar we co-directed on Romanticism and Revolution at the University of Maryland in spring 1998. As part of the syllabus, we assigned Helen Maria Williams's *Letters Written in France*, using photocopies of the first edition. Our students' enthusiasm for the book led eight members of the seminar to collaborate with us in creating this volume as both a course project and a Broadview Literary Text. Our first and greatest debt, therefore, is to this talented and dedicated group, whose names are listed as associate editors on the title page and without whom this project would not have been realized.

For the final version we owe additional debts of gratitude. Deborah Kennedy, whose research sheds new light on Williams's life and work, was enormously generous in sharing her extensive knowledge and in reviewing our introduction and chronology. Jack Undank graciously read and significantly improved our translations from the French. Curators at the Folger Shakespeare Library, the Johns Hopkins University Library, University of Maryland Library, University of North Carolina Library, the Bibliothèque nationale de France, and the British Museum were crucially cooperative. At Broadview, Don LePan, Mical Moser, Barbara Conolly, Eugene Benson, and Judith Earnshaw have been encouraging, astute, helpful, and patient editors. Finally, we thank Matthew Bray (Ph.D. Maryland, 1994), whose brilliant scholarship has informed our understanding of the *Letters* and helped inspire us to create an edition enabling students and scholars better to appreciate Williams's importance to British Romanticism and Revolutionary history.

Fédération générale des Français [Festival of Federation], 1790. Photo courtesy of the Bibliothèque nationale de France.

Introduction

Early on the morning of July 14, 1790, thousands of men and women gathered near the ruins of France's most infamous prison, the Bastille, in the Marais district on Paris's Right Bank. National guards and civic leaders from all over France, along with veterans, musicians, and schoolboys, formed an immense procession that was joined by members of the National Assembly when it reached the royal palace of the Tuileries. Some thirty thousand strong and undaunted by rain, the marchers crossed the Seine and entered the Champ de Mars, the military field where the Eiffel Tower now stands.

Thus began the Fête de la Fédération, probably the most elaborate public spectacle in European history, celebrating France's commitment to unity and harmony on the first anniversary of the fall of the Bastille. Preparations for the Festival had already displayed the new national spirit, for when a paid crew of fifteen thousand could not excavate the field on time, patriots from duchesses to day-laborers joined in, erecting a vast amphitheatre with three triumphal arches and thirty tiers of seats, and setting a National Altar upon a pavilion draped in the red, white, and blue of the Revolutionary tricolor and adorned with the royal fleur de lys.

A twenty-nine year-old English poet named Helen Maria Williams was among those present at the great Festival. An enthusiastic supporter of the Revolution even before she visited France, Williams was overwhelmed by the beauty and significance of the spectacle and later said that it sealed her political vision.[1] It is appropriate, then, that the Festival of Federation also served as the inaugural scene for Williams's eight-volume eyewitness history of the Revolution, which begins with the *Letters Written in France, in the Summer 1790*. For Williams, as for the multitude of spectators gathered at the Champ de Mars, the triumphal Festival expressed in its imagery the deeply felt aspirations for a constitutional process that was already dramatically reforming French government and transforming French society.

The revolution inaugurated in 1789 was not France's first challenge to absolutist authority, and many of the ills it sought to ameliorate had festered for decades or centuries. Demands for civil

---

1 Helen Maria Williams, *Souvenirs de la Révolution française* (Paris, 1827) 7.

liberty and government by consent had already emerged in the late sixteenth century, when bloody wars between Catholics and Protestant Huguenots, reaching their apex in the St. Bartholomew's Day Massacre of 1572, threatened but never toppled state control. The absolutist "Sun King" Louis XIV responded to discontent and rebellion during his long reign (1643-1715) by tightening his hold over church and state, ignoring food shortages and tax protests, and amassing a staggering debt when he built Europe's grandest palace at Versailles. The insouciance of Louis XV (reigned 1715-74), compounded by France's losses to England in the Seven Years' War (1756-63), further jeopardized the country's fiscal and political solvency.

But by the accession of Louis XV's grandson Louis XVI in 1774, European conceptions of government were changing rapidly. Mercantile capitalism, scientific enterprise, and a burgeoning sphere of public letters had created an educated and prosperous yet politically unempowered constituency that affirmed new Enlightenment philosophies of social contract, individual merit, and universal rights. During the thirty years before the fall of the Bastille, rebellions against absolute authority and colonial control erupted in places as far apart as Poland, Ireland, and North America, and abolition of the slave trade had become a topic of intense international debate. Despite royal censorship, French men and women read and avidly discussed the writings of Locke, Montesquieu, Voltaire, Diderot, and Rousseau, all of whom would die before the French Revolution but who would lay its intellectual cornerstones by providing reasoned grounds for liberty, equality, and participatory governance.[1]

These heady ideas spurred a new response to France's social and economic troubles, which were still mounting during the reign of Louis XVI. Although the young king was considered kinder, simpler in his pleasures, and more concerned for his people than his grandfather Louis XV, he did not exercise firm and consistent leadership, and his wife Marie Antoinette, daughter of the empress Maria Theresa of Austria, was prone to imprudence and extravagance. France's financial crisis, exacerbated by continued spending

---

1 See, for example, Locke's *Second Treatise of Government* (1689), Montesquieu's *The Spirit of Laws* (1748), Voltaire's *Philosophical Letters* (1733), Diderot and d'Alembert's *Encyclopedia* (1751-65), and Rousseau's *Social Contract* (1762).

on the part of the crown, reached a breaking point after the country's expensive involvement in the American War of Independence. In 1787 the government convened an Assembly of Notables to explore fiscal alternatives, but the nobility resisted approving the new taxes the King's ministers hoped to raise. Troubles within France's judicial system, organized as regional *parlements*, further weakened the government, while poor crops and food shortages sparked protests not only about the price of bread but about the excessive tax burden the country had long levied against its poorest citizens.

The cause of change received its greatest impetus, however, from the monarch's own decision in August 1788 to convene the Estates-General, a quasi-representative body that had not met since 1614. Delegates from every jurisdiction in France, elected in three groups representing the clergy, the nobility, and an expanded "Third Estate" of commoners,[1] were asked to bring lists of their constituents' grievances (*cahiers de doléances*) to a discussion of reforms. Within a month of its first meeting in May 1789, the Estates-General had broken ranks and formed a single and more powerful body, the National Assembly, which soon began to consider unprecedented changes in law and governance. It was in this political climate that angry Parisians, spurred by the dismissal of the popular finance minister Jacques Necker, by an alarming buildup of troops in Paris, and by the highest bread prices in twenty years, went in search of arms and ended up capturing the Bastille, almost empty at the time, but a powerful symbol of *ancien régime* power to imprison innocent people for indefinite periods on the flimsy basis of the infamous, easily procured official orders known as *lettres de cachet*.

Signaling popular support for what was now being recognized as a revolution, the fall of the Bastille encouraged even more extensive reforms of government. Within a few weeks the National Assembly, though it included many aristocratic members, had abolished the privileges traditionally accorded the nobility, effectively ending feudalism in France. It later divided the country into equi-

---

1 Although in theory "Third Estate" designated everyone who was neither clergy nor nobility, the social and economic requirements enabling people to vote or to hold office ensured that in practice most of the Third Estate's electors and delegates would be men of the educated bourgeoisie.

table jurisdictions known as *départements* and reformed local judicial and executive authority to prevent arbitrary taxes and other abuses of power. On 26 August the Revolution's fundamental principles were codified in a Declaration of the Rights of Man and Citizen (see pp. 243-46) that became a prototype for constitutions around the world and for the United Nations' 1948 Universal Declaration of Human Rights. Inspired by the U.S. Declaration of Independence and Constitution but more sweeping in its guarantees, the French Declaration granted freedom of speech, press, and belief, outlawed arrest and imprisonment without due process, made taxation a matter for legislative consent, and held all officials accountable to their constituents. Only actions deemed "harmful to society" could be forbidden by the law, which was now re-conceived as an expression of the nation's "general will," and all citizens were declared equally admissible to all honors and posts on the basis of their abilities and regardless of rank.

It is important to acknowledge that despite this grand language, civil rights were extended to some groups slowly if at all. At first, the poorest citizens could not vote and only a fraction of French men met the financial criteria for elective office. Not until mid-1791 were full citizenship rights granted to free Blacks and to Jews, although Protestants had received their rights in December 1789. France was the first country in Europe to abolish slavery, but economic self-interest delayed this act until 1794, and Napoleon would restore slavery in 1802. Women were never granted political rights despite their importance as Revolutionary activists and despite eloquent arguments, launched by distinguished members of the National Assembly as early as 1790, that their oppression was contrary to the principles of the "Rights of Man," a claim that Olympe de Gouges's "Declaration of the Rights of Woman and Female Citizen" would emphasize (see pp. 246-49).

Still, France was moving farther and faster than any government in Western history, including the United States, to expand individual and collective liberties. The elections for the Estates-General in 1788-89 had already enfranchised some six million voters, creating, in Simon Schama's words, "the most numerous experiment in political representation attempted anywhere in the world."[1] As the roster of "Beneficial Effects of the French Revolution" (see

---

1 Simon Schama, *Citizens: A Chronicle of the French Revolution* (New York: Knopf, 1989) 309.

pp. 260-62) suggests, in 1790 French citizens were hailing the many changes that had already been achieved and that were being heralded throughout Europe as a death knell to all absolutism and a new, worldwide birth of liberty and opportunity. Even the conservative counterrevolutionary Hannah More (see pp. 282-86) had to admit that at the outset every "English heart" was right to "exult at the demolition of the Bastille" and to "triumph in the warm hope, that one of the finest countries in the world would soon be one of the most free."[1]

There was much to celebrate, then, on the first anniversary of the fall of the Bastille. But the future of the new order was far from assured. Even as the Assembly was enacting peaceful reforms, the summer of 1789 also brought a wave of anti-aristocratic violence known as the "Great Fear" that spread across the French countryside, destroyed considerable property, and spurred the first major emigration of nobility. In October, several thousand angry and armed Parisians, most of them market women, had marched to Versailles demanding a reduction in the price of bread. After a day of demonstrations, they forcibly entered the sumptuous palace, killed two guards after soldiers opened fire on the people, and triumphantly escorted the royal family to Paris to take up permanent residence in the long-unused palace of the Tuileries. Throughout the year, tensions between the King and the National Assembly had plagued the process of reform; Louis was openly ambivalent toward the proposed constitution that would limit his once boundless powers, and his inconsistent demeanor had eroded his ability to lead. Marie Antoinette, long the target of political and sexual satire and already suspect as a foreigner, had become a lightning rod for public hostility, the "Autrichienne" accused of manipulating her husband, flaunting her sexuality, and marshaling foreign armies against France.[2] Clearly the success of the new government would depend on a delicate balance of power in which the crown would respect legislative authority and ordinary people would be sufficiently satisfied with their economic and political well-being to refrain from violence.

---

1 Hannah More, *Remarks on the Speech of M. Dupont* (1793), in *Works of Hannah More* (London, 1818) VI, 284.
2 "Autrichienne," which denotes a female from Austria, also operates in French as a pun signifying "Austrian bitch" since "chienne" is the feminine form for dog.

The Fête de la Fédération was designed not simply to celebrate but also to generate this unity and harmony. Festivities had begun on the previous evening with solemn services at the Cathedral of Notre Dame which included a sacred drama commemorating the capture of the Bastille. The ceremony following the procession to the Champ de Mars on the next afternoon opened with the celebration of a Catholic Mass by the bishop and statesman Talleyrand and two hundred priests clad in tricolor robes. Then the Marquis de Lafayette, commander of the National Guard, led the delegates in oaths of loyalty to nation, law, and king. Louis XVI vowed his support for the new government, the queen held up the young Dauphin, drums rolled, cannon roared, and some four hundred thousand spectators, drenched from the constant bursts of rain, rent the skies with cheers of joy. In the words of the *Gentleman's Magazine*, which printed one of many detailed accounts of the event, the crowd "baffled the eye to reckon," yet "decorum, order, peace, and concord, reigned through the immense multitude."[1] The ceremony concluded with an original "Te Deum" written expressly for the Festival by the renowned composer François-Joseph Gossec (1734-1829) and performed by more than 1200 musicians, that redirected France's Roman Catholic heritage toward a new civic faith in a future where all would live in harmony. As the ceremony ended, in what was seen as a triumphant sign from heaven, the rain ceased and the sun burst forth. The crowds joined in the Revolutionary song "Ca ira!"—*it will go forward*, proclaiming their intention to forge a new nation dedicated to the well-being of all its citizens. As the London *Times* noted in its report of the event, "Such a magnificent association of FREE MEN, emancipated from the shackles of despotism within so short a space of time," was "unparalleled in the annals of History" (see pp. 253-60).

The Fête de la Fédération set the tone for Helen Maria Williams's *Letters Written in France, in the Summer 1790*, the first and most famous of her eight eyewitness accounts designed to explain the Revolution to a British audience. Framed as twenty-six letters to a friend in England, the 1790 volume imagines the entire

---

1 "A SKETCH of the Grand National Confederation held at Paris on the 14th of July, 1790, being the Anniversary of the Downfall of Despotism by the Demolition of its dreadful Engine the BASTILE on the 14th of July, 1789," *The Gentleman's Magazine: and Historical Chronicle* 60 (August 1790): 754-58.

Revolution as a sublime spectacle carrying forth the spirit of the Federation, appealing to the noblest human sentiments, and establishing aesthetic and moral harmony across differences of sex, race, and condition. Williams opens her book by describing the solemn ceremony held at the Cathedral of Notre Dame just as she arrived in Paris on the eve of the Festival. Subsequent letters take her readers on a Revolutionary tour of Paris, visiting people, sites, and monuments, sitting in on the National Assembly, and recreating through anecdote the euphoric climate in which "distinctions of rank [are] forgotten" and princes are ready "to renounce the splendour of [their] titles for the general good" (pp. 65, 78).

Midway through the *Letters*, Williams launches the gripping history of one family's sufferings as a "form of commentary on the Declaration of the Rights of Man."[1] This tale recounts the injustices inflicted on Williams's friends the du Fossés, who suffered imprisonment, exile, injury and poverty under the legal machinery of old-regime France simply for marrying without the Baron du Fossé's consent. The father's parental tyranny serves as a powerful allegory of the old regime's capricious control of its subjects. Because it takes not only the father's death but the French Revolution to secure M. du Fossé's freedom and the reunion of the family, Williams can emphasize through this long tale the inseparability of personal fortunes from national politics.

At the same time, *Letters Written in France* emphasizes social issues important to England and hopes that the new spirit in France, which Williams sees as an extension of English liberty, will in turn infuse England and all of Europe with a new commitment to human rights that would be signified by the abolition of slavery. England's commitment to the "rights of man," egregiously compromised in Williams's eyes by the slave trade, remains an ever-present theme. Throughout her narrative, Williams exhorts her audience to "rejoice with me that tyranny is no more" (p. 114) and affirms her belief that the principles underwriting the French Revolution will secure peace and equality for the entire world. *Letters Written in France* thus inscribes not only the excitement of a single observer, but the dreams of Enlightened thinkers across Europe that this French Revolution could bring justice, liberty, and equality to all humanity. In celebrating the first year of the Revolution as a

---

1 Williams makes this comment about the *Letters Written in France* in her *Souvenirs de la révolution française*, 10.

turning point not only in French but in human history, Williams evokes an explicitly feminine sensibility as a foundation for the liberty and unity for which the Revolution stands.

Williams never wavered from her faith in the principles that her *Letters Written in France* celebrates. Even when the Revolution's turn toward violence, war, and repression tempered her early optimism, she steadfastly supported republican ideals through several French regimes and after the enthusiasm of many other English intellectuals had waned. Unique among English women writers for her long participation in French Revolutionary politics, Williams became in effect a foreign correspondent, interpreting French history to readers in England and around the continent for thirty years. Her politics made her a controversial figure in England and sometimes even in France but gained her international recognition as an eyewitness historian of world-shaking events. From the summer of 1790 until her death thirty-seven years later, Williams's personal history would be inseparable from the history of the Revolution, and her vision would remain fixed by the Festival of Federation inscribed in her *Letters Written in France*. As an architect of radical sensibility, Williams thus makes especially vivid the relationship between English Romanticism and the revolutionary politics of England's longstanding rival, France.

Helen Maria Williams and Revolutionary France

Born in London on 17 June 1761, Williams was the younger daughter of Welsh army officer Charles Williams and his second wife Helen Hay.[1] Some time after Charles Williams's death in

---

1 Knowledge about Williams's life is still sketchy, and printed sources have perpetuated various errors of fact and supposition. Our presentation is deeply indebted to the important research of Deborah Kennedy, whose *Helen Maria Williams and the Age of Revolution*, is forthcoming from Bucknell University Press. Kennedy's book, along with her entry on Williams in the new *Dictionary of National Biography*, will correct and supplement the information available in current sources including the only previous book-length biography, Lionel D. Woodward's *Une Anglaise, amie de la Révolution française* (Paris: Champion, 1930; reprinted by Slatkine in 1977 as *Helen Maria Williams et ses amis*). Kennedy's careful and extensive scholarship is an invaluable new resource for scholars of Williams's work.

December 1762, Mrs. Williams relocated the family, which included Helen's sister Cecilia and her much older half-sister Persis,[1] to Berwick-on-Tweed in Northumberland, not far from Mrs. Williams's Scottish relatives. While there is little specific information about Helen's education, Percival Stockdale records being impressed with her literary tastes and talents when she was eighteen. Certainly her works show a respectable knowledge of English literature, and Janet Todd speculates that she "must have been a voracious reader of sentimental writing, for her first literary efforts display its influence."[2]

Probably the most formative influence on Williams, however, was her family's adherence to a Dissenting religion—the term applied to those Protestant churches whose beliefs and practices differed from those of the state-sanctioned Church of England. Formally denied many civil and political liberties, Dissenters "owed most of their freedom to the non-implementation of the laws which penalized them," as Paul Langford notes.[3] It is therefore not surprising that they numbered prominently among those who sought universal civil rights, abolition of the slave trade, and reform of Parliament.[4] Williams's religious upbringing thus predisposed her to just the kind of social changes that France's Declaration of the Rights of Man would signify.

When the Williams family moved back to London in 1781, their Dissenting connections also brought them into contact with distinguished intellectuals. Helen had just completed the manuscript of what would become her first published work, *Edwin and Eltruda*, a legendary tale in verse about the War of the Roses and its devastat-

---

1 Eighteen years Helen's senior, Persis Williams was the daughter of Charles Williams and his first wife. According to Deborah Kennedy, Helen loved her as a second mother. Persis lived with Helen and Mrs. Williams in England and France, helped to raise Cecilia's children, and died in Amsterdam in 1823.

2 Janet Todd, *British Women Writers: A Critical Reference Guide* (New York: Ungar, 1989) 720.

3 Paul Langford, *A Polite and Commercial People: England 1727-1783* (Oxford/New York: Oxford University Press, 1992) 296.

4 During the last half of the eighteenth century, the most visible Dissenting sects were Presbyterians, Baptists, Congregationalists, Quakers, Unitarians and the somewhat more conservative Methodists. The civil and political rights of Dissenters remained limited even after the Toleration Act of 1689 granted them freedom of worship.

ing effects upon family relations and romantic love—a conjunction of the political and the personal that her work would continue to emphasize. With the help of the well-known Dissenting minister, author, and educator Andrew Kippis, who wrote a brief introduction, the poem was brought to press in 1782. *Edwin and Eltruda* was followed by *An Ode on the Peace* (1783), commemorating the end of England's war with the American colonies, which Williams published by subscription and which probably earned a fair profit.

By this time Williams had entered important literary and political circles, meeting such prominent figures as the writers Samuel Johnson and Charlotte Smith, Dissenting intellectuals Richard Price and Joseph Priestley, who would become central figures in England's "Revolution Debate," as well as the political theorist and novelist William Godwin and the poet Samuel Rogers, the American revolutionary Benjamin Franklin, and the Corsican independence leader Pasquale Paoli. Elizabeth Robinson Montagu, who hosted England's most famous literary salon, was an early supporter of Williams; Anna Seward and Robert Burns were among her early correspondents. As Deborah Kennedy reports, people of letters were soon congregating for evening tea at Williams's home on Southampton Row in Bloomsbury, the neighborhood that a century later would host the modernist circle of Virginia Woolf. Among the regulars were Godwin, the writers Edward Jerningham, Anna Laetitia Barbauld, and Hester Thrale Piozzi, and Whig Members of Parliament such as William Smith and Benjamin Vaughan.

Williams's reputation did not flourish simply because of her social connections; she quickly became, to use Mark Ledden's words, "a literary star of the first magnitude."[1] Her poetry was received as an epitome of the "sensibility" that gave aesthetic form to highly developed moral sentiments, thereby encouraging political reforms. For when Percy Shelley wrote in 1821 that poets were "the unacknowledged legislators of the World," he was articulating the conviction of a literary movement, already gaining strength in the 1780s, that considered social change the very purpose of poetry, and a matter not merely of poetic content but of poetic form. Writers like Williams, Charlotte Smith, Joanna Baillie, Anna Barbauld, Anna Seward, Hannah More, Mary Robinson, William

---

1 Mark Ledden, "Perishable Goods: Feminine Virtue, Selfhood and History in the Early Writings of Helen Maria Williams," *Michigan Feminist Studies* 9 (1994–95): 37.

Cowper, and George Crabbe were forging what Stuart Curran describes as "the foundation on which Romanticism was reared,"[1] a "culture of sensibility" invoking an ideal harmony between the social and the natural that was best articulated by a sensitive and gifted poetic voice. Williams's ode "To Sensibility" (see pp. 192-94) makes that quality the basis of "friendship, sympathy, and love, / And every finer thought" and praises the poet's "sacred power to weep" and "bleed" in order to heal "others wounds." Though an ideal for both sexes, sensibility was at this time associated particularly with women, who were seen as "naturally" more delicate of feeling and hence more prone to be moved by human suffering. It is a sign at once of the literary value of sensibility, the prominence of women as its practitioners, and the particular eminence of Helen Maria Williams that an admiring young William Wordsworth, without having yet met Williams, published his own first poem in tribute to her work; his 1787 "Sonnet on Seeing Miss Helen Maria Williams Weep at a Tale of Distress" (see p. 235), praises Williams's tears as proof that "in thee each virtue dwells."[2]

Williams's writings of the 1780s are indeed most often "tales of distress" in which political ills cause personal miseries. *Edwin and Eltruda* and *An Ode on the Peace* were followed by *Peru, a Poem. In Six Cantos* (1784), which opposes imperialism by depicting the dire effects of Pisarro's conquest on human lives. In 1786, Williams gathered these and other poems into a two-volume collection supported by a seventy-nine-page list of over 1500 subscribers, including figures as different as Richard Price and Hannah More whom the French Revolution would soon sharply divide. Dedicated to the popular Queen Charlotte and welcomed by both the press and the public, the *Poems* underwent a second and expanded printing in 1791. The long *A Poem on the Bill Lately Passed for Regulating the Slave Trade* (see pp. 194-203), published in 1788 and especially well received, hopes that England's recently passed Dolben Act, which institutes restraints on slave traders, will be only a step toward

---

1 Stuart Curran, "Romantic Poetry: The I Altered," in *Romanticism and Feminism*, ed. Anne K. Mellor (Bloomington: Indiana University Press, 1988) 188, 197. Meant to emphasize the importance of women, Curran's list is somewhat smaller than ours and includes only one man, Cowper.

2 Wordsworth tried to meet Williams in Paris in 1791 but she had left the city before he arrived. Two later attempts were also apparently unsuccessful, and the two did not meet until 1820.

ending British traffic in slavery. In 1790, before she left for France, Williams produced her only novel, *Julia, a novel; interspersed with some poetical pieces. Julia* can be read as a feminist reworking of two of the most popular continental novels of the later eighteenth century, Rousseau's *Julie, ou la Nouvelle Héloïse* (1761) and Goethe's *Die Leiden des jungen Werther* [*The Sorrows of Young Werther*] (1774). In Williams's rendering, a man's unbridled passion for his wife's cousin leads to his tragic death, after which the women establish a harmonious domesticity. All of her writings of the 1780s thus forge an aesthetic in which "feminine" values of mercy, attachment, and empathy displace "masculine" notions of conquest and exploitation that Williams sees as threatening to both the private and the public good.

By the dawn of the French Revolution, then, Williams was already well known for her "support of liberal causes," and, as Deborah Kennedy affirms, held "a place of some prominence in the Dissenting and Whig social circles to which she had been introduced."[1] She had also forged a personal French connection that intensified her response to the events of 1789. In 1785 or 1786, Helen and Cecilia Williams began taking French lessons from Monique Coquerel du Fossé, who was living in England with her young daughter while her husband, the son of a Baron, languished in a Rouen prison for having married against his father's will. The sufferings of the worthy du Fossés that occupy a central section of the *Letters Written in France* probably also underlie the centrality of prison imagery throughout Williams's work. Her first published response to the Revolution, a poem titled "The Bastille: A Vision" and included in *Julia*, imagines that from the chaotic "dark pile" of the famous ruins, "Freedom's sacred temple" would arise as a beacon to an "emulating world" (see pp. 203-206).

Williams's arrival in Paris on 13 July 1790 reinforced the euphoric hope that pervades the *Letters Written in France, in the Summer 1790.* As its title suggests, Williams composed her eyewitness account during the two months following the Fête as she toured France with her sister Cecilia. During that time she made a number of new French acquaintances including the writer and educator Stéphanie Félicité de Genlis, who tutored the children of the King's cousin, the Duke of Orleans (dubbed Philippe-Egalité for his sup-

---

1   Deborah Kennedy, *Helen Maria Williams and the Age of Revolution* (forthcoming).

port of the new regime). The sisters then traveled to Normandy to visit Monique du Fossé, who had been reunited with her husband after the Revolution abolished the *lettres de cachet* that had allowed a disgruntled father to imprison his own son. In September, Williams returned to England with the manuscript of her *Letters*, which the publisher Thomas Cadell brought out that November to a response that was predominantly favorable despite Williams's forebodings of anti-revolutionary sentiment in her native land. Most major English periodicals reviewed the book (see Appendix C), and if some regretted Williams's "raptures with every thing French" or thought her "too fond of revolutions," few challenged either the substance of her account or her support for a government that still appeared to be modeling itself upon English precedent.

The Williams family had now begun what would become a lifelong affiliation with France. By July of 1791 Helen's mother and sisters were again visiting the du Fossés in Rouen, cementing a friendship that would eventually lead to a marriage between Cecilia Williams and a nephew of Monique du Fossé. By September Williams herself had returned to France for a longer stay. By then, what came to be known as the "Revolution Debate" was seething in England under the impetus of Edmund Burke's *Reflections on the Revolution in France* (see pp. 266-73), which had appeared in the very same month as Williams's *Letters*. Williams's *A Farewell, for Two Years, to England* (see pp. 207-12), published just before this second trip to France, had responded to Burkean attacks on the Revolution by turning the tables, castigating Britain for failing to pass the April 1791 bill to end the slave trade. Williams would later say that by this time the course of the Revolution had already begun to dim "the rose color of the first days."[1] Although France had just adopted its new Constitution and a parliamentary monarchy still seemed possible, the King's tendency to veto key legislation angered the National Assembly, and the royal family was under virtual house arrest after its abortive attempt on 20 June to flee to Austria. Settling in Paris, Williams made or renewed acquaintance with such important elected leaders as Jacques Brissot and Pierre Vergniaud, and with Manon Roland, wife of the Interior Minister, through whose influential Paris salon she met other important French intellectuals and Revolutionary leaders. Some of these friends might well have been reading the new French translation of her *Letters*

---

1 Williams, *Souvenirs de la révolution française*, 8-9.

Written in France, which the Constitutional Society at Rouen had enthusiastically welcomed as a harbinger of English support (see pp. 224-26).[1]

In 1792 Williams returned briefly to England for the last time, presenting to her publisher the manuscript of a second volume, the *Letters from France: Containing Many New Anecdotes Relative to the French Revolution, and the Present State of French Manners*, which continues the ebullient optimism of the first volume and celebrates the King's acceptance of the new Constitution even while acknowledging some setbacks in the progress of reform, lamenting continued food shortages in the capital, and regretting the war with Austria that had begun in April of that year. Williams would now make her permanent home in France, but between 1792 and her death in 1827 she would send back many more eyewitness histories, narratives, translations, and poems. By the close of 1792, Williams's own apartment on the Rue Helvétius had become an important meeting place for French, American, and British radicals. Among the guests were the political philosopher Thomas Paine, the feminist thinker Mary Wollstonecraft (who criticized Williams for affected manners but praised her goodness of heart), the painter Benjamin West, the Whig politician Charles Fox, and the Irish independence leaders Lord Edward Fitzgerald and Wolfe Tone.

During this period when the Revolution was taking its most dramatic turns, Williams also met John Hurford Stone (1763-1818), who would become her lover and life partner. A Unitarian who had built strong friendships with Richard Price and Joseph Priestley and had joined their Society of the Friends of the Revolution, Stone became a central figure among expatriate supporters of the Revolution in France. He had managed an uncle's coal business in England; in France he involved himself in various commercial ventures, including a printing house. At the time he and Williams met, Stone was married to Rachel Coope, who had accompanied him to Paris, but both partners apparently had other intimate relation-

---

1   The French edition is titled *Lettres écrites de France, à une amie en Angleterre, pendant l'année 1790. Contenant l'histoire des malheurs de M. du F****. Traduit de l'anglais par M. de la Montagne (Paris: Garnéry, 1791). The translator has added a number of footnotes, some of which are included in this present edition of the English text, and has chosen the female gender for the unidentified "friend" of the English original. We do not know whether Williams was consulted about this choice.

ships, and Stone moved into the Williams household after his wife initiated divorce proceedings in 1794. Williams and Stone never married, although they remained together until his death; Williams erected his gravestone at Père Lachaise cemetery in Paris as a "last tribute in a long friendship" and signed it with the initials "H.M.W." Condemned as "republican morality" in a *Gentleman's Magazine* obituary for Williams's own death (see pp. 240-42), this unsanctioned relationship did not help Williams's reputation at home, which had become more controversial as British support for the Revolution began to erode under the pressure both of Burke's *Reflections* and of violent turns of events in France.

This erosion was in full flower by the end of 1792. After a violent confrontation at the Tuileries palace on 9-10 August, the royal family had been taken into custody, and on 20 September a Republic was organized under the governance of a National Convention that combined legislative and executive powers. But it was the spontaneous violence of the "September Massacres," in which hundreds of political prisoners including many clergy were gratuitously murdered, that most disenchanted English supporters for what had previously been a relatively bloodless course of reform. Sentiment against the Revolution intensified when the deposed King Louis was executed in January 1793, an act all too reminiscent of England's own murder of Charles I in 1649. Then in February France declared war on England and by March the government had established the infamous Committee on Public Safety and its Revolutionary Tribunal that would send so many of the Revolution's own allies to the guillotine. As the more radical "Jacobins" ousted the more conservative "Girondins" from power in the Convention (or legislative assembly) in late May, Williams watched many of her friends fall from leaders to prisoners. During this period, Williams began the third and fourth volumes of her *Letters* in collaboration with Stone, whose portions focus on French military action, and Thomas Christie, publisher of the *Analytical Review*, who contributed a scathing critique of Burke's *Reflections on the Revolution in France*. These volumes (excerpted in Appendix A) reveal Williams's strong criticism of the new Revolutionary government and especially of three of its most popular leaders, Maximilien Robespierre, Georges Danton, and Jean-Paul Marat, whom she sees as a fanatic "band of conspirators" perverting the Revolution's founding principles. Ironically Williams's resistance to the Jacobin leadership made her vulnerable as a "counterrevolutionary" in France even though her continued allegiance to the new Republic itself made her seem even more radical in English eyes.

By the fall of 1793, Williams's situation in France had indeed become precarious. Many of those whose political sympathies she shared were in prison, and some, including her dear friend Manon Roland, would soon go to the guillotine. Marat's assassination in July 1793 by the Girondin sympathizer Charlotte Corday had intensified radical sentiment in the capital, and the deposed queen had been scheduled for trial. The Williams household was vulnerable not only for being English citizens and therefore wartime enemies, but also for having attempted to hide at least one Girondin leader, Jean-Paul Rabaut Saint-Etienne. In the wake of mounting French pressures and a major British victory at Toulon, the Assembly passed a Law of Suspects that enabled the incarceration of anyone whose loyalty to the new regime could not be assured. The police arrested Williams, her mother, and her sister on 12 October, just four days before Marie Antoinette would be put to death. They were sent first to the Luxembourg prison and then remained in the English Conceptionist Convent until late November when Monique du Fossé's nephew Marie Martin Anathase Coquerel, who would soon marry Cecilia Williams, successfully intervened on their behalf.

The safety of both Stone and Williams was jeopardized once again in April 1794—two weeks after the execution of Danton, the journalist Desmoulins, and several of their associates—when Robespierre ordered all foreigners and nobles to leave the capital. The Williams family retreated briefly to an estate near Marly and then returned to Paris, but in June Williams and Stone, fearing arrest again, fled to Switzerland. During their six-month exile, Williams wrote her two-volume *A Tour in Switzerland; or a View of the Present State of the Governments and Manners of those Cantons: with Comparative Sketches of the Present State of Paris*, published in 1798, which sanctions a revolution in the Swiss cantons still under oligarchic rule, a Napoleonic project widely criticized in England and on the Continent. Evoking a sublime natural world as the model for a sublime social order, Williams holds out Switzerland's landscape as an idealized setting in which the Revolution is as yet incomplete, and envisions Napoleon as the embodiment of Revolutionary energy.

When she returned to Paris after the fall of the Jacobin government and the execution of Robespierre, Williams completed two further installments of her Revolutionary chronicle: the two-volume *Letters Containing a Sketch of the Politics of France, from the Thirty-first of May 1793, till the Twenty-eighth of July 1794, and of the Scenes which have Passed in the Prisons of Paris*, and a separate volume entitled *Letters Containing a Sketch of the Scenes which Passed in Various Departments of France during the Tyranny of Robespierre, and of the Events which Took Place in Paris on the 28th of July 1794*. In these works she sharply criticizes the Jacobin leaders for perverting the Revolution, celebrates the return of liberty, and steadfastly endorses what she views as the foundational principles of the Revolution. In 1796 Williams published the last of eight volumes in the series that came to be known collectively as the *Letters from France*. This last volume, *Letters Containing a Sketch of the Politics of France, from the Twenty-eighth of July 1794, to the Establishment of the Constitution in 1795, and of the Scenes which have Passed in the Prisons of Paris*, hails the new government, which would be headed by an elected five-person Directory, as a return to the Revolution's earlier course.

Williams's prolific career as a foreign correspondent continued during the desultory years of the Directory even as war raged across Europe and counterrevolutionary sentiment intensified in England. To poems and histories she now added translations, most notably the English rendition of her friend Bernardin de Saint-Pierre's wildly popular *Paul et Virginie*, a Rousseauvian tale of a fatherless boy and girl raised on an island paradise who fall in love, and whose tragic fate could be linked to the evils of the *ancien régime*. Williams had begun translating *Paul et Virginie* in prison (a contemporary turn that gave added pathos to the 1787 original), and it would become her most frequently reprinted work despite her controversial decision to interlace the novel with her own poetry.[1] Over the next two decades, she would also render into English eight volumes of her friend Alexander von Humboldt's accounts of his travels through the Americas, as well as Xavier de Maistre's "The Leper of the City of Aosta." In 1801, Williams published another book on French life, *Sketches of the State of Manners and Opinions in the French Republic, Towards the Close of the Eighteenth Century, in a Series of Letters*. She describes the *coup d'état* known as

---

1 The *Critical Review*, for example, praised this "embellishment," while the *Gentleman's Review* decried it. As Deborah Kennedy reports, the success of the translation did little to fill Williams's pocketbook: she had accepted twenty pounds for it and waived further rights.

the Eighteenth Brumaire,[1] which overthrew the ruling Directory in November 1799, and argues for Napoleon as the person now best able to advance Revolutionary ideals. Like so many of Williams's previous histories, the second volume of the *Sketches* includes an inserted story "The History of Perourou; or, The Bellows-Mender; Written by Himself," a tale of love, deception, and class struggle that was issued separately in chapbook form in 1801 and again in 1810 and that later became the basis for Bulwer Lytton's 1838 play *The Lady of Lyons*. During this period, too, several of Williams's earlier works were translated into French.[2]

For Williams as for France, the years surrounding the turn of the century were eventful ones. In September 1798, Cecilia Williams Coquerel died, leaving to Helen, her mother and her half-sister Persis the care of two young sons, Athanase-Laurent (born in 1795) and Charles-Augustin (born in 1797). The family seems to have been fairly well off in this period, living in fine quarters and maintaining a large and popular salon known for its republican sentiments, its advocacy of social causes, and its adherence to the principles of 1789. Williams's changed attitudes toward Napoleon did get her into occasional trouble with the authorities. Although the book on Switzerland had criticized the Directory and praised Napoleon as a possible savior of France, her 1802 "Ode to Peace," lauding the Peace of Amiens which temporarily ended the war between Britain and France, incurred Napoleon's anger for praising the English and failing to praise him. Notoriously hostile both to powerful women and to anyone English, Bonaparte was apparently so annoyed that he ordered Williams and her mother arrested. Although they were

---

1 From 1793 to 1806, France used a Revolutionary calendar dated back to the day in 1792 on which the Republic was proclaimed. Months were divided into ten-day weeks and renamed for natural elements appropriate to the seasons, such as wind (Ventôse), heat (Thermidor), fruitfulness (Fructidor), and fog (Brumaire). Napoleon's *coup* occurred on 18 Brumaire Year VIII, or 9 November 1799. Similarly, Robespierre was ousted and arrested on 9 Thermidor Year II, or 27 July 1794. Dates from this calendar have given permanent names to many Revolutionary events.

2 According to Deborah Kennedy, at least eight of Williams's English works were translated into French, and the *Sketches of the State of Manners and Opinions in the French Republic* was also translated into German and Dutch.

jailed for only a day, Williams remained under police surveillance for years. On grounds both personal and principled, Williams's admiration for Napoleon soon turned to disgust, which his self-coronation as emperor in 1804 only intensified. The international community that gathered at the home of Stone and Williams was known to have strong anti-Bonapartist and republican adherents, including the Polish patriot Thaddeus Kosciusko, the actor John Philip Kemble, the British politician Charles James Fox, the American poet Joel Barlow, and such figures from the founding days of the Revolution as the Abbé Henri Baptiste Grégoire, who had advanced the rights of Jews, Blacks, and other oppressed peoples, and the Jacobin Lazare Carnot, who had stood up to Robespierre during the Terror and aided his fall at Thermidor.

The period of Napoleon's ascendancy seems to have been for both Stone and Williams an especially trying time. The resumption of war with England in 1803 prevented Williams from receiving her English friends. In that same year, she published an English translation of what she believed comprised *The Political and Confidential Correspondence of Lewis the Sixteenth; with Observations on Each Letter.* The work stirred Napoleon's fear of a Bourbon restoration by suggesting that Louis could have been a just constitutional monarch, and he ordered all copies of the book to be seized and destroyed. The work was eventually released, in part thanks to friends in high places, but to Williams's great embarrassment the letters supposedly written by the king turned out to be forgeries. The book was widely criticized in both England and France, and Williams, though ultimately exonerated, was forced to appear in court. This professional humiliation, along with the difficulty of commerce between her native country and her adopted one, and the vehement attacks upon Williams for her continued adherence to France by an increasingly reactionary English press, may explain why Williams did not publish anything of her own for the next eleven years. Partly for this reason, the 1810s seem to have been financially troubled ones for the Williams-Stone household, especially after a failed printing venture forced Stone to declare bankruptcy in 1813. The death of Williams's mother in April 1812 was yet another loss during this period.

Napoleon's final defeat at Waterloo in June 1815 permanently restored travel between France and England, so that Williams was again able to receive British visitors and catch up on British literary affairs. She was now also free to publish a critical account of

Napoleon's empire, which appeared as *A Narrative of the Events which have Taken Place in France, from the Landing of Napoleon Bonaparte on the 1st of March 1815, till the Restoration of Louis XVIII* ... Here Williams chronicles her disillusionment with Napoleon, piling up so many grievances, including his treatment of women, that with no apparent consciousness of irony she is able to hail the Bourbon Restoration as a return of happiness to France. The volume did not sell well, however, and Williams may have found herself too pressed for money to maintain regular literary gatherings. She did resume her history of contemporary France, producing in 1816 *On the Late Persecution of the Protestants in the South of France* and in 1819 *Letters on the Events which have Passed in France since the Restoration in 1815*, her last completed book on current French conditions, which once again enthusiastically champions the cause of French liberty.

Williams and Stone became naturalized French citizens in 1817; just a year later, on 22 May 1818, Stone died and was buried near Williams's mother in Père Lachaise cemetery. For a brief time after Stone's death, Williams went to live with her nephew Athanase-Laurent in Amsterdam, where Persis Williams, who would die in 1823, had also taken up residence. But Helen soon returned to her beloved France; her nephews, Athanase now a Protestant minister and Charles a journalist, provided financial support during the last years of her life. In 1823 Helen collected the poems she had written over the past several years and brought them out as *Poems on Various Subjects; with Introductory Remarks on the Present State of Science and Literature in France.* Her final work, published in the year of her death, looks back to the French Revolution and joins its cataclysmic history to her own. It appeared only in French, translated from the English manuscript by her nephew Charles as *Souvenirs de la Révolution française.* Williams died in Paris on 14 December 1827, at the age of sixty-six; she was buried next to Stone beneath a headstone erected by her nephews that commemorates her literary accomplishments.

When the news of Williams's death reached England, the *Gentleman's Magazine* acknowledged her poetic successes and her large circle of admirers but also emphasized her "pre-eminen[ce] among the violent female devotees of the French revolution" and her out-of-wedlock relationship with Stone (see pp. 240-42). If English conservatives tried, as Janet Todd suggests, to transform her "from a young heroine of sensibility into the militant supporter of blood-soaked France,"[1] liberal thinkers recalled her as an influential interpreter of politics and history. These intensely divergent responses to Williams reflect a larger controversy, known as the English "Pamphlet Wars" or "Revolution Debate" launched in the very month that Williams's *Letters Written in France, in the Summer 1790* appeared. The catalyst, however, was not Williams's book, which was quite well received, but Edmund Burke's counterrevolutionary *Reflections on the Revolution in France*, which became one of the most influential political discourses in English history. Evoking England's own recent history of revolt and regicide and tapping ancient rivalries that constructed England as the antithesis of France, English responses to the French Revolution became, in J.G.A. Pocock's words, "the most counter-revolutionary in Europe."[2] Both Williams's writings about the Revolution and their reception in her native land are best understood within the framework of this debate.

Letters Written in France and The English "Revolution Debate"

When Helen Maria Williams left England in July 1790, her enthusiasm for the Revolution was commonplace. As one Member of Parliament told a friend in Geneva, the Revolution "has produced a very sincere and very general joy here. It is the subject of all conversations; and even all the newspapers, without one exception, though they are not conducted by the most liberal or most philosophical of men, join in sounding forth the praises of the Parisians, and in rejoicing at an event so important for mankind."[3] Many considered the Revolution a fulfillment of Enlightenment ideals and expected a speedy end to feudal governments across the European continent. "Bliss was it in that dawn to be alive," wrote a rapturous William Wordsworth of those first heady months when almost no one was predicting the Revolutionary violence that was

---

1 Janet Todd, *The Sign of Angellica: Women, Writing and Fiction 1660-1800* (New York: Columbia University Press, 1989) 195.
2 J.G.A. Pocock, "Political Thought in the English-speaking Atlantic, 1760-1790" in *The Varieties of British Political Thought, 1500-1800*. Ed. J.G.A. Pocock, with Gordon J. Schochet and Lois G. Schwoerer (Cambridge: Cambridge University Press, 1993) 304.
3 Samuel Romilly, Letter to Etienne Dumont of 28 July 1789, from *Memoirs of Sir S. Romilly* (London, 1840) I, 356.

still over three years away. Even Edmund Burke declared in October 1789 his hopes for "the establishment of a solid and rational scheme of liberty in France."[1]

Indeed, most British support for the Revolution assumed that France was simply importing "English liberties" rooted in the principles of shared governance proclaimed by the Magna Carta in 1215. England's own constitutional monarchy had been affirmed just a century earlier during the bloodless "Glorious Revolution" of 1688-89, when the Catholic ruler James II was exiled and his Protestant daughter and son-in-law, Mary Stuart and William of Orange, were brought to the throne in a coalition that gave new powers to Parliament and established a Bill of Rights for English citizens. But the very name "Glorious Revolution" screened out the grim civil war that began in 1642, when parliamentary leaders under Oliver Cromwell battled royalist forces, beheading King Charles I in 1649 and establishing a short-lived Commonwealth in which radical "Levellers" agitated to extend civil rights to ordinary citizens. Resemblances between this period of English history and events in France would deeply disturb a nation already unsettled by new episodes of civil unrest in the 1770s and especially by the largest and most injurious of these, the Gordon Riots that terrorized London in 1780.[2] English support for the Revolution rested in no small degree on the nonviolent cooperation of people, legislators, and royalty so visibly affirmed at the Festival of Federation.

Some supporters, however, were less sanguine about their own country's record of civil rights and looked to the French Revolution to set a new standard for English liberties. Williams's *Letters* suggests this possibility when she personifies English liberty as a middle-aged matron and French liberty as a maiden with the "freshness of youth" (p. 93). English radicals who had been calling for abolition of slavery and religious freedom were overjoyed when the French National Assembly began debating these concerns. When

---

1 Burke, Letter to M. Dupont, October 1789, from *Correspondence* (1844) III, 104–08.

2 The Gordon Riots grew out of agitation by the popular Protestant Association after Parliament passed a bill removing civil disabilities of Roman Catholics. A week of violence, directed first at the homes and chapels of Catholics and their supporters, eventually resulted in indiscriminate pillaging, the burning of jails, and widespread damage to persons and property that ended only through military intervention.

the French National Assembly considers abolition, Williams hopes that the rest of Europe is also "hastening towards a period too enlightened for the perpetuation of such monstrous abuses"; exploiting the longstanding rivalry between the two nations, she cautions England not to "submit to be taught by another nation the lesson of humanity" and warns that "if our senators continue to doze over this affair as they have hitherto done, the French will have the glory of setting us an example" (p. 84).

The fortuitous proximity of the fall of the Bastille to the centennial of England's Glorious Revolution enhanced these rhetorical links between English and French liberties. The Society for Commemorating the [Glorious] Revolution in Great Britain was one of the first organized bodies to view the events in France as a clarion call for British reform. A sermon to that Society by the Dissenting preacher, moral philosopher, and government financial advisor Richard Price, delivered on 4 November 1789 and subsequently published to enthusiastic responses from sympathizers like Mary Wollstonecraft, catalyzed what would become the Revolution Debate. Price contended that the Glorious Revolution had failed to deliver on its promises of religious liberty and participatory governance (see pp. 263-66). With apocalyptic urgency, he exhorted the British to look to France, where "THIRTY MILLIONS of people" were "demanding liberty with an irresistible voice," and he warned the "oppressors of the world," clearly including the English government, to "restore to mankind their rights, and consent to the correction of abuses, before they and you are destroyed together."

Price's inflammatory discourse galvanized the Anglo-Irish statesman and philosopher Edmund Burke, a Whig member of Parliament who had supported the American Revolution and championed other causes of human rights, to write his *Reflections on the Revolution in France*. Burke's first public response to Price's sermon had been an "impassioned denunciation" in Parliament in February 1790 that, as the historian William Doyle puts it, "left his fellow Whigs dumbfounded."[1] Burke followed up with an account of ideas and events in France that was as alarming and bloody as Williams's *Letters Written in France* was peaceful and harmonious. Burke's *Reflections* would set off British anxieties and

---

1 William Doyle, *The Oxford History of the French Revolution* (Oxford/New York: Oxford University Press, 1989) 167.

polarize English debate at least as much as would the subsequent violence in France.

Burke's full-scale attack sets out to rupture the connection between the French Revolution and the Glorious Revolution that underlay English support. He explains the French Revolution as the upstart behavior at once of a "swinish multitude" and of "monied interests," fueled by atheistic philosophies and further debased by the inferior character of the French populace. To this Burke opposed an English tradition of genteel governance according to codes of mannerly behavior enacted by landed aristocrats in alliance with the established Church. Burke feared a contagion by which the beneficial ecclesiastical, aristocratic and commercial institutions that England had developed and nourished for centuries would be destroyed in a revolutionary fervor that subverted codes of manners and social behavior, for "when ancient opinions and rules of life are taken away … we have no compass to govern us; nor can we know distinctly to what port we steer" (1790, p. 117). Skeptical of the grand claims of Enlightenment rationalism, Burke privileges the authority of tradition and insists that historical precedence far outweighs individual reason as the foundation for social morality. He thus redefines human rights not as universal guarantees accorded by nature but as station-specific properties, so that the authority to establish a government, "though made in the name of the whole people," belongs by right only to "gentlemen." Where Williams hailed French liberty as the epitome of the "natural," Burke saw it as a dangerous abstraction that would set madmen free of their chains; English liberty, in contrast, was a pragmatic deployment of power by officials, clergy, and kings who would inspire reverence and respect. "Prejudice," rather than being demolished, was to remain the safe basis for judgments and acts, and property would be the bedrock value on which to base civil authority. While Williams rhapsodized about the Revolution's spirit of cooperative generosity, Burke stirred England's memories of riot and regicide with his overblown account of the October 1789 Women's March on Versailles (see pp. 271-73).

Burke's *Reflections*, as the historian Alfred Cobban notes, was at once a brilliant elaboration of conservative political philosophy and a "violently unfair" and "grossly unhistorical" narrative rife with inaccurate information and hyperbolic language.[1] Initially,

---

1 Alfred Cobban, *The Debate on the French Revolution 1789-1800* (London: Nicholas Kaye, 1950) 5.

Williams's *Letters Written in France* was far more persuasive to English readers than Burke's ill-informed account, which shocked even the young Frenchman to whose inquiry Burke's *Reflections* is purportedly a response. Stirring English anxieties, which were being fueled by stories of violence in the French countryside from aristocrats who had fled during the Great Fear of 1789, and probably also tapping into longstanding rivalries between England and France, the *Reflections* became a best-seller in England and, speedily translated into several European languages, touched off a storm of debate.

One of the most immediate responses to the *Reflections* was Mary Wollstonecaft's *Vindication of the Rights of Men*, which appeared anonymously just four weeks after the publication of Burke's book (see pp. 273-76). Wollstonecraft harshly criticizes Burke's "mortal antipathy to reason" and charges him with defending a corrupt feudal order and an English Constitution "shackled by the grossest prejudices and most immoral superstition." She characterizes Burke's argument as nothing more than "sentimental exclamations" and criticizes his theatrical emotional appeal, maintaining that the rational mind rather than the emotional heart should guide moral and political acts. Wollstonecraft's philosophy here sets her apart from Williams who, like Burke if for drastically different purposes, stresses the priority of sensibility.

But among Burke's many opponents, the secular republican Thomas Paine would most dramatically polarize the English debate. Paine's *The Rights of Man* (see pp. 276-82), the first half of which appeared in February 1791, was a runaway best-seller, far outstripping Burke's very popular *Reflections* in sales (200,000 to 19,000 copies in the first six months). Paine had already established himself as a radical force in American politics through his 1776 pamphlet, *Common Sense*. Having returned to England, he now charged Burke with "an outrageous abuse on the French Revolution, and the principles of Liberty." Correcting what he considered Burke's "flagrant misrepresentations," Paine also disagreed with Burke's conceptions of individual rights, state authority, and republican governance. For Paine, government must derive its power from the people through election and representation, not from royal succession: "the exercise of Government requires talents and abilities," and "talents and abilities cannot have hereditary descent." Each generation must therefore "be as free to act for itself in all cases as the age and generations which preceded it" and no one should be allowed to govern "beyond the grave." Paine upholds France's Declaration of the

Rights of Man as a far stronger protection than England's unwritten constitution, which could be changed or revoked by Parliament. The Glorious Revolution so acclaimed by Burke is thus to Paine simply the transfer of tyrannical power from the monarchy to a landed aristocracy. Given this democratic rhetoric, it is not surprising that Paine, like Williams, became an active Revolutionist in France, serving in the French National Assembly before and after his imprisonment during the Terror.

The opposing philosophies of Burke and Paine structured the Revolution Debate into one of the most important political discussions in English history. The controversy raged for over a decade in books, pamphlets, newspapers and journals, in public meetings and ultimately in the courts, with powerful consequences for friendships, fortunes, and futures well into the next century. Dozens of writers and statesmen joined Burke, Williams, Paine, and Wollstonecraft in creating the published record, among them Arthur Young, Anna Barbauld, Charles Stanhope, James Mackintosh, William Godwin, Thomas Holcroft, Thomas Christie, William Cobbett, Robert Burns, John Thelwall, William Wordsworth, Robert Southey, Samuel Taylor Coleridge, Hannah More, Joseph Priestley, Joel Barlow, and many others both identified and anonymous. Speeches in Parliament abounded, and Revolutionary societies sprang up both in London and in provincial towns, dedicating themselves to English reforms, among which the most volatile was the expansion of representation in Parliament. The government found especially threatening groups such as the London Corresponding Society and the Society for Constitutional Information, which boasted large working-class memberships and became the proving ground for British class politics. A few counterrevolutionary societies such as the Association for Preserving Liberty and Property Against Republicans and Levellers also emerged, and in July 1791 England experienced its first direct Revolutionary violence in Birmingham when Dissenting meeting-houses and the home of Joseph Priestley were sacked and burned by conservative "Church and King" mobs after a dinner commemorating Bastille Day.

Meanwhile, events in France, especially the September massacres, the execution of King Louis, and France's declaration of war with England joined with fears of working-class radicalism in England to tip governmental and popular opinion to Burke's side of the debate. The ironic upshot was that by the mid 1790s, "English liberties" were being abrogated by laws that restricted civil rights in a fashion much more modest in magnitude but not much different in logic from the repressive politics England was deploring in France. Freedoms of speech, press and assembly were suspended or curtailed. In December 1792 Thomas Paine's *Rights of Man* was prosecuted under a new Libel Act passed earlier that year by Parliament. In 1794 the government suspended the Habeas Corpus Act and arrested several prominent radicals including the activist leaders Thomas Hardy and Horne Tooke and the publisher Joseph Johnson. Although most of those tried in London were acquitted, Edinburgh trials led to the deportation of five prominent radicals, at least one of whom died as a result.

The Seditious Meetings and Treasonable Practices Acts of 1795 further restricted press and assembly. Letters from English citizens who had remained in France, including both Williams and Stone, were intercepted and sometimes published. The word "Jacobin" became a damning label indiscriminately applied, much like the term "Communist" in the United States in the 1950s, to almost anyone with liberal values; "reform" was now seen as a code word for "mob rule"; and the satiric journal *The Anti-Jacobin* maintained for a decade a practice of personalized ridicule. Many people who had earlier supported the Revolution, including poets like Southey and Wordsworth, recanted or at least minimized their revolutionary past, while others, such as Arthur Young, insisted that the Revolution itself was so altered that anyone who supported it at the outset was morally obliged to oppose it after 1792. This swing toward Burkean values, which survived Burke's death in 1797, set back for decades the cause of reform: by the time the Revolutionary Wars finally ended in 1815, Britain was far more conservative than it had been in 1790, when Williams's *Letters Written in France* was generally supported and Burke's *Reflections on the Revolution in France* greeted mostly with shock.

Although the *Letters Written in France* could not of course engage in direct dialogue with Burke's *Reflections* because the two works went simultaneously into print, the book already shows Williams's awareness of an incipient "Revolution controversy" in her native land. When Williams returned to England with her manuscript in September 1790, she was shocked to hear wild rumors of mass bloodshed in France; her dismay at English reference to the "barbarous," "republican," and "levelling" French who were leaving "every highway deluged with blood" makes clear that such images were being disseminated in England even before Burke published his book. Williams's last entry in the *Letters* thus anticipates public criticism and predicts that she will be attacked for not sympathizing with upper-class *émigrés* who have lost property: "Must I be told that my mind is perverted, that I am become dead to all sensations of sympathy, because I do not weep with those who have lost a part of their superfluities, rather than rejoice that the oppressed are protected, that the wronged are redressed, that the captive is set at liberty, and that the poor have bread?" (p. 148). Such a statement already sets Williams in implicit dialogue with the *Reflections*, which criticizes English supporters of the Revolution for their indifference to the sufferings of *émigré* aristocrats and clergy and condemns French revolutionists for threatening the rights of property.

Williams would respond to Burke implicitly and occasionally explicitly, however, in subsequent works. Her 1791 *Farewell, for Two Years, to England* locates English hostility to the Revolution in just the anti-French bigotry Burke deployed, and in a proprietary attitude to liberty and a nationalist intolerance of difference. It also chastises England for its dalliance about abolition and turns to "Gallia" to take up the cause that "Britain's sons decline." In her "Epistle to Dr. Moore," Williams proclaims that France's new "temple" of government is a "manship worthy of the human race." And a frontal assault on Burke appears in Letter V of her fourth volume of *Letters from France* (see pp. 166-67) in a passage actually written by Thomas Christie, who had also authored an anti-Burkean *Letters on the Revolution in France* in 1791, which recognizes that Burke has "always seen government through the spectacles of old establishments, and not as it ought to be founded in the nature of man." In place of what had become a common judgment by hindsight that credited Burke for having predicted the violent course of the Revolution, this passage argues instead that Burke's inflammatory predictions actually *fostered* the events he feared. He is even accused of helping to bring about the death of King Louis XVI "by persuading [the King] that he [was] ill-treated" and thus turning him against the Revolutionary cause.

Responses to Williams's own work stem, like the Revolution Debate itself, as much from English anxieties as from turns of events in France. From the outset some readers read the *Letters Written in France* in opposition to Burke's *Reflections*. Anna Seward, for example, expressed her hope that her friend Helen Williams's "interesting epistolary pamphlet" would shed beams of light to disperse "the clouds with which [Burke's] imagination seeks to eclipse the sun of liberty."[1] But from the start Williams's sex also permeated and complicated responses to her work. Most of the reviews, whether for Williams or against her, read the book as "characteristically 'feminine,'" as Gary Kelly observes, or responded to the woman rather than to the text.[2] Those who liked the work felt compelled either to place it "above the common female range" or to trivialize it as an "amusement"; some declared "the seductive insinuations of miss Williams" harder to resist than the energetic arguments of men.[3] As the Revolution progressed and the Burkean position became more widespread, gender took on even more significance in rhetoric about Williams's histories; reviewing a narrative of the Terror in 1795, the *Gentleman's Magazine* complained that Williams had "debased her sex, her heart, her feelings, her talents" merely by "recording such a tissue of horror and villainy."[4] Later that magazine's obituary would label Williams a "violent female devotee" of the Revolution, transferring the violence from the events to the woman who reported them (see p. 240). And there may well be an edge of sexual jealousy in comments such as the *Critical Review*'s that "because Miss Williams has written well and successfully" about the Revolution, now "none but a *lady*" can do so, as if Williams is making history itself a woman's work.[5] Williams's sex almost surely underlies the egregious omission of her influential writings from most discussions of the Revolution Debate even though it is clear that Williams's volumes of eyewitness history were very widely read, excerpted, cited, and used.

This gendered response to Williams extended to other women who supported the Revolution, especially those known to be living with men out of wedlock. Indeed, complex links of gender and politics led English conservatives to deplore what Steven Blakemore describes as "the scandalous promotion of the French Revo-

---

1 Anna Seward, *Letters of Anna Seward*, ed. A. Constable (Edinburgh, 1811) III, 47.

2 Gary Kelly, *Women, Writing, and Revolution* (Oxford: Clarendon, 1993) 78–79.

3 *Critical Review* (September 1792): 65–66, cited in Kelly *Women, Writing and Revolution*, 40.

4 *Gentleman's Magazine* 55 (1795): 1030.

5 *Critical Review* 19 (1797): 265, cited in Deborah Kennedy, "Spectacle of the Guillotine: Helen Maria Williams and the Reign of Terror," *Philological Quarterly* 73 (1994): 95.

lution by fallen British women" and to inaugurate "a sexual counterrevolution" against women like Wollstonecraft, Williams, Charlotte Smith, Annabel Plumptre, and Mary Hays by representing
them as "traitorous, ideological whore[s]."[1] These women, including Williams, would come to be satirized most famously in Richard
Polwhele's 1798 "The Unsex'd Females."

In reality, however, women participated on all sides of the Revolution Debate. Hannah More, for example, who preached
women's domestic subordination to husband and church though
she was also a strong abolitionist like Williams, took up Burke's
gauntlet with a vengeance, directing her attack on the *Rights of Man*
to working-class readers by writing poems and dialogues in working-class voices and publishing them in cheap editions circulated
through evangelical networks (see pp. 282-86). Two other poems in
Appendix G, both probably written late in 1792 when the British
reaction had become more intense, embody the divergent responses that came from women's pens: Anna Barbauld's "To a Great
Nation" calls on France to fulfill its Revolutionary promise as it
"deals" its "dreadful vengeance round," while Mary Alcock's
"Instructions for the Mob" presents revolutionary activity as mind-
less thug violence.

Ironically, the most extensive assault on the *Letters Written in
France* was not only written by a woman but it attacks Williams on
the grounds of her sex—Laetitia Matilda Hawkins's two-volume
Letters on the Female Mind (excerpted on pp. 226-29), written in
1793 with all the benefit of historical hindsight. Establishing
through complex rhetorical maneuvers her own credibility despite
her sex, Hawkins accuses Williams of impropriety for dabbling in
the world of politics: "every *female* politician is a *hearsay* politician."
Refuting the first and second volumes of Williams's *Letters* point for
point, Hawkins rewrites Williams's images as scenes of a Burkean
mob violence that Williams's "poetical imagination" has obscured.
In a backhanded compliment to Williams's rhetorical effectiveness,
Hawkins accuses her of instigating Revolutionary violence, "exciting republican opinions" through her "democratic effusions" and
thus helping to determine the course of history.

Hawkins recognizes here Williams's unique position among participants in the Revolution Debate, few of whom experienced the

---

1   Steven Blakemore, "Revolution and the French Disease: Laetitia Matilda
    Hawkins's *Letters* to Helen Maria Williams," *SEL* 36 (1996): 675.

events in France at first hand. Williams was unique in establishing permanent residence in France, involving herself deeply in French politics, and then taking on a long-lasting commitment to give her compatriots in England what she saw as an accurate rendering of French happenings. In this sense, the Revolution gave Williams a professional opportunity and a political importance that were unavailable in her native land. And most reviewers and readers seem to have accepted Williams's veracity even when they did not share her enthusiasm or her point of view; the 1790 *Letters Written in France* established for Williams an eyewitness credibility, doubtless bolstered by her already high literary reputation, that she never really lost. A considerable segment of English society was gaining its knowledge and understanding of the Revolution from her pen; her volumes were so widely distributed that they became one of the chief sources for creating English opinion about events in Revolutionary France. Gary Kelly provides extensive evidence that even in the late 1790s, when anti-Jacobin rhetoric raged, her histories received admiration and respect as an important and distinctive "picture of the times" and a leading Revolutionary history. Mary Pilkington's 1804 *Memoirs of Celebrated Female Characters* identifies Williams as "a female possessed of superior abilities" who is "no less celebrated than admired, although it is evident that her political sentiments are rather of the republican kind." Pilkington goes on to quote a reviewer who praises Williams's "powers of description, political discernment, her vivacity, her sensibility, her patriotism, and her wit," affirms her "perfectly established" fame, and praises her "masculine" style.[1]

Williams herself seems conscious of both her importance and her responsibility. Later volumes continue to correct what she considers erroneous impressions in England, a practice that may help to explain her tendency to circle back over events she has covered in previous volumes in order to provide further clarity. And the debate over not just the French *Revolution* but the French *character* spurred Williams to challenge "the opinions which are formed in England of the public characters of France, not by the enemies but by the friends of the French revolution."

Maintaining her place in English eyes as the Revolution continued was also a challenge for Williams, especially since her choice to reside in France meant that she was living with the

---

1 Mary Pilkington, *Memoirs of Celebrated Female Characters* (London: Albion Press, 1804) 341.

enemy. But despite the English rhetoric that sometimes associated Williams with Revolutionary violence, her writings are as critical of bloodshed as any Burkean text. After the September massacres she wonders whether the current anarchy may be even worse than the despotism of the old regime (see pp. 168-69), and she acknowledges that the Revolution came "into the hands of fools." Yet she continues to insist that the *foundation* of the Revolution "was laid in wisdom," and taking up Burke's famous metaphor of the state as edifice, she predicts that even if the superstructure should fall, the foundation would remain: "The BASTILLE, though honoured by Mr. Burke with the title of the king's castle (a shocking satire on every humane and just prince), will never be rebuilt in France; and the declaration of the rights of man will remain eternal, as the truth it contains."

It is fitting that Williams locates in the power of the new print culture the possibility that what the French Revolution sowed will be reaped at some future date. At the time of Williams's death, the ultraroyalist Charles X sat on the French throne; it would take half a century, and several more French revolutions, before a republic firmly displaced monarchy and empire to reinstate the Rights of Man. Nor was the cause of reform swift in England, though British conscience was jolted in 1819 by the shocking massacre of demonstrating workers and their families at St. Peter's Field, Manchester. Not until five years after Williams's death would some of the principles of 1789 come to fruition in England in the 1832 Reform Bill, which so redistributed parliamentary seats and reduced the qualifications for suffrage as nearly to triple the electorate and effected a dramatic transfer of power from landowners to an expanding middle class. If the Revolution set back the timing of such major change, Williams was right to believe that the seeds of reform had been preserved in the print record to which she herself was such an important contributor.

Romanticism and Revolution in the *Letters Written in France, in the Summer 1790*

Writing in a "Romantic" age that would be constructed by twentieth-century scholars almost entirely in masculine terms, Helen Maria Williams is just now regaining her place of influence and achievement as an early Romantic writer who helped to set the aesthetic and political grounds for new literary practices. It is not insignificant that the young William Wordsworth, whose contribution to the *Lyrical Ballads* of 1798 would be considered a foundational text of British Romanticism, revered such women poets as Helen Williams and Charlotte Smith. Yet Wordsworth's own 1802 preface to the *Lyrical Ballads* would re-fashion the values of subjectivity, sincerity, emotional depth, and republican principles into a calling as "manly" as the one Burke sought in the *Reflections*, so that sensibility, formerly tied to femininity, would become a hallmark of the poet, who was reimagined as "a man among men." Such a gendering of genius set the stage for a scholarship that overlooked women and came to focus primarily on the poetic writings of six men—Blake, Wordsworth, Coleridge, Keats, Shelley, and Byron—whose art was argued to "transcend" history.

Williams's place in Romanticism has become even more important as recent scholarship has reaffirmed the French Revolution as the central event of the period not only politically but also culturally and aesthetically. This recognition has also propelled an expansion of the Romantic canon to embrace discourses beyond the privileged and supposedly transcendent category of poetry. As scholars re-establish both the place of women in history and the place of the French Revolution in Romantic literature, Williams emerges as a key figure in understanding the cultural practices of her age. None of Williams's works, and few other works of the period, articulate as clearly as the *Letters Written in France* the convergence of aesthetics and politics that lies at the heart of those practices.

In this light, the simultaneous publication in 1790 of treatises on the Revolution by Williams and Burke is more than coincidence. The two works stand in implicit dialogue as much on grounds of aesthetic theory and conceptions of gender as on Revolutionary ideology. Both structured as letters across the Channel, these volumes are rhetorically more like one another than either of them resembles works more politically congenial: Burke and Williams share an affective approach to the Revolution that ultimately sets sensibility and sympathy above reason as the foundation of moral and political agency, distancing them from the Enlightenment rationalism of Paine and Wollstonecraft and from the deconstructive dialogues of More.

If Williams was a poet of the new sensibility, Burke was one of its philosophical architects. Taking up arguments articulated by such important Enlightenment thinkers as David Hume and Adam Smith, Burke, like Williams, saw sensibility or sympathy as a necessary foundation for moral goodness.[1] In his widely influential *Philosophical Enquiry into the Origin of Our Ideas of the Sublime and Beautiful* (1757) Burke distinguishes not only between the terrifying and awe-inspiring masculine sublime and the pleasing, feminine beautiful—a distinction of gender and genre that Williams's *Letters Written in France* will implicitly critique—but also between visual and verbal art. Literature, Burke argued, was the best medium for inspiring sensibility: "the proper manner of conveying the *affections* of the mind from one to another, is by words."[2]

This is precisely Williams's project in the *Letters Written in France, in the Summer 1790*: to communicate her own affection for the Revolution through stories and images of the scenes whose sublimity had inspired both her own and the French people's enthusiasm for the new government and its values of liberty and harmony. In order to evoke these same emotions in her readers, Williams has recourse to a number of specific strategies to create an aesthetic suitable for a new Revolutionary politics. Central to this aesthetic are the recourse to images of nature and especially of light, the representation of the Revolution as a participatory spectacle, a new version of the sublime that deconstructs the opposition between sublime and beautiful established by Burke and Kant, and a project of displacement whereby Revolutionary icons and practices are explicitly substituted for those of the old regime. Underlying these various strategies is Williams's assertion of "feminine" values as the foundation for Revolutionary possibility.

These practices show that for Williams and for Romanticism in general, the representation of history was a literary enterprise. If Williams attributes the Revolution and her friendship with the du Fossés with turning her pen "from the annals of imagination to the records of politics; from the poetry to the prose of human life" (p. 100), her French Revolution, like that of all Romantic writers, would have to be rendered poetically in order to be true and transformative. The French government also understood the importance of art as a means not only for expressing but for achieving political

---

1 See, for example, David Hume, *Treatise of Human Nature* (1739-40) and Adam Smith, *Theory of Moral Sentiments* (1759).
2 Edmund Burke, *A Philosophical Enquiry into the Origin of Our Ideas of the Sublime and Beautiful* (London: R. and J. Dodsley, 1757), 45-46.

solidarity; as the Festival of Federation makes evident, music, pageantry, and iconography were central to the project of Revolutionary change.

Participatory spectacle and popular spontaneity, official events and patriotic anecdotes blend to give shape and substance to the *Letters Written in France*. Williams's epistolary form provides both a sense of immediacy and the rationale for structuring her history as a tour of France in which sites, events, and individual encounters converge as testimony to the new spirit of liberty and humanity she wants her English readers to endorse. At the same time, this loose form masks omissions: the events and topics Williams does not address—for example, elitism, poverty, popular discontent, political conflict within the Revolution, weaknesses in the political process, and counterrevolutionary sentiment—seem absent simply because Williams has not contemplated them at first hand. The epistolary strategy also allows the writer's own vision to inform and even displace the empirical: when she visits the palace at Versailles, for example, Williams artfully substitutes "the gloomy dungeons of the Bastille, which still haunt my imagination," for the otherwise dazzling "splendour of this superb palace," and when she carefully describes "the memorable night when the *Poissardes* visited Versailles," she imagines the queen standing on the balcony "with the Dauphin in her arms" (pp. 98-99) where Burke portrayed a queen nearly slaughtered in her bed.

Structurally, the *Letters Written in France* divides into three unequal parts. The fifteen letters comprising the first half of the book take us from a mass at Notre Dame on the eve of the Festival of Federation to the author's journey some weeks later from Paris to Rouen. After the Festival, Williams's first desire is to "contemplate the ruins" of the Bastille, which occasions an extended meditation on the Revolution's beginnings. Subsequent letters recount visits to the writer Madame de Genlis, tutor for the Duc d'Orléans's children, to the National Assembly, to the royal palace at Versailles, to the theatre, and through the French countryside en route to Rouen. Each visit provides an occasion for contemplating the Revolution: anecdotal encounters reinforce the virtues of the new government and of the French people, and allusions to places, persons, and past events layer the text with historical resonance, realistic detail, and a sense of both continuity and distinction between old and new France. Thus Williams describes the statue on the Pont Neuf of France's most beloved king, Henry IV, now decorated with the Revolutionary tricolor and surrounded with images of Bailly and Lafayette, while that of Louis XIV is "stripped of its former ostentatious ornaments" (pp. 103–104).

The section beginning with Letter XVI and continuing over the next six letters recounts at length the history of M. and Mme. du Fossé, their sufferings under the old regime, and their salvation by the almost simultaneous death of M. du Fossé's father and the birth of Revolutionary justice. A true history with "the air of romance," this family narrative permits Williams to illustrate with vivid specificity the effects of absolutist authority on one imprisoned man, on his exiled and impoverished wife, and on their children, who become literary characters with whom Williams's readers can identify and to whose liberation through the Revolution they can assent.

The four final letters restore the eyewitness epistolarity of the first section while looking more intensely toward England as Williams prepares for her journey home. Concluding the *Letters Written in France* with her return to London, Williams articulates her dismay at the sharp differences between her own happy experience of the Revolution and English distrust. Her last letter hopes for a new ship of politics, "built upon principles that defy the opposition of the tempestuous elements," that will sail "sublimely over the untracked ocean" to "[unite] those together whom nature seemed for ever to have separated, and [throw] a line of connection across the divided world" (p. 149). Williams here seems to be seeking not only the political unity of the French, but a spiritual union between the two countries, England and France, she has identified earlier as the mature matron and the fresh maiden of Liberty.

Williams's image of a sailing ship points as well to a complex and pervasive use of "nature" in her text. In an age when nature often signified the highest social possibilities, Williams strives to show the Revolution as an embodiment, restoration, or redefinition of the natural. Images of light, for example, pervade the text, and when the sun bursts forth at the end of the Festival of Federation, it is the assent of the universe that Williams wants to emphasize. Thus "philosophy" is itself a kind of light, shedding its "benign beams," while images of chains, iron, stone, and darkness characterize Williams's depictions of the old regime. Nature affirms the rightness of Revolutionary ideals: the aristocracy is figured as a distorted and twisted tree, while the tree of patriotism is tall and straight.

At the same time and somewhat paradoxically, Williams produces much of this "natural" effect through tableaus and scenarios that allow her to aestheticize the Revolution as spectacle. Importantly, this is not the theatricality one might associate with Burke's representation, for example, of the supposed attack on Marie Antoinette at Versailles (p. 271). The October march on Versailles as Burke renders it, might be said to represent a conventional, tragic staging in which audiences look on in horror as evil forces attempt to bring down the leadership. Marie-Hélène Huet has suggested that the Revolution constructed a new notion of sublime drama that turns spectators into participants and brings everyone present together into a transformed community that enacts in spectacle what it also lives out beyond the staged event.[1] This is precisely the kind of sublime spectacle Williams represents in her rendering of the Festival of Federation and goes on to recreate in several more episodes throughout the *Letters Written in France*: a living out of sublimity through reaffirmations that are at the same time stylized, yet everyday and commonplace.

In creating her particular sense of Revolutionary spectacle, however, Williams must exploit and ultimately alter the widely accepted notions of the sublime and beautiful established by Burke and Kant. Burke's *Enquiry*, which influenced Kant's *Observations on the Feeling of the Beautiful and Sublime* (1764) and *Critique of Judgment* (1790), was one of the most important aesthetic treatises of the eighteenth-century. Burke defines the sublime as the "strongest emotion which the mind is capable of feeling" and locates its source in objects that turn potential terror into awe and respect. The beautiful, on the other hand, originates merely in pleasure and does not require the mental exertion demanded by the sublime. Burke, and Kant after him, applied these aesthetic categories to political and social relationships, so that beautiful qualities such as tenderness and affection assume a subordinate position to sublime qualities such as the awe and respect shown by subjects to their rulers and state. Moreover, sublime qualities of nobility, reason, and awe are also associated with men; beautiful qualities of tenderness, friendship, and elegance with women. And for Burke (though not quite for Kant) the feudal order of England and France represents a sublime political structure that inspires awe, admiration, and respect for a powerful patriarchal authority founded on centuries of tradition.

---

1 See Marie-Hélène Huet, *Mourning Glory: The Will of the French Revolution* (Philadelphia: University of Pennsylvania Press, 1997) Ch. 3.

Williams interprets the Revolution through a set of fluid aesthetic categories that privilege the beauty and harmony of the Revolution as a new kind of sublimity, shifting the terrible aspects of the sublime—terror and horror—to an inhumane *ancien régime*. The Bastille, the arch-symbol of old-regime terror, is no edifice of awe or reverence; rather, the *ruins* of the Bastille becomes a site of beauty that can be experienced by all. Sublimity is possible only through revolutionary principles in which a shared emotional state reflects a shared politics.[1] Williams thus synthesizes the sublime with the beautiful by liberating the sublime from pain and terror and allowing its grandeur to be informed with pleasurable participatory sympathy. As the Revolution dissolves hierarchies of sex, condition, and structures of governance, so it collapses the old aesthetic dichotomy: "If the splendour of a despotic throne can only shine like the radiance of lightning, while all around is involved in gloom and horror, in the name of heaven let its baleful lustre be extinguished for ever. May no such strong contrast of light and shade again exist in the political system in France!" (p. 74). Thus, too, Williams envisions a "ship" of government that can "defy" rather than toss in tempests and thereby "sail sublimely" across "untracked" seas.

Williams also enacts this transformation of the sublime through a practice that the French revolutionists adopt as well: she projects a series of substitutions whereby *ancien régime* forms and practices are explicitly displaced and replaced by parallel Revolutionary icons, words, images, and artifacts. Williams makes clear that these substitutions are a deliberate project of the Revolutionary government; popular consciousness is transformed, for both Williams and the government, by adapting or replacing old-regime forms already familiar to the populace. Thus, for example, the Bastille itself becomes Revolutionary art, both through its ruins, which Williams recreates as "a scene of beauty and pleasure" (p. 72), and in its replicas, when she tells us that "eighty-three complete models" of the Bastille are presented "with a true patriotic spirit, to the eighty-three departments of the kingdom" that replaced the old Parlement, and presented "by way of hint to his countrymen to take care of their liberties in future" (p. 77). The term "aristocrat" becomes a political label, so that "Every thing tiresome or unpleas-

---

1 Mary Favret, "Spectatrice as Spectacle: Helen Maria Williams at Home in the Revolution," *Studies in Romanticism* 32:2 (1993): 282.

ant," from the badly paved streets of Paris to bad weather, is "une aristocracie," "and every thing charming and agreeable is 'à la nation.'" (p. 95). Williams's *Letters* extends the same project to the English; her text offers a set of icons, images, and anecdotes designed to instill in the British not only the principles of liberty and equality but the signifiers that bring them vividly to life.

Williams's most extensive effort to transform the images and symbols of the *ancien régime* into revolutionary icons is enacted through her "romantic" story of the du Fossés. Her narrative charts the ultimate fall of the manipulative old order, whose law allows a cruel father to abuse patriarchal prerogative and bring extensive suffering to his own son and to the woman his son has defied him by marrying, even causing the death of an innocent child. The elder Baron du Fossé incarnates the despotism of the government: "Formed by nature for the support of the antient government of France, he maintained his aristocratic rights with unrelenting severity, ruled his feudal tenures with a rod of iron, and considered the lower order of people as a set of beings whose existence was tolerated merely for the use of the nobility." (p. 115) Here Williams embodies in a single person the evils that the Revolution must remedy—a rigid patriarchal political structure, a feudal commercial system ruled by the landed aristocracy, and a class structure in which the nobility show little benevolence toward their subjects. This is indeed the reality of the political structure Burke aestheticizes, and Williams effectively transforms it from the sublime to the simply "terrible" by narrating a "true" story in which there are "real sufferings" (p. 119).

Williams replaces this hierarchical setup with the horizontal structure of a partnership between husband and wife that is meant to represent the new egalitarian ideals of revolutionary France. Here she creates a microcosm of what Lynn Hunt describes as the "family romance of the French Revolution,"[1] in which sons overthrow tyrannical fathers and establish new structures of relationship based on love and unity rather than on fear. M. du Fossé the younger, in contrast to his heartless father, "possessed the most amiable dispositions, and the most feeling heart" (p. 115). Williams links M. du Fossé's sensibility to that of the enlightened Revolutionary leaders who, "well acquainted with the human heart," have "not

---

1 See Lynn Hunt, *The Family Romance of the French Revolution* (Berkeley: University of California Press, 1992).

trusted merely to the force of reason, but have studied to interest in their cause the most powerful passions of human nature, by the appointment of solemnities perfectly calculated to awaken the general sympathy which is caught from heart to heart with irresistible energy, fills every eye with tears, and throbs in every bosom" (p. 90). This is also the project of sensibility of the *Letters Written in France*: to make a revolutionary passion "irresistible" to English readers by a "calculated" representation of Revolutionary "solemnities." Williams's choice to frame her history as a set of letters "to a friend" whose sex is not specified reinforces this sense that principles are not simply or primarily rational, but are matters to be "caught from heart to heart."

Underlying Williams's understanding of revolutionary transformation, then, is a language and a vision in which values that have been culturally marked "feminine" predominate. Williams seeks to universalize this sensibility across gender boundaries, opposing the Burkean notion of "manly morals" by establishing the human hearts of both men and women as the "natural terrain of politics."[1] She thus insists on a crucial and public role not only for "feminine" sensibility but for women themselves: "The women have certainly had a considerable share in the French revolution: for, whatever the imperious lords of the creation may fancy, the most important events which take place in this world depend a little on our influence; and we often act in human affairs like those secret springs in mechanism, by which, though invisible, great movements are regulated" (p. 79). For Williams democracy itself is a feminine structure: "The number of those who have murmured at the loss of rank, bears a very small proportion to those who have acted with a spirit of distinguished patriotism; who, with those generous affections which belong to the female heart, have gloried in sacrificing titles, fortune, and even the personal ornaments, so dear to female vanity, for the common cause" (pp. 78-79). It is also true that while she lauds France for allowing women to observe the National Assembly, Williams ignores the actual limitations on women's formal political activity.

The consistent identification of femininity with the Revolution that threads itself throughout the volumes of Williams's *Letters*, however, helps to resolve what might otherwise seem to be contradictions in Williams's politics. Some critics have wondered how

---

1 Favret, "Spectatrice as Spectacle," 289.

Williams could support a range of rather different French regimes without acknowledging a change in her own position. But if one recognizes with Gary Kelly that Williams was a consistent advocate of "feminized politics," it becomes clear that for Williams it was not the regime itself, but its values and practices, that won or lost her support. Lynn Hunt argues that eventually the Revolution's "family romance" became a romance of brothers fighting one another and excluding their sisters, and Williams's criticisms of French leaders evoke just this kind of scenario. As Gary Kelly observes, one of the ways in which Williams figures the Terror is through its departure from the feminizing values of the earlier Revolutionary period. While the gentle confederation once united people and vindicated the virtuous, the brutal Jacobin rulership divides families, sets citizen against citizen, and punishes the innocent.[1] As Deborah Kennedy describes it, under the Terror, Liberty, whom Williams herself embodies in a tableau represented in the 1790 *Letters*, now becomes "a woman of sensibility, wounded by the ill-usage of the Jacobins."[2] And Williams is also consistent in never foregoing the dual consciousness wrought by her double allegiances to England and France. In the last volume of her *Letters from France*, published in 1796, she continues to reproach England as a slave-trader nation that has no right to chastise France for its sins: "Ah, let us, till the slave-trade no longer stains the British name, be more gentle in our censures of other nations!" In such a moment we see the consistency of Williams's view and the stability of the values that structured her judgments of events in both England and France.

This does not mean that Williams's view of the Revolution was static. When she looks back on the Fête de la Fédération in the *Souvenirs de la Révolution française*, published in the last year of her life, Williams acknowledges both the lasting power of that "sublime spectacle" and its dissonance with events that followed it: "In those days, the evils the Revolution would produce seemed impossible, as if France had nothing more to do than to rejoice in her happiness." She now sees the Festival of Federation as a beautiful dream, and its lesson the difficulty of changing human consciousness. In a poignant statement that challenges her own aesthetic agenda by deconstructing a central image through which she figures the Fes-

---

1 Kelly, *Women, Writing and Revolution* 60 and *passim*.
2 Kennedy, "Spectacle of the Guillotine," 97.

tival, she acknowledges that "one cannot create liberty as God created light." The National Assembly, she says, would have been better off promoting strong laws that would direct "all this beautiful energy" toward a "stable end." Instead, the Revolutionaries "got lost in debating the rights it would establish, and seemed to forget to learn the art of keeping them once they were established." Here Williams soberly questions the efficacy of words to effect change, and it is a sad irony that her own words would long remain buried beneath a masculinization of literary merit that she would have deplored.

But Williams's place on the landscape of Romanticism and Revolution is now being recognized as both an early and a lasting one. She is, in fact, one of the few courageous writers who did not cave in to the pressures of English counterrevolution and misogynist attack. As many poets hurriedly disavowed their support for the Revolution in ways for which more radical writers of the next generation, like Shelley and Byron, would have contempt, Williams re-inscribed the principles she had carried into her first published works, even when those principles seemed doomed or ridiculous. Where Wordsworth retrenched into "transcendence," Williams remained immersed in history. She thus gives us a rare opportunity to see how literature, politics, gender, and history may come together in the production of a distinct and daring Romantic voice.

Helen Maria Williams: A Brief Chronology

1761   Born 17 June.

1762   Death of father, Charles Williams.

1781   Moves to London and enters intellectual circles.

1782   *Edwin and Eltruda.*

1783   *An Ode on the Peace.*

1784   *Peru, a Poem. In Six Cantos.*

1785   Meets Monique du Fossé.

1786   *Poems.*

1788   *A Poem on the Bill Lately Passed for Regulating the Slave Trade.*

1790   *Julia, a Novel*; Williams travels in France (June–September); *Letters Written in France* (November).

1791   *A Farewell, for Two Years, to England*; return to France (September); *Poems* (2nd and enlarged edition).

1792   Brief and final return to England; *Letters from France: Containing Many New Anecdotes*; in France meets John Hurford Stone.

1793   Imprisoned by French authorities (Oct-Nov); *Letters from France: Containing ... Interesting and Original Information.*

1794   Williams and Stone flee to Switzerland (June).

1795   Return to France; *Letters Containing a Sketch of the Politics of France* [May 1793-July 1794]; *Letters Containing a Sketch of the Scenes ... during the Tyranny of Robespierre*; *Paul and Virginia.*

1796   *Letters containing a Sketch of the Politics of France* [July 1794–1795].

1798   Death of Helen's sister Cecilia; *A Tour in Switzerland.*

1801   *Sketches of the State of Manners and Opinions in the French Republic*; *The History of Perourou.*

1802   "Ode to Peace" angers Napoleon, prompting one-day imprisonment.

1803 Napoleon attempts to confiscate *The Political and Confidential Correspondence of Lewis XVI*.

1812 Death of Williams's mother.

1814 Begins publishing translations of Humboldt's writings.

1815 *A Narrative of the Events which have Taken Place in France, from the Landing of Napoleon ... till the Restoration of Louis XVIII*.

1816 *On the Late Persecution of the Protestants in the South of France*.

1817 Williams and Stone become French citizens.

1818 Death of John Hurford Stone.

1819 *Letters on the Events which have Passed in France since the Restoration in 1815*.

1823 Death of Persis Williams; *Poems on Various Subjects; with Introductory Remarks on the Present State of Science and Literature in France*.

1827 *Souvenirs de la Révolution française*; death of Williams (14 December).

Contemporary Historical Events

	France 1760–1832	Great Britain 1760–1832
1760		Death of King George II and accession of his grandson as George III.
1762	Publication of Rousseau's *Social Contract*.	
1763	Treaty of Paris ends Seven Years War with England.	Treaty of Paris ends Seven Years War with France.
1770	Marriage of the Dauphin to Marie Antoinette of Austria.	
1772		Mansfield Decision undermines slavery on British soil.
1774	Death of Louis XV and accession of his grandson as Louis XVI.	
1775	"Flour Wars" in Paris (April–May).	War with American colonies begins (April).
1778	France enters American war against Britain.	
1780		Gordon Riots in London (June).
1782		American War of Independence ends.
1783		Peace of Versailles ends war between Britain and France in North America; William Pitt elected Prime Minister.
1785		Burke leads corruption charges against Warren Hastings, governor of India.
1788	Louis XVI calls for elections to Estates-General.	Temporary insanity of George III precipitates first Regency Crisis; Warren Hastings tried for corruption.
1789	Estates-General convenes at Versailles (5 May) and becomes National Assembly (20 June); capture of the Bastille (14 July); *Declaration of the Rights of Man and Citizen* (26 August); women march to Versailles and return royal family to Paris (5-6 October).	Richard Price gives sermon to London Revolution Society (5 November).

France	Great Britain
1790	Monasteries and convents dissolved; nobility abolished; Fête de la Fédération celebrates fall of the Bastille (14 July); clergy required to take oath supporting civil control of the Church.	English debate over French Revolution begins.
1791	Royal family, fleeing France, is arrested at Varennes (20 June); Champ de Mars Massacre of republican protestors (17 July); Slave revolts in Saint Domingue; Louis XVI accepts French Constitution (18 Sept).	Thomas Paine responds to Burke in *Rights of Man*, part 1; Birmingham Riots: against radicals on "Bastille Day."
1792	France declares war on Austria; Prussia declares war on France; monarchy overthrown after storming of Tuileries Palace (9-10 August); September Massacres; first French victory at Valmy: France becomes a Republic (20 September).	London Corresponding Society founded; George III issues royal proclamation against seditious writings; Paine prosecuted under new Libel Act; Wollstonecraft, *Vindication of the Rights of Woman*.
1793	Louis XVI guillotined for treason (21 January); France declares war on Britain, Dutch Republic and Spain (Feb-Mar); Girondins ousted (May-June); Marat assassinated by Charlotte Corday (13 July); Marie Antoinette executed (16 October).	Formal mourning by British Court for Louis XVI's death; war declared by France; Godwin, *Enquiry Concerning Political Justice*.
1794	Slavery abolished (4 February); Danton guillotined (5 April); Robespierre and Jacobin leaders overthrown (27-28 July) to end Terror.	Habeas Corpus suspended; prominent radicals in London and Edinburgh tried for treason.
1795	Vendemaire uprisings; Convention restores freedom of worship and decrees separation of church and state; peace treaty with Spain; Five-member Directory established as France's governing body.	Bread riots; Seditious Meetings Act and Treasonable Practices Act outlaw mass meetings and lectures.
1796	Napoleon leads invasions of Italy.	

France	Great Britain
1797 Fructidor: anti-royalist coup by Directors with military support; peace agreement with Austria.	Mutinies in the British Navy at Spithead and Nore.
1798 Napoleon lands in Egypt; Britain, Austria, and Russia form alliance against France.	Irish Rebellion supported by France yields massive casualties; Wordsworth and Coleridge publish *Lyrical Ballads*.
1799 Coup d'état of 18 Brumaire: Napoleon overthrows Directory; Constitution of Year VII creates 3-person consulate.	Britain conquers Surinam; Sierra Leone made a British colony.
1801 As Chief Consul Napoleon negotiates Concordat with Pope, re-establishing French church; truces with Britain and Austria.	Union with Ireland takes effect by proclamation; truce with France.
1802 Napoleon restores slave trade; Peace of Amiens (25 March).	Peace of Amiens re-opens Continent to British travel (25 March).
1803 U.S. makes Louisiana Purchase from Napoleon; war renewed with England.	Peace of Amiens ends, war is renewed between France and Britain (12 May).
1804 Saint Domingue declared independent and becomes Haiti; Napoleonic Code enacted in France; Napoleon crowns himself Emperor of the French (2 December).	Spain declares war on Britain.
1805 Napoleon defeats Austrians and Russians at Austerlitz; Treaty of Pressburg between France and Austria forces Austria out of coalition with Britain.	Coalition of Austria, Russia, Sweden and Britain against France and Spain; British navy under Horatio Nelson defeats French Navy at Cape Trafalgar.
1806 Wars with Prussia and Russia; Continental blockade of Britain.	Lord Grenville elected Prime Minister.
1807 French invade Portugal; Treaty of Tilsit with Russia and Prussia.	Abolition of African slave trade (does not prohibit continuance of slavery).
1808 French invade Spain, withdraw from Portugal.	Peninsular Campaign begins; British troops land in Portugal.
1809 Napoleon annexes Papal states.	Senegal, Martinique and Cayenne captured by British.

	France	Great Britain
1811		Prince of Wales made regent after George III declared permanently insane (5 February); Luddite uprisings in Midlands against textile mechanization.
1812	Napoleon invades Russia, then retreats.	U.S. declares war on Britain (June).
1814	Napoleon abdicates and is exiled to Elba; Bourbons restored, with brother of Louis XVI reigning as Louis XVIII (April).	Treaty of Ghent ends war with U.S. after British capture and burn Washington, D.C.
1815	The "Hundred Days": Napoleon escapes from Elba and regains power (April–June); Napoleon defeated at Waterloo (18 June) and exiled to St. Helena; monarchy restored.	Corn Law Bill protects British landlords by regulating corn import and export.
1816		Spa Field Riot: mass meeting and march on the Tower of London.
1818		Habeas Corpus restored and never again suspended.
1819		Massacre of Corn Law protesters at Manchester ("Peterloo").
1820	Revolts in Spain and Italy against Bourbons.	Death of George III and accession of George IV (January).
1821	Napoleon dies on St. Helena (5 May).	
1824	Death of Louis XVIII and accession of his ultraconservative brother Charles X.	
1830	Citizens of Paris revolt (July); Charles X abdicates and Louis–Philippe, son of the Duc d'Orléans, comes to power; new Constitution provides for elected monarch.	
1832	Uprisings in Paris.	Reform Bill extends the vote to middle class, doubling the electorate; representation in Parliament is reapportioned (June).

Paris in 1790: Sites Mentioned in *Letters Written in France*

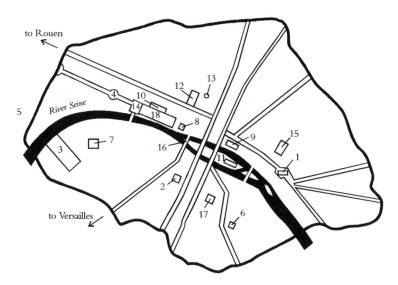

1. Bastille (site)
2. Carmelite Convent
3. Champ de Mars
4. Champs-Elysées
5. Chateau de La Muette
6. Gobelins Manufacture
7. Hôpital (Hôtel) des Invalides
8. Louvre
9. Maison de Ville and Place de Grève (Hôtel de Ville)
10. National Assembly Meeting Hall
11. Notre Dame Cathedral
12. Palais Royal
13. Place des Victoires and Statue of Louis XIV
14. Place Louis XV (Concorde)
15. Place Royale (Place des Vosges)
16. Pont Neuf and Statue of Henri IV
17. Sainte-Geneviève
18. Tuileries Palace and Gardens

A Note on the Text

This text is based on the first edition of 1790, published in London by T. Cadell. During the next six years, Cadell published four more editions of the 1790 *Letters Written in France*, all of which vary only negligibly from the first. An edition was also published in Dublin in 1791 by G. Burnet, P. Wogan, P. Byrne, et al., which essentially reproduced the original London edition. Also appearing in 1791 were the first American edition, printed by J. Belknap and A. Young in Boston, and the first French edition, titled *Lettres écrites de France: à une amie en Angleterre, pendant l'année 1790: contenant l'histoire des malheurs de M. du F****, published in Paris by Garnéry.

We have silently corrected obvious typographical errors in both the English and the French. We have retained, however, spellings that were acceptable by the conventions of Williams's own day. Thus, for example, we retain "chuse" "croud" "desart" and "controuled," but emend "poeple" to "people" and "patrioque" to "patriotique." Although Williams's French was imperfect, we have retained her translations from French to English and the syntax of her French as textual information valuable in its own right. We correct accent marks in Williams's French to conform to the standard usage of her day.

In general we follow the typographical format of the first edition, except for its use of long indented passages and of quotation marks placed at the beginning of each line of a quotation. Williams's own footnotes appear at the bottom of the relevant page and are followed by her name within brackets.

We have treated the contextual material in the Appendices diplomatically, transcribing them verbatim, without correction, and calling attention only to significant errors in the source document. In the Appendices, all translations from the French are our own.

LETTERS

WRITTEN IN

FRANCE,

IN THE SUMMER 1790,

TO A

FRIEND IN ENGLAND;

CONTAINING,

VARIOUS ANECDOTES

RELATIVE TO THE

FRENCH REVOLUTION;

AND

MEMOIRS

OF

MONS. AND MADAME DU F——.

—————

BY

HELEN MARIA WILLIAMS.

—————

LONDON:

PRINTED FOR T. CADELL, IN THE STRAND.

M.DCC.XC.

Title page, first edition of *Letters Written in France*. From the copy in the Hoyt Collection, Rare Book Collection, the University of North Carolina at Chapel Hill.

LETTER I.

I ARRIVED at Paris, by a very rapid journey, the day before the federation;[1] and when I am disposed to murmur at the evils of my destiny, I shall henceforth put this piece of good fortune into the opposite scale, and reflect how many disappointments it ought to counterbalance. Had the packet[2] which conveyed me from Brighton to Dieppe failed a few hours later; had the wind been contrary; in short, had I not reached Paris at the moment I did reach it, I should have missed the most sublime spectacle which, perhaps, was ever represented on the theatre of this earth.

I shall send you once a week the details which I promised when we parted, though I am well aware how very imperfectly I shall be able to describe the images which press upon my mind. It is much easier to feel what is sublime than to paint it; and all I shall be able to give you will be a faint sketch, to which your own imagination must add colouring and spirit. The night before the federation, by way of prelude to the solemnities of that memorable day, the Te Deum was performed at the church of Notre Dame, by a greater number of musicians than have ever been assembled together, excepting at Westminster Abbey.[3] The overture which preceded the Te Deum was simple and majestic: the music, highly expressive, had the power of electrifying the hearers: and near the conclusion of the piece, the composer, by artful discords, produced a melancholy emotion, and then, by exciting ideas of trouble and inquietude, prepared the mind for a recitative[4] which affected the audi-

---

1 The Fête de la Fédération (Festival of Federation) held on 14 July 1790 was a spectacular celebration of the first anniversary of the fall of the Bastille. See Introduction, pp. 7 and 14.
2 A boat regularly ferrying mail, cargo, and passengers between ports. Williams had traveled from southeastern England to northwestern France.
3 The Te Deum is a Latin hymn of praise to God. Notre Dame de Paris is located on the eastern end of the Ile de la Cité, the oldest part of Paris. Begun in 1163 and completed around 1330, Notre Dame is perhaps the most celebrated of medieval Gothic churches. Desacralized and renamed a "Temple of Reason" during the Revolution, Notre Dame was the site of Napoleon's coronation in 1804. Westminster Abbey, founded in 1245 by Henry III, sits immediately opposite London's Houses of Parliament and has served for centuries as the site of Britain's coronations and memorials for its honored dead.
4 This "recitative" was the hiérodrame (sacred drama) called The Taking of the Bastille [La Prise de la Bastille], composed for the occasion by Marc-Antoine Desaugiers (1742-93) and performed by over six hundred musicians.

ence in a very powerful manner, by recalling the images of that consternation and horror which prevailed in Paris on the 13th of July, 1789, the day before that on which the Bastille was taken.[1] The words were, as well as I can recollect, what follows:—"People, your enemies advance, with hostile sentiments, with menacing looks! They come to bathe their hands in your blood! Already they encompass the walls of your city! Rise, rise from the inaction in which you are plunged, seize your arms, and fly to the combat! God will combat with you!" These words were succeeded by a chorus of instruments and voices, deep and solemn, which seemed to chill the soul. But what completed the effect was, when the sound of a loud and heavy bell mixed itself with this awful concert, in imitation of the alarm-bell, which, the day before the taking of the Bastille, was rung in every church and convent in Paris, and which, it is said, produced a confusion of sounds inexpressibly horrible. At this moment the audience appeared to breathe with difficulty; every heart seemed frozen with terror; till at length the bell ceased, the music changed its tone, and another recitative announced the entire defeat of the enemy; and the whole terminated, after a flourish of drums and trumpets, with an hymn of thanksgiving to the Supreme Being.

LETTER II.

I Promised to send you a description of the federation: but it is not to be described! One must have been present, to form any judgment of a scene, the sublimity of which depended much less on its external magnificence than on the effect it produced on the minds of the spectators. "The people, sure, the people were the sight!"[2] I may tell you of pavilions, of triumphal arches, of altars on which incense was burnt, of two hundred thousand men walking in procession; but how am I to give you an adequate idea of the behaviour of the spectators? How am I to paint the impetuous feelings of that immense, that exulting multitude? Half a million of people assembled at a spectacle, which furnished every image that can ele-

---

1 Located in the eastern part of Paris, this medieval fortress with its notorious dungeons and political prisoners became the symbol of arbitrary and oppressive state power. Letter IV describes Williams's visit to the Bastille.
2 Alexander Pope, *First Epistle of the Second Book of Horace, Imitated* (1737), line 323.

vate the mind of man; which connected the enthusiasm of moral sentiment with the solemn pomp of religious ceremonies; which addressed itself at once to the imagination, the understanding, and the heart! *(Eiffel Tower)*

The Champ de Mars[1] was formed into an immense amphitheatre, round which were erected forty rows of seats, raised one above another with earth, on which wooden forms were placed. Twenty days labour, animated by the enthusiasm of the people, accomplished what seemed to require the toil of years. Already in the Champ de Mars the distinctions of rank were forgotten; and, inspired by the same spirit, the highest and lowest orders of citizens gloried in taking up the spade, and assisting the persons employed in a work on which the common welfare of the state depended. Ladies took the instruments of labour in their hands, and removed a little of the earth, that they might be able to boast that they also had assisted in the preparations at the Champ de Mars; and a number of old soldiers were seen voluntarily bestowing on their country the last remains of their strength. A young Abbé of my acquaintance told me, that the people beat a drum at the door of the convent where he lived, and obliged the Superior to let all the Monks come out and work in the Champ de Mars. The Superior with great reluctance acquiesced, "Quant à moi," said the young Abbé, "je ne demandois pas mieux."[2]

At the upper end of the amphitheatre a pavilion was built for the reception of the King, the Queen, their attendants, and the National Assembly,[3] covered with striped tent-cloth of the national colours, and decorated with streamers of the same beloved tints,

---

1 Literally, "Field of Mars." Currently the site of the Eiffel Tower, this military parade ground on the Left Bank of the Seine was the setting for massive gatherings during the Revolution. If the 1790 Fête marked the most euphoric of these occasions, the antithesis was the Champ de Mars Massacre on 17 July 1791, when the National Guard opened fire on protestors petitioning for an end to the monarchy.

2 As for me, I desired nothing better. [Williams's note]

3 Legislative body of revolutionary France established on 17 June 1789, when members of the Estates-General—composed of elected representatives from the nobility, the clergy, and the mostly middle-class group known as the "Third Estate"—rejected representation by strict class distinctions and constituted themselves as a National Assembly. This was dissolved on 30 September 1791 and replaced by the Legislative Assembly created by the new constitution.

and fleur de lys.[1] The white flag was displayed above the spot where the King was seated. In the middle of the Champ de Mars L'Autel de la Patrie[2] was placed, on which incense was burnt by priests dressed in long white robes, with sashes of national ribbon. Several inscriptions were written on the altar, but the words visible at the greatest distance were, La Nation, la Loi, et le Roi.[3]

At the lower end of the amphitheatre, opposite to the pavilion, three triumphal arches were erected, adorned with emblems and allegorical figures.

The procession marched to the Champ de Mars, through the central streets of Paris. At La Place de Louis Quinze, the escorts, who carried the colours, received under their banners, ranged in two lines, the National Assembly, who came from the Tuileries.[4] When the procession passed the street where Henry the Fourth was assassinated,[5] every man paused as if by general consent: the cries of joy were suspended, and succeeded by a solemn silence. This tribute of regret, paid from the sudden impulse of feeling at such a moment, was perhaps the most honourable testimony to the virtues of that amiable Prince which his memory has yet received.

In the streets, at the windows, and on the roofs of the houses, the people, transported with joy, shouted and wept as the procession passed. Old men were seen kneeling in the streets, blessing God that they had lived to witness that happy moment. The people ran to the

---

1 Heraldic emblem consisting of three petals or leaves, traditionally associated with French royalty.
2 The National Altar.
3 The Nation, the Law, and the King. [Williams's note]
4 Royal residence in Paris (adjacent to the Louvre), long unoccupied by French kings, to which Louis XVI and his family were brought on 6 October 1789 after a large crowd composed primarily of women marched to Versailles and demanded the royal family's removal to Paris, where they could be watched more closely.
5 Henry of Navarre (1533-1610) became King of France in 1589. The first Bourbon to assume the French throne, Henry converted to Catholicism to win Paris after failing to take it by force. He remained sympathetic to French Protestants, however, and his 1598 Edict of Nantes (revoked by Louis XIV in 1685), granted them the right to hold public office and retain their property. Assassinated by François Ravaillac, a Roman Catholic zealot, on 14 May 1610, Henry IV was a particularly beloved monarch and was revered by many revolutionaries in 1790 for his legendary concern for the people. Williams describes him as her "favourite hero" in Letter XII below.

doors of their houses loaded with refreshments, which they offered to the troops; and crouds of women surrounded the soldiers, and holding up their infants in their arms, and melting into tears, promised to make their children imbibe, from their earliest age, an inviolable attachment to the principles of the new constitution.

The procession entered the Champ de Mars by a long road, which thousands of people had assisted in forming, by filling up deep hollows, levelling the rising grounds, and erecting a temporary bridge across the Seine, opposite to the triumphal arches. The order of the procession was as follows:

A troop of horse, with trumpets.
A great band of music.
A detachment of grenadiers.[1]
The electors chosen at Paris in 1789.
A band of volunteers.
The assembly of the representatives of the people.
The military committee.
Company of chasseurs.[2]
A band of drums.
The Presidents of sixty districts.
The Deputies of the people sent to the Federation.
The Administrators of the municipality.
Bands of music and drums.
Battalion of children, carrying a standard, on which was written, L'Espérance de la Patrie.[3]
Detachment with the colours of the national guard of Paris.
Battalion of veterans.
Deputies from forty-two departments, arranged alphabetically.
The Oriflamme, or grand standard of the Kings of France.
Deputies from the regular troops.
Deputies from the navy.
Deputies from forty-one departments, arranged also alphabetically.[4]

---

1 Soldiers specially trained to hurl grenades, a feat demanding great courage and strength.
2 Infantry equipped with light weapons.
3 The Hope of the Country. [Williams's note]
4 In order to create more equitable legislative and judicial systems, Revolutionary France was divided into eighty-three *départements*, which replaced the provinces of the ancien régime.

Band of volunteer chasseurs.
Troop of horse, with trumpets.

The procession, which was formed with eight persons abreast, entered the Champ de Mars beneath the triumphal arches, with a discharge of cannon. The deputies placed themselves round the inside of the amphitheatre. Between them and the seats of the spectators, the national guard of Paris were ranged; and the seats round the amphitheatre were filled with four hundred thousand people. The middle of the amphitheatre was crouded with an immense multitude of soldiers. The National Assembly walked towards the pavilion, where they placed themselves with the King, the Queen, the royal family, and their attendants; and opposite this group, rose in perspective the hills of Passy and Chaillot, covered with people. The standards, of which one was presented to each department of the kingdom, as a mark of brotherhood, by the citizens of Paris, were carried to the altar to be consecrated by the bishop. High mass was performed, after which Monsieur de la Fayette,[1] who had been appointed by the King Major General of the Federation, ascended the altar, gave the signal, and himself took the national oath.[2] In an instant every sword was drawn, and every arm lifted up. The King pronounced the oath, which the President of the National Assembly repeated, and the solemn words were re-echoed by six hundred thousand voices; while the Queen raised the Dauphin[3] in her arms, shewing him to the people and the army. At the moment the

---

1 Marie-Joseph-Yves-Gilbert du Motier, Marquis de Lafayette (1757-1834), the renowned military leader who fought with the colonists against the British during the American Revolutionary War. In 1790 he was a member of the National Assembly and commander of the National Guard who was often asked to mediate conflicts between the people and the King. Although Lafayette was a progressive supporter of social reform early in the Revolution, he was branded a royalist after the Champ de Mars massacre on 17 July 1791.

2 A declaration of loyalty to the principles of the new constitutional monarchy. For King Louis XVI, taking the oath was a dramatic concession of royal power to the National Assembly.

3 Heir to the throne. The four-year-old Louis-Charles, duc de Normandie, became Dauphin after the death of his brother Louis-Joseph in 1789. Upon the death of Louis XVI on 21 January 1793, the imprisoned Dauphin was proclaimed Louis XVII by émigré royalists. The pawn and hope of constitutional monarchists, he is believed to have died in 1795 of scrofula.

consecrated banners were displayed, the sun, which had been obscured by frequent showers in the course of the morning, burst forth, while the people lifted their eyes to heaven, and called upon the Deity to look down and witness the sacred engagement into which they entered. A respectful silence was succeeded by the cries, the shouts, the acclamations of the multitude: they wept, they embraced each other, and then dispersed.

You will not suspect that I was an indifferent witness of such a scene. Oh no! this was not a time in which the distinctions of country were remembered. It was the triumph of human kind; it was man asserting the noblest privileges of his nature; and it required but the common feelings of humanity to become in that moment a citizen of the world. For myself, I acknowledge that my heart caught with enthusiasm the general sympathy; my eyes were filled with tears; and I shall never forget the sensations of that day, "while memory holds her seat in my bosom."[1]

The weather proved very unfavourable during the morning of the federation; but the minds of people were too much elevated by ideas of moral good, to attend to the physical evils of the day. Several heavy showers were far from interrupting the general gaiety. The people, when drenched by the rain, called out with exultation, rather than regret, "Nous sommes mouillez à la nation."[2] Some exclaimed, "La révolution Françoise est cimentée avec de l'eau, au lieu de sang."[3] The national guard, during the hours which preceded the arrival of the procession, amused the spectators d'une dance round,[4] and with a thousand whimsical and playful evolutions, highly expressive of that gaiety which distinguishes the French Character. I believe none but Frenchmen would have diverted themselves, and half a million of people, who were waiting in expectation of a scene the most solemn upon record, by circles of ten thousand men galloping en dance ronde.[5] But if you are disposed to think of this gaiety with the contempt of superior

---

1 Line 68 of William Hayward Roberts, "To G.A.S. Esq. On his Leaving Eton School": "Even in thy heart while memory holds her seat" in *Poems* (1774).
2 We are wet for the nation. [Williams's note]
3 The French revolution is cemented with water, instead of blood. [Williams's note]
4 With dancing in a circle. [Williams's note]
5 In the round dance. [Williams's note]

gravity, for I will not call it wisdom, recollect that these dancers were the very men whose bravery formed the great epocha of French liberty; the heroes who demolished the towers of the Bastille, and whose fame will descend to the latest posterity.

Such was the admirable order with which this august spectacle was conducted, that no accident interrupted the universal festivity. All carriages were forbidden during that day, and the entrances to the Champ de Mars were so numerous, that half a million of people were collected together without a croud.

The people had only one subject of regret: they murmured that the king had taken the national oath in the pavilion, instead of performing that ceremony at the foot of the altar; and some of them, crouding round Mons. de la Fayette, conjured him to persuade the king to go to the altar, and take the oath a second time. "Mes enfans," said Mons. de la Fayette, "le serment n'est pas une ariette, on ne peut pas le jouer deux fois."[1]

Mons. de la Fayette, after the Federation, went to the Chateau de la Muette,[2] where a public dinner was prepared for the national guard. An immense croud gathered round him when he alighted from his horse, at a little distance from the chateau, and some Aristocrates, mixing themselves with the true worshippers of him who is so justly the idol of the French nation, attempted to stifle him with their embraces. He called out *"Mais, mes amis, vous m'étouffez!"*[3] and one of his aides de camp, who perceived the danger of his general, threw himself from his horse, which he intreated Mons. de la Fayette to mount. He did so, and hastened to the chateau.

This incident reminds me of a line in Racine's fine tragedy of Britannicus,[4] where Nero says,

"J'embrasse mon rival, mais c'est pour l'étouffer."[5]

Adieu.

---

1 My friends, the oath is not an air which can be played twice over. [Williams's note]

2 Some twenty-thousand official participants in the Fête de la Fédération were invited to dine after the ceremonies in the gardens of the Chateau de la Muette, situated in the Bois de Boulogne at Paris's western edge. In 1783, the grounds at la Muette had been the launch site for the first human flight in a balloon.

3 But, my friends, you stifle me. [Williams's note]

4 Jean Racine (1639-99), often considered France's greatest dramatic poet, staged in Paris the first performance of *Britannicus*, a political tragedy based on Tacitus, in 1669. Williams cites line IV.iii.10.

5 I embrace my rival, but it is to destroy him. [Williams's note]

LETTER III.

THE rejoicings at Paris did not terminate with the ceremony of the Federation. A succession of entertainments, which lasted several days, were prepared for the deputies from the provinces, who were all quartered in the houses of the bourgeois, where they were received with the most cordial hospitality.

The night of the 14th of July the whole city of Paris was illuminated, and the next day le ci-devant Duc, now Mons. d'Orleans,[1] gave a public dinner to the national guard in the hall of the Palais Royal.[2] We walked in the evening round the gallery, from which we saw part of the croud below amusing themselves by dancing, while others were singing in chorus the favourite national songs.

On the following Sunday the national guards were reviewed by Mons. de la Fayette in the Champ de Mars, which was again filled with spectators, and the people appeared more enthusiastic than ever in their applauses of their general. The Champ de Mars resounded with repeated cries of "Vive Mons. de la Fayette."[3] On this day carriages were again forbidden, and the evening displayed a scene of general rejoicing. The whole city was illuminated, and crouds of company filled the gardens of the Tuileries, from which we saw the beautiful façade of the Louvre lighted in

---

1 Louis Phillipe Joseph, duc d'Orléans (1747-93), cousin of King Louis XVI and leader of the group in the Estates-General who defected from the ranks of the nobility in order to join the Third Estate in forming the National Assembly. Williams's reference to the "former Duke" ("*le ci-devant Duc*") alludes to the abandonment of titles and privileges that began early in the Revolution. Orléans forsook his title and adopted the name Philippe-Egalité. In 1793, amid rumors that he had aspirations to assume the throne, he was arrested as a counter-revolutionary and sent to the guillotine.

2 Property of Louis Phillipe that became a center of revolutionary sentiment and activity in the years leading up to and immediately following the fall of the Bastille. A rectangle one side of which was formed by the Duke's palace walls, the Palais Royal contained cafés, theaters, and shops that attracted pleasure-seekers both wealthy and poor. Williams describes it appreciatively in Letter X.

3 Long live Mons. de la Fayette. [Williams's note]

the most splendid manner.[1] In the Champs Elysées,[2] where a fête was given to the Deputies, innumerable lamps were hung from one row of trees to another, and shed the most agreeable brilliance on those enchanting walks; where the exhilarated croud danced and sung, and filled the air with the sound of rejoicing. Several parties of the national guard came from the Champs Elysées, dancing along the walks of the Tuileries with a woman between every two men; and all the priests, whom they met in their way, they obliged to join in the dance, treating them as women, by placing them between two soldiers, and sometimes sportively dressing them in grenadiers caps. Fire-works of great variety and beauty were exhibited on the Pont Neuf,[3] and the statue of Henry the Fourth was decorated with the ornament of all others the most dear in the eyes of the people, a scarf of national ribbon. Transparencies of Mons. de la Fayette and Mons. Bailly[4] were placed, as the highest mark of public favour, on each side of this revered statue.

But the spectacle of all others the most interesting to my feelings, was the rejoicings at the Bastille. The ruins of that execrable fortress were suddenly transformed, as if with the wand of necromancy, into a scene of beauty and of pleasure. The ground was covered with fresh clods of grass, upon which young trees were placed in rows, and illuminated with a blaze of light.[5] Here the minds of the people took a higher tone of exultation than in the other scenes of festivity. Their mutual congratulations, their reflections on

---

1 The French translator of Williams's *Letters* notes that from the garden of the Tuileries one saw not the facade of the Louvre but that of the less beautiful Tuileries palace.

2 Literally, "Elysian Fields." Grand avenue in Paris that now runs between the Arc de Triomphe and the Place de la Concorde, leading at its lower end to the Tuileries Gardens.

3 Bridge constructed during the reign of Henry IV that unites the two banks of the Seine across the tip of the Ile de la Cité. Lined with shops, it was at the heart of Parisian daily life.

4 Jean Sylvain Bailly (1736-93), a distinguished scientist, was elected President of the National Assembly and also Mayor of Paris in 1789. He fell out of favor as a result of the Champ de Mars massacre and was ultimately sent to the guillotine by the Revolutionary Tribunal.

5 At this point in the French version, the translator expresses surprise that Williams ignores the fact that these trees are arranged in a pattern that imitates the shape of the Bastille itself.

the horror of the past, their sense of present felicity, their cries of "Vive la Nation,"[1] still ring in my ear! I too, though but a sojourner in their land, rejoiced in their happiness, joined the universal voice, and repeated with all my heart and soul, "Vive la nation!"

LETTER IV.

BEFORE I suffered my friends at Paris to conduct me through the usual routine of convents, churches, and palaces, I requested to visit the Bastille; feeling a much stronger desire to contemplate the ruins of that building than the most perfect edifices of Paris. When we got into the carriage, our French servant called to the coachman, with an air of triumph, "A la Bastille—mais nous n'y resterons pas."[2] We drove under that porch which so many wretches have entered never to repass, and alighting from the carriage descended with difficulty into the dungeons, which were too low to admit of our standing upright, and so dark that we were obliged at noon-day to visit them with the light of a candle. We saw the hooks of those chains by which the prisoners were fastened round the neck, to the walls of their cells; many of which being below the level of the water, are in a constant state of humidity; and a noxious vapour issued from them, which more than once extinguished the candle, and was so insufferable that it required a strong spirit of curiosity to tempt one to enter. Good God! and to these regions of horror were human creatures dragged at the caprice of despotic power. What a melancholy consideration, that

—— "Man! proud man,
Drest in a little brief authority,
Plays such fantastic tricks before high heaven,
As make the angels weep."——[3]

There appears to be a greater number of these dungeons than one could have imagined the hard heart of tyranny itself would

---

1 Long live the Nation. [Williams's note]
2 To the Bastille,—but we shall not remain there. [Williams's note]
3 Lines spoken by Isabella in Shakespeare's *Measure for Measure* (II.ii.117-18, 121-22). The two intervening lines omitted by Williams read: "Most ignorant of what he's most assur'd, / (His glassy essence), like an angry ape...."

contrive; for, since the destruction of the building, many subterraneous cells have been discovered underneath a piece of ground which was inclosed within the walls of the Bastille, but which seemed a bank of solid earth before the horrid secrets of this prison-house were disclosed. Some skeletons were found in these recesses, with irons still fastened on their decaying bones.

After having visited the Bastille, we may indeed be surprized, that a nation so enlightened as the French, submitted so long to the oppressions of their government; but we must cease to wonder that their indignant spirits at length shook off the galling yoke.

Those who have contemplated the dungeons of the Bastille, without rejoicing in the French revolution, may, for aught I know, be very respectable persons, and very agreeable companions in the hours of prosperity; but, if my heart were sinking with anguish, I should not fly to those persons for consolation. Sterne says, that a man is incapable of loving one woman as he ought, who has not a sort of an affection for the whole sex;[1] and as little should I look for particular sympathy from those who have no feelings of general philanthropy. If the splendour of a despotic throne can only shine like the radiance of lightning, while all around is involved in gloom and horror, in the name of heaven let its baleful lustre be extinguished for ever. May no such strong contrast of light and shade again exist in the political system of France! but may the beams of liberty, like the beams of day, shed their benign influence on the cottage of the peasant, as well as on the palace of the monarch! May liberty, which for so many ages past has taken pleasure in softening the evils of the bleak and rugged climates of the north, in fertilizing a barren soil, in clearing the swamp, in lifting mounds against the inundations of the tempest, diffuse her blessings also on the genial land of France, and bid the husbandman rejoice under the shade of the olive and the vine!

The Bastille, which Henry the Fourth and his veteran troops assailed in vain, the citizens of Paris had the glory of taking in a few hours. The avarice of Mons. de Launay[2] had tempted him to guard this fortress with only half the complement of men ordered by

---

1 Laurence Sterne (1713-68), major English novelist, author of *A Sentimental Journey* (1768), whose narrator Yorick claims to be "firmly persuaded that a man who has not a sort of an affection for the whole sex, is incapable of ever loving a single one as he ought" (2nd ed. [1768]: II, 64).

2 Bernard René Jordan, Marquis de Launay (1740-89), Governor of the Bastille, who failed in his defense of the prison against the revolutionary crowds assailing it on 14 July 1789 and was executed by them.

government; and a letter which he received the morning of the 14th of July, commanding him to sustain the siege till the evening, when succour would arrive, joined to his own treachery towards the assailants, cost him his life.

The courage of the besiegers was inflamed by the horrors of famine, there being at this time only twenty-four hours provision of bread in Paris. For some days the people had assembled in crouds round the shops of the bakers, who were obliged to have a guard of soldiers to protect them from the famished multitude; while the women, rendered furious by want, cried, in the resolute tone of despair, "Il nous faut du pain pour nos enfans."[1] Such was the scarcity of bread, that a French gentleman told me, that, the day preceding the taking of the Bastille, he was invited to dine with a Negotiant,[2] and, when he went, was informed that a servant had been out five hours in search of bread, and had at last been able to purchase only one loaf.

It was at this crisis, it was to save themselves the shocking spectacle of their wives and infants perishing before their eyes, that the citizens of Paris flew to arms, and, impelled by such causes, fought with the daring intrepidity of men who had all that renders life of any value at stake, and who determined to die or conquer. The women too, far from indulging the fears incident to our feeble sex, in defiance of the cannon of the Bastille, ventured to bring victuals to their sons and husbands; and, with a spirit worthy of Roman matrons, encouraged them to go on. Women mounted guard in the street, and, when any person passed, called out boldly, "Qui va là?"[3]

A gentleman, who had the command of fifty men in this enterprize, told me, that one of his soldiers being killed by a cannon-ball, the people, with great marks of indignation, removed the corpse, and then, snatching up the dead man's hat, begged money of the bystanders for his interment, in a manner characteristic enough of that gaiety, which never forsakes the French, even on such occasions as would make any other people on earth serious. "Madame, pour ce pauvre diable qui se fait tué pour la Nation!— Mons. pour ce pauvre chien qui se fait tué pour la nation!"[4] This

---

1 We must have bread for our children. [Williams's note]
2 A financier.
3 Who goes there? [Williams's note]
4 Madam, for this poor devil, who has been killed for the Nation!—Sir, for this unfortunate dog, who has been killed for the Nation! [Williams's note]

mode of supplication, though not very pathetic, obtained the end desired; no person being sufficiently obdurate to resist the powerful plea, "qu'il se fait tué pour la Nation."[1]

When the Bastille was taken, and the old man, of whom you have no doubt heard, and who had been confined in a dungeon thirty-five years, was brought into day-light, which had not for so long a space of time visited his eyes, he staggered, shook his white beard, and cried faintly, "Messieurs, vous m'avez rendu un grand service, rendez m'en un autre, tuez moi! je ne sais pas où aller."—"Allons, allons," the croud answered with one voice, "la Nation te nourrira."[2]

As the heroes of the Bastille passed along the streets after its surrender, the citizens stood at the doors of their houses loaded with wine, brandy, and other refreshments, which they offered to these deliverers of their country. But they unanimously refused to taste any strong liquors, considering the great work they had undertaken as not yet accomplished, and being determined to watch the whole night, in case of any surprize.

All those who had assisted in taking the Bastille, were presented by the municipality of Paris with a ribbon of the national colours, on which is stamped inclosed in a circle of brass, an impression of the Bastille, and which is worn as a military order.

The municipality of Paris also proposed a solemn funeral procession in memory of those who lost their lives in this enterprize; but, on making application to the National Assembly for a deputation of its members to assist at this solemnity, the assembly were of opinion that these funeral honours should be postponed till a more favourable moment, as they might at present have a tendency to inflame the minds of the people.

I have heard several persons mention a young man, of a little insignificant figure, who, the day before the Bastille was taken, got up on a chair in the Palais Royal, and harangued the multitude, conjuring them to make a struggle for their liberty, and asserting, that now the moment was arrived. They listened to his eloquence with the most eager attention; and, when he had instructed as many as could hear him at one time, he requested them to depart, and repeated his harangue to a new set of auditors.

---

1 Had been killed for the Nation. [Williams's note]
2 Gentlemen, you have rendered me one great service; render me another, kill me! for I know not where to go.—Come along, come along, the Nation will provide for you. [Williams's note]

Among the dungeons of the Bastille are placed, upon a heap of stones, the figures of the two men who contrived the plan of this fortress, where they were afterwards confined for life. These men are represented chained to the wall, and are beheld without any emotion of sympathy.

The person employed to remove the ruins of the Bastille, has framed of the stones eighty-three complete models of this building, which, with a true patriotic spirit, he has presented to the eighty-three departments of the kingdom, by way of hint to his countrymen to take care of their liberties in future.

LETTER V.

I AM just returned from a visit to Madame Sillery,[1] whose works on education are so well known and so justly esteemed in England, and who received me with most engaging politeness. Surely the French are unrivalled in the arts of pleasing; in the power of uniting with the most polished elegance of manners, that attentive kindness which seems to flow warm from the heart, and which, while it sooths our vanity, secures our affections. Madame Sillery and her pupils are present at St. Leu, a beautiful spot in the rich valley of Montmorenci. Mons. d'Orleans has certainly conferred a most essential obligation upon his children, by placing them under the care of this lady. I never met with young people more amiable in their dispositions, or more charming in their manners, which are equally remote from arrogance, and from those efforts of condescension which I have seen some great people make, with much difficulty to themselves, and much offence to others. The Princess, who is thirteen years of age, has a countenance of the sweetest expression, and appears to me to be Adelaide, the heroine of Madame Sillery's Letters on Education, personified. The three

---

1 Madame Sillery (1746-1830), best known as Stéphanie Félicité la Comtesse de Genlis (but also known as Madame Brulart), a renowned author of books for adults and children, including several treatises on educating the children of nobility, among which is *Adelaide and Theodore, or Letters on Education* (1782). Appointed to educate the children of Louis Phillippe, duc d'Orléans, she may well, as Williams surmises, have based her fictional heroine on Adelaide, the daughter of Louis Phillipe and Louise Marie Adélaide.

princes, though under Madame Sillery's superintendence, have also preceptors who live in the house, and assist in their education. The eldest prince, Mons. de Chartres,[1] is nearly eighteen years of age, and his attentive politeness formed a striking contrast in my mind, to the manners of those fashionable gentlemen in a certain great metropolis, who consider apathy and negligence as the test of good-breeding. But if I was pleased with the manners of this young Prince, I was still more delighted to find him a confirmed friend to the new constitution of France, and willing, with the enthusiasm of a young and ardent mind, to renounce the splendour of his titles for the general good. When he heard that the sacrifice of fortune also was required, and that the immense property, which he had been taught to consider as his inheritance, was to be divided with his brothers, he embraced them with the utmost affection, declaring that he should rejoice in such a division. To find a democratic Prince, was somewhat singular: I was much less surprized that Madame Sillery had adopted sentiments which are so congenial to an enlarged and comprehensive mind. This lady I have called Sillery, because it is the name by which she is known in England; but, since the decree of the National Assembly, abolishing the nobility, she has renounced with her title the name of Sillery, and has taken that of Brulart.

She talked to me of the distinctions of rank, in the spirit of philosophy, and ridiculed the absurdity of converting the rewards of personal merit into the inheritance of those who had perhaps so little claim to honours, that they were a sort of oblique reproach on their character and conduct. There may be arguments against hereditary rank sufficiently convincing to such an understanding as Madame Brulart's: but I know some French ladies who entertain very different notions on this subject; who see no impropriety in the establishments of nobility; and who have carried their love of aristocratical rights so far as to keep their beds, in a fit of despondency, upon being obliged to relinquish the agreeable epithets of Comtesse or Marquise, to which their ears had been so long accustomed.

But let me do justice to the ladies of France. The number of those who have murmured at the loss of rank, bears a very small

---

1 Louis Philippe, duc d'Orleans (1773-1850), the son of Philippe-Egalité, would assume the throne of France in 1830, though like his father he had earlier renounced his titles.

proportion to those who have acted with a spirit of distinguished patriotism; who, with those generous affections which belong to the female heart, have gloried in sacrificing titles, fortune, and even the personal ornaments, so dear to female vanity, for the common cause. It was the ladies who gave the example of le don patriotique,[1] by offering their jewels at the shrine of liberty; and, if the women of ancient Rome have gained the applause of distant ages for such actions,[2] the women of France will also claim the admiration of posterity.

The women have certainly had a considerable share in the French revolution: for, whatever the imperious lords of the creation may fancy, the most important events which take place in this world depend a little on our influence; and we often act in human affairs like those secret springs in mechanism, by which, though invisible, great movements are regulated.

But let us return to Madame Brulart, who wears at her breast a medallion made of a stone of the Bastille polished. In the middle of the medallion, *Liberté* was written in diamonds; above was marked, in diamonds, the planet that shone on the 14th of July; and below was seen the moon, of the size she appeared that memorable night. The medallion was set in a branch of laurel, composed of emeralds, and tied at the top with the national cockade,[3] formed of brilliant stones of the three national colours.

Our conversation on the subject of the Bastille, led Madame Brulart to relate an action of Mons. de Chartres, which reflects the highest honour on his humanity. Being in Normandy, he visited Mont St. Michel, a fortress built on a rock which stands a league and a half from the coast of Normandy. The tide covers this space twice every twenty-four hours; but when it is low-water, a person can pass over on foot. Mont St. Michel was originally a church, founded by a good bishop in the seventh century, in honour of St. Michel, who, it seems, appeared to him in a vision on this spot. Richard, the first Duke of Normandy of that name, afterwards converted the church into an abbey, and this abbey gave rise to the military order des Chevaliers de St. Michel, instituted by Louis the

---

1 The patriotic donation. [Williams's note]
2 Williams is referring to women's legendary patriotism during the second Punic War between Rome and Carthage (218-201 BCE).
3 A tricolor bow or knot of ribbons—royal white and municipal red and blue—worn in the hat by sympathizers of the French Revolution.

Eleventh. After having seen the precious relics of the abbey, the square buckler, and the short sword found in Ireland near the body of the well-known dragon, whose destruction is attributed to the prowess of St. Michel, Mons. de Chartres was conducted, through many labyrinths, to the subterraneous parts of the edifice; where he was shewn a wooden cage, which was made by order of Louis the Fourteenth, for the punishment of an unfortunate wit, who had dared to ridicule his conquests in Holland, no sooner gained than lost. Mons. de Chartres beheld with horror this instrument of tyranny, in which prisoners were still frequently confined; and, expressing in very strong terms his indignation, he was told, that, as a prince of the blood, he had a right, if he thought proper, to order the cage to be destroyed. Scarcely were the words pronounced, when the young Prince seized a hatchet, gave the first stroke himself to this execrable machine, waited to see it levelled with the ground, and thus may claim the glory of having, even before the demolition of the Bastille, begun the French revolution.

We found at St. Leu a young English lady, who is the companion of the Princess, and whose appearance is calculated to give the most favourable idea of English beauty. I never saw more regular features, or an expression of countenance more lovely: Madame Brulart, by whom she has been educated, assured me that "the mind keeps the promise we had from the face." This young lady talked of her own country with a glow of satisfaction very grateful to my feelings. She seems to,

"Cast a look where England's glories shine.
And bids her bosom sympathise with mine."[1]

LETTER VI.

I Have been at the National Assembly, where, at a time when the deputies from the provinces engrossed every ticket of admission, my sister[2] and I were admitted without tickets, by the gentleman who had the command of the guard, and placed in the best seats,

---

1 Cf. Oliver Goldsmith's *The Traveller, or A Prospect of Society* (1764), lines 421–22, which reads "his bosom" for Williams's "her bosom."
2 Helen Williams was accompanied on this first visit to France by her elder sister Cecilia.

before he suffered the doors to be open to other people. We had no personal acquaintance with this gentleman, or any claim to his politeness, except that of being foreigners and women; but these are, of all claims, the most powerful to the urbanity of French manners.

My sister observed to me, that our seats, which were immediately opposite the tribune from which the members speak, reminded her of our struggles to attain the same situation in Westminster Hall.[1] But you must recollect, I answered, that we have attained this situation without any struggle. I believe, however, that if the fame of Mr. Fox's eloquence[2] should lead a French woman to present herself at the door of Westminster Hall without a ticket, she might stand there as long as Mr. Hastings's trial[3] has lasted, without being permitted to pass the barrier.

The hall of the National Assembly is long and narrow; at each end there is a gallery, where the common people are admitted by applying very early in the morning for numbers, which are distributed at the door; and the persons who first apply secure the first numbers. The seats being also numbered, all confusion and disorder are prevented. The galleries at the side of the hall are divided into boxes, which are called tribunes. They belong to the principal members of the National Assembly, and to these places company are admitted with tickets.[4] Rows of seats are placed round the hall, raised one above another, where the members of the Assembly are seated; and immediately opposite the chair of the

---

1 Meeting place of Britain's Houses of Parliament.
2 Charles James Fox (1749-1806), a longtime member of British Parliament and leader of the Whigs, was known for his eloquence and for his outspoken support of the French Revolution in the face of heavy political opposition in England.
3 Warren Hastings (1732-1818), Governor General of Bengal, was accused of extortion and corruption in his management of Bengal by his political adversaries, led by Edmund Burke. Hastings was impeached in 1786, after he returned to England, and stood trial in the House of Lords from 1788-95, at the end of which time he was finally acquitted.
4 Here the French translator takes exception to Williams's use of the phrase "principal members of the Assembly"; he says that "all members of the assembly, like all French citizens, are equal; they are no principals except in talent and in patriotism. The tribunes belong to everyone who presents an entrance ticket. Only M. de Gouy-d'Arcy, for some reason, has one all to himself."

president, in the narrow part of the hall, is the tribune which the members ascend when they are going to speak. One capital subject of debate in this Assembly is, who shall speak first; for all seem more inclined to talk than to listen; and sometimes the president in vain rings a bell, or with the vehemence of French action stretches out his arms, and endeavours to impose silence;[1] while the six Huissers, persons who are appointed to keep order, make the attempt with as little success as the president himself. But one ceases to wonder that the meetings of the National Assembly are tumultuous, on reflecting how important are the objects of its deliberations. Not only the lives and fortunes of individuals, but the existence of the country is at stake: and of how little consequence is this impetuosity in debate, if the decrees which are passed are wise and beneficial, and the new constitution arises, like the beauty and order of nature, from the confusion of mingled elements! I heard several of the members speak; but I am so little qualified to judge of oratory, that, without presuming to determine whether I had reason to be entertained or not, I shall only tell you that I was so.

And this, repeated I with exultation to myself, this is the National Assembly of France! Those men now before my eyes are the men who engross the attention, the astonishment of Europe; for the issue of whose decrees surrounding nations wait in suspence, and whose fame has already extended through every civilized region of the globe: the men whose magnanimity invested them with power to destroy the old constitution, and whose wisdom is erecting the new, on a principle of perfection which has hitherto been thought chimerical, and has only served to adorn the page of the philosopher; but which they believe may be reduced to practice, and have therefore the courage to attempt. My mind, with a sensation of elevated pleasure, passing through the interval of ages, anticipated the increasing renown of these legislators, and the period when, all the nations of Europe following the liberal system which France has adopted, the little crooked policy of the present times shall give place to the reign of reason, virtue, and science.

---

1 Another objection from the translator, who says that Williams is mis-characterizing the current president and the behaviors of the delegates.

The most celebrated characters in the National Assembly were pointed out to us. Monsieur Barnave de Dauphine,[1] who is only six and twenty years of age, and the youngest member of the Assembly, is esteemed its first orator, and is the leader of the democratic party. I believe Mons. Barnave does not owe all his reputation to his talents, however distinguished: his virtues also claim a considerable share of that applause which he receives from his country. He has shewn himself as stedfast in principle, as he is eloquent in debate. With firm undeviating integrity he has defended the cause of the people. Every motion he has made in the Assembly has passed into a law, because its beneficial tendency has been always evident; and it was he who effected that memorable decree which deprived the King of the power of making war, without the consent of the nation. Mons. Barnave is adored by the people; who have two or three times taken the horses from his carriage, and drawn him in triumph along the streets of Paris.

We also saw Mons. Mirabeau l'ainé,[2] whose genius is of the first class, but who possesses a very small share of popularity. I am, however, one of his partizans, though not merely from that enthusiasm which always comes across my heart in favour of great intellectual abilities. Mons. Mirabeau has another very powerful claim on my partiality: he is the professed friend (and I must and will love him for being so) of the African race. He has

---

1 Antoine-Pierre-Joseph-Marie Barnave (1761-93), a lawyer and delegate from Dauphiné popular and powerful at the time of Williams's visit to the National Assembly, would become president of that body in October 1790. Initially more radical than Mirabeau and Lafayette, he was tried and executed in 1793 after having reversed his earlier political position and argued for a constitutional monarchy.

2 Honoré Gabriel Riqueti, Comte de Mirabeau (1749-91), a powerful proponent of a constitutional monarchy and chief opponent of Barnave in the National Assembly. He was a talented writer and orator for progressive causes, including the abolition of slavery, and he was so generally beloved it was said that had he lived, the constitutional monarchy would have had a better chance of succeeding. Williams names him "*l'ainé*" (the elder) to distinguish him from his younger brother, André-Boniface-Louis Riqueti Mirabeau (1754-92), a leading reactionary at the outbreak of the French Revolution.

proposed the abolition of the slave trade[1] to the National Assembly, and, though the Assembly have delayed the consideration of this subject, on account of those deliberations which immediately affect the country, yet, perhaps, if our senators continue to doze over this affair as they have hitherto done, the French will have the glory of setting us an example, which it will then be our humble employment to follow. But I trust the period will never come, when England will submit to be taught by another nation the lesson of humanity. I trust an English House of Commons will never persist in thinking, that what is morally wrong, can be politically right; that the virtue and the prosperity of a people are things at variance with each other; and that a country which abounds with so many sources of wealth, cannot afford to close one polluted channel, which is stained with the blood of our fellow-creatures.

But it is a sort of treason to the honour, the spirit, the generosity of Englishmen, to suppose they will persevere in such conduct. Admitting, however, a supposition which it is painful to make; admitting that they should abide by this system of inhumanity, they will only retard, but will not finally prevent the abolition of slavery. The Africans have not long to suffer, nor their oppressors to triumph. Europe is hastening towards a period too enlightened for the perpetuation of such monstrous abuses. The mists of ignorance and error are rolling fast away, and the benign beams of philosophy are spreading their lustre over the nations.— But whither have these children of captivity led me? I perceive I have wandered a great way from the National Assembly, where I was so happily seated, and of which I will tell you more in my next letter.

---

1   Although a topic of constant debate in the early months of the Revolution, the French slave trade was not abolished until 1793. In February 1794, slavery was ended in all French colonies, only to be reinstated by Napoleon in 1802. The slave trade was not finally outlawed in France until 1817, and slavery itself not until 1848.

LETTER VII.

THE Abbé Maury[1] is one of the most distinguished members of the National Assembly. He possesses astonishing powers of eloquence; but he has done his talents the injustice to make them subservient to the narrow considerations of self-interest. Had he displayed that ability in defence of civil and religious liberty, which he has employed in the service of the exorbitant pretensions of the church, he would have deserved the highest applause of his country; instead of which, he has called to the aid of his genius an auxiliary it ought to have scorned; that subtlety which tries "to make the worse appear the better reason;"[2] and he is still more detested than admired. I am not surprized that a little mind is sometimes tempted by interest to tread in a mean and sordid path; but I own it does astonish me that genius can be seduced from the fair field of honourable fame into those serpentine ways where it can meet with no object worthy of its ambition. "Something too much of this."[3] You shall hear a repartee of the Abbé Maury, who, after having made a very unpopular motion in the Assembly, was insulted as he was going out; the people crying, as they are too apt to do, "A la lanterne."[4] The Abbé, turning to the croud, answered, with equal indignation and spirit, "Eh! Messieurs, si j'étois à la lanterne, serez vous plus éclairer?"[5] The Abbé Maury, before the revolution, was in possession of eight hundred farms, and has lost sixty

---

1 Jean-Sifferein, Abbé Maury (1746-1817), a writer, monarchist, and defender of the Church. He emigrated to Rome after the National Assembly dissolved in 1791, having already earned many enemies, as much because of his satiric attacks on his opponents as for his early beliefs.

2 John Milton, *Paradise Lost*, II.113-14. Milton is speaking here of the demon Belial: whose "Tongue / Dropt Manna, and could make the worse appear / The better reason."

3 *Hamlet* III.ii.74.

4 To the lantern [Williams's note]. Lamp posts were conventional places for hangings and were on a few occasions actually used to hang opponents of the Revolution. The term "aristocrat" came to designate a person of whatever class who resisted the Revolution, and the phrase "à la lanterne" became a battle cry against perceived enemies. For Williams's reaction to seeing the lamp post opposite La Maison de Ville upon which the first victims were hanged, see Letter X.

5 If I were at the lantern, would you be more enlightened? [Williams's note]

thousand livres a year in consequence of that event. But enough of Mons. l'Abbé, whose picture I have just purchased in a snuff-box. You touch a spring, open the lid of the snuff-box, and the Abbé jumps up, and occasions much surprize and merriment. The joke, however, is grown a little stale in France: but I shall bring the Abbé with me to England, where I flatter myself his sudden appearance will afford some diversion.

A singular but very respectable figure in the National Assembly is a Deputy from Britany, called Le Père Gerard. This venerable old man is a peasant, and his appearance reminds one of those times when Generals were called from the plough to take the command of armies. The dress of Le Père Gerard is made of a coarse woollen cloth, which is worn by the peasants of Britany, and is of such strong texture that a coat often descends from one generation to another. This cloth is called Pinchina; and the King, to whom the old Breton has presented several addresses from the Assembly, calls him, en badinage, Le Père Pinchina.[1] When I saw him, he had on this everlasting coat, and wore worsted stockings gartered above the knees. But, what pleased me most in his appearance, were the long white hairs which hung down his shoulders; an ornament for which you know I have a particular predilection.

The respectable Père Gerard boasts that he is descended from a race of deputies, his great grandfather having been chosen as a deputy to Les Etats Généraux in 1614,[2] the last time the States were held, before that memorable period when they effected the revolution.

At the time when the ladies set the example of Le don patriotique,[3] by offering their jewels, and the members of the National Assembly, in a moment of enthusiasm, took the silver buckles out of their shoes, and laid them on the President's table, the Pere Gerard rose, and said, that he had no such offering to give, his buckles being made of brass, but that his don patriotique should be that of rendering his services to his country unpaid. The old man was

---

1 In pleasantry, Father Pinchina. [Williams's note]
2 Representatives of the three estates first met as "Les Etats Généraux" in April 1302, but were thereafter convened only infrequently. The meeting in 1614, which collapsed into a deadlock of competing interests among the three estates, was the last before the final one held at the outset of the Revolution in 1789.
3 The patriotic donation. [Williams's note]

heard by the Assembly with the applause he merited; and the people, on the day of the Federation, carried him from the Champ de Mars to his own house in triumph on their shoulders. Messieurs Charles and Alexander Lameth, two brothers, and Mons. Rabeau de St. Estienne,[1] are among the first patriots of the National Assembly, and have a very high reputation for talents. The French, who love what they call an équivoque,[2] tell you, que Mons. Rabeau vaut deux d'Mirabeau.[3]

The meetings of the Assembly, though still tumultuous, are much less so than they were at their first commencement. A gentleman, who was present when the motion was made for abolishing monasteries,[4] told me, that the minds of the members were, on that occasion, inflamed to such a height, that it appeared to him very probable, that the debate would end in a massacre. He mentioned a circumstance very characteristic of French vivacity. One of the members was expressing himself in these words, "What is a

---

1 Charles (1757-1832) and Alexandre (1760-1829) Lameth, brothers who had fought in the American War of Independence (along with a third brother Theodore), were both elected to the Estates General in 1789 and were political allies of Barnave. Progressive revolutionaries in 1789 who abandoned the ranks of the nobility to join the Third Estate, they desired a constitutional monarchy and emigrated from France after the monarchy fell. Jean Paul Rabaut de Saint Etienne (1743-93), a Protestant deputy and a monarchist before the ill-fated flight of Louis XVI in June 1791, wrote a history of the Revolution. When the Girondins were purged from the Convention in the Spring of 1793, the Williams family attempted to hide him, but Rabaut was arrested and, later that year, sent to the guillotine.

2 A play upon words. [Williams's note]

3 The play on words can be translated, "One Rabeau is worth two Mirabeaus," or "One Rabeau is worth two half-Rabeaus." The reviewer of the *Letters Written in France* for the *Critical Review* laments: "We are sorry, however, to find our young lady so idle as to have left the translation of the French quotations to some incompetent assistant. If she had attended to it herself she would undoubtedly have explained 'Mons. Rabeau vaut deux de Mi—rabeau,' even by printing it in the manner we have done, for *mi* is an abbreviation of *demi* [half]." See p. 217.

4 One of several measures taken to limit the property and rights of the Catholic Church. Monastic recruitment was suspended on 28 October 1789; Church property was nationalized in November 1789; and monastic vows were outlawed in February 1790.

Monk? A man who has renounced his father, his mother, every tie, every affection that is dear in nature! and for whom?"—before the speaker could finish his sentence, a member from the other end of the hall seized the moment while the orator was drawing his breath, and called out "Pour une puissance étrangère,"[1] to the great horror of le côté noir, for so the clergy are called.[2]

The Democrates place themselves on one side of the hall, and the Aristocrates on the other. The spectators in the galleries take such a part in the debate, as frequently to express their applause by clapping their hands with great violence. An old Marechal[3] of France rose, the day I was at the Assembly, when they were debating on the military pensions, and declared, that in recompense for the services which he had rendered his country, he desired honours and not pay. The Assembly clapped him, and the galleries joined in this mark of approbation. A young Frenchman, who sat next me, whispered to me, "Mons. trouve apparemment que l'argent l'incommode."[4]

The members of the National Assembly are paid three crowns a day for their attendance; while in England a candidate for a seat in parliament often spends many thousand pounds, and, with magnificent generosity, makes a whole county drunk for a week, merely to enjoy the privilege of serving his country without pay.

The qualification requisite for a member of the National Assembly, is that of possessing sufficient property in land or houses to pay taxes to the amount of a marc d'argent, which is the value of four louis.[5] Every hundred of the citizens, who pay taxes to government of three days labour, or three livres, have a right to vote for an elector, whose qualification is that of paying taxes to the amount of ten livres, or ten days labour. The electors of one department meet together in one assembly, and chuse from among their own body the persons who are to direct the administration of that department.

---

1 For a foreign power. [Williams's note]
2 Literally, "the black side," to designate the body of clergy who, dressed predominantly in black, would have been seated together (as the Second Estate) at the opening of the Estates General.
3 Marshall.
4 I suppose that gentleman finds money troublesome. [Williams's note]
5 A gold coin, also known as a *louis d'or*, named after the French monarchs. Napoleon continued the practice, but called the coins "*napoleons*."

Those electors will also chuse in the same manner the deputies sent by that department to the National Assembly. There will therefore be only one intermediate degree between the lowest order of active citizens, and the members of the National Assembly.

I was interrupted by a visitor,[1] who related a little incident, which has interested me so much, that I can write of nothing else at present, and you shall therefore have it warm from my heart. While the National Assembly were deliberating upon the division of property among brothers, a young man of high birth and fortune, who is a member of the Assembly, entered with precipitation, and, mounting the tribune, with great emotion informed the Assembly, that he had just received accounts that his father was dying; that he himself was his eldest son, and had come to conjure the Assembly to pass, without delay, that equitable decree, giving the younger sons an equal share of fortune with the eldest, in order, he said, that his father might have the satisfaction, before he breathed his last, of knowing that all his children were secure of a provision. If you are not affected by this circumstance, you have read it with very different feelings from those with which I have written it: but if, on the contrary, you have fallen in love with this young Frenchman, do not imagine your passion is singular, for I am violently in love with him myself.

LETTER VIII.

YOU have not heard, perhaps, that on the day of the Federation at Paris, the national oath was taken throughout the whole kingdom, at the hour of twelve.

A great number of farmers and peasants walked in the procession at Rouen, bearing in their hands the instruments of their husbandry, decorated with national ribbons. The national guard cut down branches from the trees, and stuck them in their hats; and a French gentleman of my acquaintance, who understands English, and reads Shakespeare, told me, that it seemed like Birnham Wood coming to Dunsinane.[2]

---

1 The French translator suggests that this visitor is a M. de Croy.
2 In Act V of *Macbeth*, Malcolm instructs his troops to carry boughs from the Woods of Birnam to disguise their attack on Macbeth (at Dunsinane) who was secure in his crown until "Great Birnam wood to high Dunsinane hill / Shall come against him" (IV.i.93-94).

The leaders of the French revolution, are men well acquainted with the human heart. They have not trusted merely to the force of reason, but have studied to interest in their cause the most powerful passions of human nature, by the appointment of solemnities perfectly calculated to awaken that general sympathy which is caught from heart to heart with irresistible energy, fills every eye with tears, and throbs in every bosom.

I have heard of a procession, which took place not long ago in one of the districts of Paris, in which five hundred young ladies walked dressed in white, and decorated with cockades of the national ribbon, leading by silken cords a number of prisoners newly released from captivity; and who, with their faces covered by long flowing veils, were conducted to a church, where they returned thanks for their deliverance.

Thus have the leaders of the revolution engaged beauty as one of their auxiliaries, justly concluding, that, to the gallantry and sensibility of Frenchmen, no argument would be found more efficacious than that of a pretty face.

I have just read a private letter from a little town about two leagues from Montauban, called Nègre-Pelisse, where the inhabitants, on the day of the Federation, displayed a liberality of sentiment, which reflects honour, not only on themselves, but on the age in which we live. The national guard of this little town and its environs, were assembled to take the national oath. Half of the inhabitants being Protestants, and the other half Catholics, the Curé[1] and the Protestant Minister ascended together one altar, which had been erected by the citizens, and administered the oath to their respective parishioners at the same moment, after which, Catholics and Protestants joined in singing Te Deum.

Surely religious worship was never performed more truly in the spirit of the Divine author of Christianity, whose great precept is that of universal love! Surely the incense of praise was never more likely to ascend to heaven, than when the Catholics and Protestants of Nègre-Pelisse offered it together!

This amiable community, when their devotions were finished, walked in procession to a spot where fire-works had been prepared; and, it being considered as a mark of honour to light the fire-works, the office was reserved for Mons. le Curé, who, however, insisted on the participation of the Protestant Minister in this

---

1 Parish priest.

distinction; upon which the Minister received a wax taper from the Curé, and with him led the procession. The fire-works represented two trees. One, twisted and distorted, was emblematical of aristocracy, and was soon entirely consumed; when a tall straight plant, figurative of patriotism, appeared to rise from the ashes of the former, and continued to burn with undiminished splendour.

When we look back on the ignorance, the superstition, the barbarous persecutions of Gothic times, is it not something to be thankful for, that we exist at this enlightened period, when such evils are no more; when particular tenets of religious belief are no longer imputed as crimes; when the human mind has made as many important discoveries in morality as in science, and liberality of sentiment is cultivated with as much success as arts and learning; when, in short, (and *you* are not one of those who will suspect that I am not all the while a good Englishwoman) when one can witness an event so sublime as the French revolution?

LETTER IX.

YESTERDAY I received your letter, in which you accuse me of describing with too much enthusiasm the public rejoicings in France, and prophesy that I shall return to my own country a fierce republican. In answer to these accusations, I shall only observe, that it is very difficult, with common sensibility, to avoid sympathizing in general happiness. My love of the French revolution, is the natural result of this sympathy, and therefore my political creed is entirely an affair of the heart; for I have not been so absurd as to consult my head upon matters of which it is so incapable of judging. If I were at Rome, you would not be surprized to hear that I had visited, with the warmest reverence, every spot where any relics of her ancient grandeur could be traced; that I had flown to the capitol, that I had kissed the earth on which the Roman senate sat in council: And can you then expect me to have seen the Federation at the Champ de Mars, and the National Assembly of France, with indifference? Before you insist that I ought to have done so, point out to me, in the page of Roman history, a spectacle more solemn, more affecting, than the Champ de Mars exhibited, or more magnanimous, more noble efforts in the cause of liberty than have been made by the National Assembly. Whether the new form of government, establishing in France, be more or less perfect than our own,

"Who shall decide, when doctors disagree,
And soundest casuists doubt, like you and me?"[1]

I fancy we had better leave the determination of this question in the hands of posterity. In the mean time, I wish that some of our political critics would speak with less contempt, than they are apt to do, of the new constitution of France, and no longer repeat after one another the trite remark, that the French have gone too far, because they have gone farther than ourselves; as if it were not possible that that degree of influence which is perfectly safe in the hand of the executive part of our government, might be dangerous, at this crisis, to the liberty of France. But be this as it may, it appears evident that the temple of Freedom which they are erecting, even if imperfect in some of its proportions, must be preferable to the old gloomy Gothic fabric which they have laid in ruins. And therefore, when I hear my good countrymen, who guard their own rights with such unremitting vigilance, and who would rather part with life than liberty, speak with contempt of the French for having imbibed the noble lesson which England has taught, I cannot but suspect that some mean jealousy lurks beneath the ungenerous censure. I cannot but suspect, that, while the fair and honourable traders of our commercial country act with the most liberal spirit in their ordinary dealings with other nations, they wish to make a monopoly of liberty, and are angry that France should claim a share of that precious property;[2] by which, however, she may surely be enriched, without our being impoverished. The French, on the contrary, seem to have imbibed, with the principles of liberty, the strongest sentiments of respect and friendship towards that people, whom they gratefully acknowledge to have been their masters in this science. They are, to use their own phrase, "devenus fous des Anglois,"[3] and fondly imagine that the applause they have received from a society of philosophers in our country, is the general voice of the nation.

Whether the new constitution be composed of durable materials or not, I leave to politicians to determine; but it requires no

---

1 The opening lines of Pope's "Epistle III. To Allen Lord Bathurst" (1733).
2 At this point the French translator remarks, "Here, in few words, is a complete response to all the sophisms of Mr. Burke."
3 Become madly fond of the English. [Williams's note]

extraordinary sagacity to pronounce, that the French will hence-forth be free. The love of liberty has pervaded all ranks of the people, who, if its blessings must be purchased with blood, will not shrink from paying the price:

> "While ev'n the peasant boasts his rights to scan,
> And learns to venerate himself as man."[1]

The enthusiastic spirit of liberty displays itself, not merely on the days of solemn ceremonies—occupies not only every serious deliberation—but is mingled with the gaiety of social enjoyment. When they converse, liberty is the theme of discourse; when they dance, the figure of the cotillon is adapted to a national tune; and when they sing, it is but to repeat a vow of fidelity to the constitution, at which all who are present instantly join in chorus, and sportively lift up their hands in confirmation of this favourite sentiment.

In every street, you see children performing the military exercise, and carrying banners made of paper of the national colours, wearing grenadiers caps of the same composition, and armed, though not like Jack the Giant-killer, with swords of sharpness.

Upon the whole, liberty appears in France adorned with the freshness of youth, and is loved with the ardour of passion. In England she is seen in her matron state, and, like other ladies at that period, is beheld with sober veneration.

With respect to myself, I must acknowledge, that, in my admiration of the revolution in France, I blend the feelings of private friendship with my sympathy in public blessings; since the old constitution is connected in my mind with the image of a friend confined in the gloomy recesses of a dungeon, and pining in hopeless captivity; while, with the new constitution, I unite the soothing idea of his return to prosperity, honours, and happiness.

This person is Mons. du F—,[2] whose lady I am come to France to visit. They are friends with whom I wept in the day of their

---

1 Another couplet culled from Oliver Goldsmith's *The Traveller, or A Prospect of Society* (lines 333-34).

2 Augustin François Thomas du Fossé (1750-1833), whose sufferings under the old regime Williams recounts in Letters XVI-XXII. Williams first met Monique du Fossé in England in 1785 or 1786 through the French lessons she gave in order to support herself and her daughter while in exile.

adversity, and with whom in their prosperity I have hastened to rejoice. Their history is most affecting; and, when I leave the hurry of Paris, to accompany them to their Chateau in Normandy, I will make you acquainted with incidents as pathetic as romance itself can furnish.   Adieu!

LETTER X.

WE have been driving at a furious rate, for several days past, through the city of Paris, which I think bears the same resemblance to London (if you will allow me the indulgence of a simile) that the grand natural objects in a rude and barren country bear to the tame but regular beauties of a scene rich with cultivation. The streets of Paris are narrow, dark, and dirty; but we are repaid for this by noble edifices, which powerfully interest the attention. The streets of London are broad, airy, light, and elegant; but I need not tell you that they lead scarcely to any edifices at which foreigners do not look with contempt. London has, therefore, most of the beautiful, and Paris of the sublime, according to Mr. Burke's definition of these qualities;[1] for I assure you a sensation of terror is not wanting to the sublimity of Paris, while the coachman drives through the streets with the impetuosity of a Frenchman, and one expects every step the horses take will be fatal to the foot-passengers, who are heard exclaiming, "Que les rues de Paris sont aristocrates."[2] By the way, *aristocracie*, and *à la nation*, are become cant terms, which, as

---

1 Published in 1757, Edmund Burke's *A Philosophical Enquiry into the Origin of Our Ideas of the Sublime and Beautiful* helped to make his reputation as a literary critic and man of letters. For Burke, the comforting realm of the beautiful is feminine, founded in pleasure, and associated with the comparatively small, the light, the polished, and the delicate, whereas the disconcerting realm of the sublime is masculine, founded in pain, and associated with the great, the terrible, the obscure, the dark, and the powerful.

   At this point in the French version of Williams's *Letters*, the translator makes a sharp contrast between Burke's *Enquiry* and his anti-Revolutionary *Reflections*: written when he was twenty-five, the essay on the sublime "earned him a reputation far different from what he has just acquired through the work that dishonors his white hair."

2 That the streets of Paris are aristocrates. [Williams's note]

Sterne said of *tant pis*, and *tant mieux*,[1] may now be considered as two of the great hinges in French conversation. Every thing tiresome or unpleasant, "c'est une aristocracie!" and every thing charming and agreeable is "à la nation."

I have seen all the fine buildings at Paris, and fancy I should have admired the façade of the Louvre, the beautiful new church of St. Genevieve, and some other edifices, even if I had not been told previously, by a connoisseur in these matters, the precise degree of admiration which it was proper to bestow on every public building in Paris: but, having received such minute instructions on this subject, I can form but an imperfect notion of my own taste for architecture.

At the request of Madame Brulart, Mons. de Chartres sent orders for our admission to the Palais Royal, which is not at present shewn to the public. Of the collection of pictures I am incapable of saying any thing, and enough has been already said by those who understand its merits. Fine painting gives me considerable pleasure, but has not the power of calling forth my sensibility like fine poetry; and I am willing to believe that the art I love is the most perfect of the two; and that it would have been impossible for the pencil of Raphael to convey all those ideas to the mind, and excite all those emotions in the heart, which are awakened by the pen of Shakespeare.

I confess, the only picture in Paris which has cost me any tears, is that of La Valliere,[2] in the convent of the Carmelites. She is represented in the habit of a Carmelite; all the former ornaments of her person lie scattered at her feet; and her eyes are cast up to Heaven with a look of the deepest anguish. While I gazed at her picture, I lamented that sensibility which led into the most fatal errors a mind that seems to have been formed for virtue, and

1 A second reference to Sterne's *Sentimental Journey Through France and Italy*, in which the narrator, an English tourist named Yorick, advises "that *tant pis* [so much the worse] and *tant mieux* [so much the better] being two of the great hinges in French conversation, a stranger would do well to set himself right in the use of them, before he gets to Paris" (I, 93).
2 Louise-Françoise de La Baume le Blanc, duchesse de Vallière (1644-1710), was the mistress of Louis XIV, until the King cast her aside for the more worldly and ambitious Marquise de Montespan. La Vallière retreated to a Carmelite convent in Paris, where she lived under a series of self-imposed penances until her death thirty-six years later.

which, even in the bosom of pleasure, bewailed its own weakness. How can one forbear regretting, that the capricious inconstant monarch, to whom she gave her heart, should have inspired a passion of which he was so unworthy; a passion which appears to have been wholly unmixed with interest, vanity, or ambition? And how can one avoid pitying the desolate penitent, who, for so many years, in the dismal gloom of a convent, deplored her errors, and felt at once the bitterness of remorse, and the agony of disappointed love? while, probably,

"In every hymn she seem'd his voice to hear,
And dropt with every bead, too soft a tear!"[1]

If the figure of this beautiful Carmelite had not come across my imagination, I should have told you sooner, that the Palais Royal is a square, of which the Duc de Orleans's palace forms one side. You walk under piazzas round this square, which is surrounded with coffee-houses, and shops displaying a variety of ribbons, trinkets, and caricature prints, which are now as common at Paris as at London. The walks under the piazzas are crouded with people: and in the upper part of the square, tents are placed, where coffee, lemonade, ices, &c. are sold. Nothing is heard but the voice of mirth; nothing is seen but chearful faces; and I have no doubt that the Palais Royal is, upon the whole, one of the merriest scenes under the sun. Indeed, what is most striking to a stranger at Paris, is that general appearance of gaiety, which it is easy to perceive is not assumed for the moment, but is the habit of the mind, and which is, therefore, so exhilarating to a spectator of any benevolence. It is this which gives such a charm to every public place and walk in

---

1 Paraphrased from a couplet written in the first person by Eloisa in Alexander Pope's *Eloisa to Abelard* (1717; lines 269-70). Pierre Abelard was a twelfth-century French scholar who fell in love with his pupil Héloïse. After Héloïse became pregnant, the two married secretly; when the marriage became known, Héloïse's uncle, a prominent cleric, had Abelard castrated. As LaVallière was later to do, Héloïse and Abelard sought refuge in monastic life, but they maintained a lifelong correspondence that brought them fame as tragic lovers. Jean-Jacques Rousseau's extremely popular *Julie, ou la Nouvelle Héloïse* (1761) intensified the mythology of Héloïse and Abelard by creating a modern and secular version of their romantic history.

Paris. Kensington Gardens can boast as fine verdure, as majestic trees, as noble walks, and perhaps more beautiful women than the gardens of the Tuileries; but we shall look in vain for that sprightly animation, that everlasting chearfulness, which render the Tuileries so enchanting.

We have just returned from the Hôpital des Invalides,[1] a noble building, adorned with fine paintings which record the history of some celebrated saints, whose exploits were recounted with incredible rapidity by the man who conducted us through the chapels, and who seemed to think that nothing could be more absurd than our curiosity, after having heard these stories from his lips, to observe how they were told by the painters.

As we passed through the church, we saw several old soldiers kneeling at the confessionals, with that solemn devotion which seemed undisturbed by our intrusion, and fixed upon "the things that are above."

A few days before the taking of the Bastille, a croud of the Parisians assembled at the Hôpital des Invalides, and demanded arms of the old soldiers; who answered, that they were the friends of their fellow citizens, but durst not deliver up their arms without the appearance of a contest; and therefore desired that the people would assemble before the gates in greater numbers the next day, when, after firing a little powder upon them, they would throw down their arms. The people accordingly returned the following day; and the invalids, after a faint shew of resistance, threw down their arms, which the citizens took up, embraced the old men, and then departed.

We stopped yesterday at La Maison de Ville,[2] and went into a large apartment where the mayor and corporation assemble. The walls are hung round with pictures of Kings and Dukes, which I looked at with much less respect than at the chair on which Mons.

---

1 Louis XIV founded The Hôpital or Hôtel des Invalides west of the Faubourg Saint-Germain on the Left Bank of Paris to shelter and aid 7,000 aged or invalid veterans (1671-76). Williams passes through the church of Saint-Louis, whose gold-plated dome towers above the other buildings in the large complex, and which now houses the tomb of Napoleon.

2 La Maison de Ville, or Hôtel de Ville, was the City Hall of Paris, located on the Right Bank and situated at what was then called La Place de Grève. It was the center of popular uprising during the French Revolution, as it was later in 1830, 1848, 1871, and 1944.

Bailly sits. If his pictures should ever be placed in this apartment, I fancy that, in the estimation of posterity, it will obtain precedency over all the Princes in the collection.

As we came out of La Maison de Ville, we were shewn, immediately opposite, the far-famed lanterne,[1] at which, for want of a gallows, the first victims of popular fury were sacrificed. I own that the sight of La Lanterne chilled the blood within my veins. At that moment, for the first time, I lamented the revolution; and, forgetting the imprudence, or the guilt, of those unfortunate men, could only reflect with horror on the dreadful expiation they had made. I painted in my imagination the agonies of their families and friends, nor could I for a considerable time chase these gloomy images from my thoughts.

It is for ever to be regretted, that so dark a shade of ferocious revenge was thrown across the glories of the revolution. But, alas! where do the records of history point out a revolution unstained by some actions of barbarity? When do the passions of human nature rise to that pitch which produces great events, without wandering into some irregularities? If the French revolution should cost no farther bloodshed, it must be allowed, notwithstanding a few shocking instances of public vengeance, that the liberty of twenty-four millions of people will have been purchased at a far cheaper rate than could ever have been expected from the former experience of the world.

LETTER XI.

WE are just returned from Versailles,[2] where I could not help fancying I saw, in the back ground of that magnificent abode of a despot, the gloomy dungeons of the Bastille, which still haunt my imagination, and prevented my being much dazzled by the splendour of this superb palace.

We were shewn the passages through which the Queen escaped

---

1 The lamp-iron. [Williams's note]
2 Built as royal residence for Louis XIV, chiefly by Louis Le Vau and Jules Hardouin-Mansart during the last half of the 17th century, Versailles was the largest and most opulent of palaces, virtually a city in itself, and came to signify the splendor and extravagance of the *ancien régime*. It stands twenty-two kilometers southwest of Paris.

from her own apartment to the King's, on the memorable night when the *Poissardes* visited Versailles,[1] and also the balcony at which she stood with the Dauphin in her arms, when, after having remained a few hours concealed in some secret recess of the palace, it was thought proper to comply with the desire of the croud, who repeatedly demanded her presence. I could not help moralizing a little, on being told that the apartment to which this balcony belongs, is the very room in which Louis the Fourteenth died; little suspecting what a scene would, in the course of a few years, be acted on that spot.

All the bread which could be procured in the town of Versailles, was distributed among the *Poissardes*; who, with savage ferocity, held up their morsels of bread on their bloody pikes, towards the balcony where the Queen stood, crying, in a tone of defiance, "Nous avons du pain!"[2]

During the whole of the journey from Versailles to Paris, the Queen held the Dauphin in her arms, who had been previously taught to put his infant hands together, and attempt to soften the enraged multitude by repeating, "Grâce pour maman!"[3]

Mons. de la Fayette prevented the whole Gardes du Corps from being massacred at Versailles, by calling to the incensed people, "Le Roi vous demande grâce pour ses Gardes du Corps."[4] The voice of Mons. de la Fayette was listened to, and obeyed. The Gardes du Corps were spared; with whom, before they set out for Paris, the

---

1 The *Poissardes*, fishwives and market women, would on ceremonial occasions offer their greetings and pledge their loyalty to the King and Queen at Versailles. However, on the night of 5 October 1789, a group of approximately 7,000 "*Poissardes,*" after having gathered at the Hôtel de Ville, marched on Versailles joined by others, to demand bread. The next morning, a few Parisians from the still-assembled crowd made their way into the precincts of the palace and were fired upon by royal bodyguards, enraging the crowd, which stormed the palace, killed two guardsmen, and almost reached the queen's apartments. Lafayette, who had arrived from Paris to attempt to restore order, placed the royal family under his personal protection. When the King finally acceded to the crowd's demand that he be brought to Paris, Lafayette escorted the royal family, accompanied by a procession estimated at 60,000.
2 We now have bread. [Williams's note]
3 Spare mama! [Williams's note]
4 The King begs of you to spare his body-guards. [Williams's note]

people exchanged clothes, giving them also national cockades; and, as a farther protection from danger, part of the croud mounted on the horses of the Gardes du Corps, each man taking an officer behind him. Before the King came out of La Maison de Ville, Mons. de la Fayette appeared, and told the multitude, who had preserved an indignant silence the whole way from Versailles to Paris, that the King had expressed sentiments of the strongest affection for his people, and had accepted the national cockade; and that he (Mons. de la Fayette) hoped, when his Majesty came out of la Maison de Ville, they would testify their gratitude. In a few minutes the King appeared, and was received with the loudest acclamations.

When the Queen was lately asked to give her deposition on the attempt which, it is said, was made to assassinate her, by the *Poissardes* at Versailles, she answered, with great prudence,[1] "Jai tout vu, tout entendu, et tout oublié!"[2]

The King is now extremely popular, and the people sing in the streets to the old tune of "Vive Henri quatre! &c." "Vive Louis seize!"[3]

The Queen is, I am told, much altered lately in her appearance, but she is still a fine woman. Madame is a beautiful girl;[4] and the Dauphin, who is about seven years of age, is the idol of the people.[5] They expect that he will be educated in the principles of the new constitution, and will be taught to consider himself less a king than a citizen.[6] He appears to be a sweet engaging child, and I have just heard one of his sayings repeated. He has a collection of animals, which he feeds with his own hand. A few days ago, an

---

1 The French translator here questions the aptness of the word "prudence," but concludes that "it's a foreigner who is writing this."

2 I saw every thing, heard every thing, and have forgot every thing. [Williams's note]

3 Long live Henry the Fourth. Long live Lewis the Sixteenth. [Williams's note]

4 The firstborn of Louis XVI and Marie-Antoinette's children, Marie-Therese Charlotte (1778-1851) was dubbed "Madame Royale" in her infancy. The only member of the royal family to have survived the Revolution, she later married Louis-Antoine de Bourbon duc D'Angoulême, son of France's last Bourbon king, Charles X.

5 The French translator comments that "idol" is an inappropriate, old-regime word, for "the French have broken their idols."

6 Another wry comment from the translator: "But have they changed a single one of the [Dauphin's] old tutors?"

ungrateful rabbit, who was his first favourite, bit his finger when he was giving him food. The Prince, while smarting with the pain, called out to his petit lapin, "Tu es Aristocrate."[1] One of the attendants enquired, "Eh! Monseigneur, qu'est-ce que c'est qu'un Aristocrate." "Ce sont ceux," answered the Prince, "qui font de la peine à Papa."

The King lately called the Queen, en badinage, Madame Capet; to which she retorted very readily, by giving his Majesty the appellation of "Monsieur *Capot*."[2]

When Les gardes Françoises laid down their arms at Versailles, their officers endeavoured to persuade them to take them up. An officer of my acquaintance told me, that he said to his soldiers, "Mes enfans, vous allez donc me quitter, vous ne m'aimez plus?" "Mon officier," they answered, "nous vous aimons tous, si il s'agit d'aller contre nos ennemis, nous sommes tous prêts à vous suivre, mais nous ne tirerons jamais contre nos compatriotes."[3] Since that period, whenever any of les Gardes Françoises appear, they are followed by the acclamations of the people, and "Vive les Gardes Françoises!"[4] resounds from every quarter.

While we were sitting, after dinner, at the inn at Versailles, the door was suddenly opened, and a Franciscan friar entered the room. He had so strong a resemblance to Sterne's monk,[5] that I am persuaded he must be a descendant of the same family. We could not, like Sterne, bestow immortality; but we gave some alms: and the venerable old monk, after thanking us with affecting simplicity, added, spreading out his hands with a slow and solemn movement, "Que la paix soit avec vous,"[6] and then departed. I have been frequently put in mind of Sterne since my

---

1 Little rabbit, Thou art an Aristocrate.—And pray, my Lord, what is an Aristocrate?—Those who make my papa uneasy. [Williams's note]

2 Capot is the French term at picquet, when the game is lost. [Williams's note]

3 My friends, you are going then to forsake me; I possess none of your affection.—Captain, they answered, we all love you; and, if you will lead us against our enemies, we are all ready to follow you: but we will never fire at our fellow citizens. [Williams's note]

4 Long live the French guards. [Williams's note]

5 A Franciscan monk, who appears at the opening of Sterne's *A Sentimental Journey* asking alms from the narrator Yorick, who finds several amusing ways to rationalize his decision to deny the Monk's request.

6 Peace be with you. [Williams's note]

arrival in France; and the first post-boy I saw in jack-boots, appeared to me a very classical figure, by recalling the idea of La Fleur mounted on his bidet.[1]

LETTER XII.

WE have been at all the Theatres, and I am charmed with the comic actors. The tragic performers afforded me much less pleasure. Before we can admire Madame Vestris, the first tragic actress of Paris, we must have lost the impression (a thing impossible) of Mrs. Siddons's performance; who, instead of "tearing a passion to rags,"[2] like Madame Vestris, only tears the hearts of the audience with sympathy.

Most of the pieces we have seen at the French theatres have been little comedies relative to the circumstances of the times, and, on that account, preferred, in this moment of enthusiasm, to all the wit of Moliere. These little pieces might perhaps read coldly enough in your study, but have a most charming effect with an accompany-ment of applause from some hundreds of the national guards, the real actors in the scenes represented. Between the acts national songs are played, in which the whole audience join in chorus. There is one air, in particular, which is so universal a favourite, that it is called "Le Carrillon National:"[3] the burden of the song is "Ça ira."[4] It is sung not only at every theatre, and in every street of Paris, but in every town and village of France, by man, woman, and child. "Ça ira" is every where the signal of pleasure, the beloved sound which

---

1 In Sterne's *A Sentimental Journey*, La Fleur is a local Frenchman hired as a servant by Yorick. Williams is recalling a comic episode in which the jack-booted La Fleur is unable to get his "bidet," or post-horse, to pass by a dead ass. Eventually, the bidet throws the hapless, exasperated La Fleur and runs away, providing the ever-observant Yorick with a fit occasion to anatomize the various exclamations available in the French language (I, 117-22).

2 Sarah Siddons (1755-1831; née Kemble), one of the greatest British tragic actresses. The passage is from *Hamlet* III.ii.9.

3 The National anthem. In 1790 France, like most other countries, had no official national anthem, and "Ça ira" gained the informal status of a national song. "La Marseillaise," composed in April 1792 by Rouget de Lisle, quickly became the most popular marching song of the Revolution-ary Armies and was later adopted as the French anthem.

4 It will go on. [Williams's note]

animates every bosom with delight, and of which every ear is enamoured. And I have heard the most serious political conversations end by a sportive assurance, in allusion to this song, que "Ça ira!"

Giornowiche, the celebrated player on the violin, who was so much the fashion last winter at London, I am told, sometimes amused himself at Paris, by getting up into one of the trees of the Palais Royal, after it was dark, and calling forth tones from his violin, fit to "take the prison'd soul, and lap it in Elysium."[1] He has frequently detained some thousands of people half the night in the Palais Royal, who, before they discovered the performer, used to call out in rapture, "Bravo, bravo; c'est mieux que Giornowiche."[2]

I am just returned from seeing the Gobelin tapestry,[3] which appears the work of magic. It gave me pleasure to see two pictures of Henry the Fourth. In one, he is placed at supper with the miller's family; and in the other, he is embracing Sully,[4] who is brought forward on a couch, after having been wounded in battle. Nothing has afforded me more delight, since I came to France, than the honours which are paid to my favourite hero, Henry the Fourth, whom I prefer to all the Alexanders and Frederics that ever existed. They may be terribly sublime, if you will, and have great claims to my admiration; but as for my love, all that portion of it which I bestow on heroes, is already in Henry's possession.

Little statues of Henry the Fourth and Sully are very common. Sully is represented kneeling at the feet of this amiable Prince, who holds out his hand to him; and on the base of the statue, are written the words which Sully records in his Memoirs: "Mais levez vous, levez vous donc, Sully, on croiroit que je vous pardonne."[5]

While the statue of Henry the Fourth, on the Pont-Neuf, is illuminated and decorated with national ribbon, that of Louis the

---

1 Milton, *Comus*, lines 256–57.
2 This is better than Giornowiche. [Williams's note]
3 The Manufacture Nationale Des Gobelins was established in Paris in 1663 as a royal tapestry works to provide tapestries for the royal residences. By the time of the Revolution, the weavers were set to copying oil paintings by artists of the day.
4 Maximilien de Béthune, duc de Sully (1560–1641), a Protestant, was a devoted soldier and minister to Henry IV. In his role as Finance Minister, he restored financial equilibrium during Henry's reign.
5 But rise, pray rise, Sully; they will believe I am forgiving you. [Williams's note]

Fourteenth, in the Place Victoire, is stripped of its former ostentatious ornaments;[1] the nations, which were represented enchained at his feet, having been removed since the revolution. The figure of Fame is, however, still left hovering behind the statue of the King, with a crown of laurel in her hand, which, it is generally supposed, she is going to place upon his head. But I have heard of a French wit, who enquired whether it was really her intention to place the laurel on his Majesty's head, or whether she had just taken it off.

In our ride this morning, we stopped at the Place Royale, where I was diverted by reading, on the front of a little shop under the piazzas, these words: "Robelin, ecrivain.—Mémoires et lettres écrites à juste prix, à la nation."[2] I am told, that Mons. Robelin is in very flourishing business; and perhaps I might have had recourse to him for assistance in my correspondence with you, if I did not leave Paris to-morrow. You shall hear from me from Rouen.

LETTER XIII.

WE had a most agreeable journey from Paris to Rouen, travelling a hundred miles along the borders of the Seine, through a beautiful country, richly wooded, and finely diversified by hill and valley. We passed several magnificent chateaus, and saw many a spire belonging to Gothic edifices, which, it would seem, were built of such lasting materials, with the moral purpose of leading the mind to reflect on the comparatively short duration of human life. Frequently an old venerable cross, placed at the side of the road by the piety of remote ages, and never passed by Roman Catholics without some mark of respect, throws a kind of religious sanctity over the landscape.

We stopped to look at the immense machine which conveys water to Versailles and Marly. The water is raised, by means of this machine, sixty feet, and is carried the distance of five hundred. I never heard a sound which filled my mind with more horror than the noise occasioned by the movements of this tremendous machine; while, at the same time, the vast chasms, where the water

---

1 Known as the "Sun King," Louis XIV reigned in France from 1643 to 1715 and epitomized the monarch as absolute ruler.
2 Writer.—Memoirs and letters written at a moderate price, for the Nation. [Williams's note]

foams with angry violence, make the brain giddy, and I was glad to leave these images of terror.

Part of our journey was performed by moon–light, which slept most sweetly upon the bank,[1] and spread over the landscape those softened graces which I will not attempt to describe, lest my pen should stray into rhyme.

We passed the chateau of Rosni, a noble domain given to Sully by Henry the Fourth; a testimony of that friendship which reflects equal honour on the King and the Minister.

About three leagues from Rouen stands a convent, of which Abelard was for some time the superior. It is still inhabited by a few monks, and is called Le Couvent de deux Amans.[2] Had it been the monastery of the Paraclete, the residence of Eloisa, I should have hastened to visit the spot,

"Where, o'er the twilight groves and dusky caves,
Long sounding isles, and intermingled graves,
Black Melancholy sits, and round her throws
A death–like silence, and a dread repose;
Her gloomy presence saddens all the scene,
Shades ev'ry flow'r, and darkens ev'ry green,
Deepens the murmur of the falling floods,
And breathes a browner horror on the woods."[3]

If it were not very difficult to be angry with such a poet as Pope, particularly after having just transcribed these exquisite lines, I should be so when I recollect how clearly Mr. Berington[4] shows, in his History of Abelard and Eloisa, the cruel injustice done by Pope to the sentiments of Eloisa, who is too often made to speak a very different language in the poem, from that of her genuine letters.

On our way to Rouen we slept at Gallon, a town about five leagues distant. Our inn was close to the castle, which formerly belonged to the Archbishop of Rouen, and which is now the prop-

---

1 Paraphrase of Shakespeare, *The Merchant of Venice*: "How sweet the moon-light sleeps upon this bank!" (V.i.54).
2 The Convent of Two Lovers.
3 Pope, *Eloisa to Abelard*, lines 163-70.
4 Joseph Berington (1746-1827), a liberal English Catholic priest who was trained in France, wrote *The History of the Lives of Abeillard and Heloisa* (1787).

erty of the nation. The castle is a venerable gothic building, with a fine orangery, and parks which extend several leagues. The Archbishop, who is the Cardinal de la Rochefoucault,[1] brother to that distinguished patriot the ci-devant Duc de la Rochefoucault, has lost a very considerable revenue since the revolution. He had an immense train of servants, whom it is said he dismissed, upon the diminution of his income, with all possible gentleness, giving horses to one, a carriage to another, and endeavouring to bestow on all some little alleviation of the pain they felt at quitting so good a master. It is impossible not to regret that the property of the Cardinal de la Rochefoucault is diminished, by whom it was only employed in dispensing happiness.

After visiting the castle, I returned somewhat in mournful mood to the inn, where there was nothing calculated to convey one chearful idea. The ceiling of our apartment was crossed with old bare beams; the tapestry, with which the room was hung, displayed, like the dress of Otway's old woman, "variety of wretchedness;"[2] the canopied beds were of coarse dirty stuff; two pictures, in tawdry gilt frames, slandered the sweet countenances of the Dauphin and Madame; and the floor was paved with brick. In short, one can scarcely imagine a scene more remote from England, in accommodation and comfort, than the country inns of France: yet, in this habitation, where an Englishman would have been inclined to hang himself, was my rest disturbed half the night by the merry songs which were sung in an adjoining apartment, as gloomy as my own. But those local circumstances, which affect English nerves, never disturb the peace of that happy people, by whom, whether engaged in taking the Bastille, or sitting with their friends after supper, tout se fait en chantant.[3]

---

1 Dominique de La Rochefoucauld, comte de Saint-Elpis (1713-1800), a member of the National Assembly, who argued against new laws regarding the clergy and Church, emigrated to Germany after the fall of the monarchy. His "patriot" brother was François-Alexandre-Frédéric, duc de La Rochefoucauld-Liancourt (1747-1827), who served on the Estates-General and the National Assembly. A sympathizer of Louis XVI, he emigrated to England in 1792 until 1799, when he returned to France.

2 A disturbing figure in Thomas Otway's (1652-85), *The Orphan: or, the Unhappy-Marriage*, as described by Chamont, a young soldier of fortune, who sees her in a prophetic dream (II.i.244-54): "her lower weeds were all o'er coarsely patched / With diff'rent colored rags, black, red, white, yellow, / And seemed to speak variety of wretchedness" (II.i.252-54).

3 Every thing is done singing. [Williams's note]

LETTER XIV.

ROUEN is one of the largest and most commercial towns of France. It is situated on the banks of the Seine, has a fine quay, and a singular bridge, of barges placed close together, with planks fixed upon them: the bridge rises and sinks with the tide, and opens for vessels to pass.

The streets of Rouen are so narrow, dark, and frightful, that, to borrow an expression from Madame Sévigné,[1] "elles abusent de la permission qu'ont les rues Françoises d'être laides."[2] There are many figures of Saints to be seen from these ugly streets, placed in little niches in the walls. The Virgin Mary is seated in one of these niches, with the infant in her arms; and in the neighbourhood is St. Anne, who has the credit of having taught the Virgin to read. Every night the general darkness of the town is a little dispelled by the lamps which the people place in the niches, "pour éclairer les Saints."[3]

Rouen is surrounded by fine boulevards, that form very beautiful walks. On the top of the hill of Ste Catharine, which overlooks the town, are the ruins of a fort called St. Michel, from which Henry the Fourth besieged Rouen. I love to be put in mind of Henry the Fourth, and am therefore very well pleased, that whenever I go to walk, I can fix my eyes on the hill of Ste Catharine.

I always feel a little ashamed of my country, when I pass the spot where the Maid of Orleans[4] was executed, and on which her statue stands, a monument of our disgrace. The ashes of her persecutor, John Duke of Bedford, repose at no great distance, within a

---

1 Marie de Rabutin-Chantal, Marquise de Sévigné (1626-96), whose fame as an author was based on her letters, which revolutionalized the epistolary genre.
2 "They abuse the permission the French streets have of being ugly." [Williams's note]
3 "To light the Saints." [Williams's note]
4 Jeanne d'Arc or Joan of Arc (1412-31), French peasant girl who, at the age of seventeen, led the French army to a major victory over the English at the Siege of Orléans (1429). This battle marked a turning point in the English war against France (another episode of the Hundred Years' War), which was being led by John Plantagenet, Duke of Bedford (1389-1435), brother of Henry V and an able military strategist. Joan was tried and executed as a heretic by the English in May 1431.

tomb of black marble, in the cathedral, which was built by the English. One cannot feel much respect for the judgment of our ancestors, in chusing, of all places under the sun, the cathedral of Rouen for the tomb of him whose name is transmitted to us with the epithet of the *good* Duke of Bedford: for you have scarcely left the cathedral, before the statue of Jean d'Arc stares you in the face, and seems to cast a most formidable shade over the *good* Duke's virtues.

The cathedral is a very magnificent edifice, and the great bell is ten feet high, and weighs thirty-six thousand pounds. But in France it is not what is *antient*, but what is *modern*, that most powerfully engages attention. Nothing in this fine old cathedral interested me so much as the consecrated banner, which, since the Federation, has been placed over the altar, and on which is inscribed, "Vivons libres, ou mourir!"[1] I hope every Frenchman, who enters the cathedral of Rouen, while he reads the inscription on this consecrated banner, repeats from the bottom of his soul, "Vivons libres ou mourir!"[2] But the French will, I trust, escape the horrors of civil war, notwithstanding the gloomy forebodings of the enemies of the new constitution.

A people just delivered from the yoke of oppression, will surely have little inclination to resume their shackles; to rebuild the dungeons they have so lately demolished; to close again those gloomy monastic gates which are now thrown open; to exchange their new courts of judicature, founded on the basis of justice and humanity, for the caprice of power, and the dark iniquity of lettres de cachet;[3] to quench the fair star of liberty, which has arisen on their hemisphere, and suffer themselves to be once more guided by the meteor of despotism.

A very considerable number, even among the nobility of France, have had the virtue to support the cause of freedom; and,

---

1 Let us live free, or die! [Williams's note]
2 Let us live free, or die! [Williams's note]
3 Sealed letters signed by the King that could relegate someone to prison for an unspecified time. Such letters were often abused by those in power, and they thus came to symbolize the despotism of the *ancien régime* and were abolished during the Revolution by the Constituent Assembly in March 1790. Williams dramatically illustrates just such an abuse in the Du Fossé story below.

forgetting the little considerations of vanity, which have some importance in the ordinary course of human affairs, but which are lost and annihilated when the mind is animated by any great sentiment, they have chosen to become the benefactors rather than the oppressors of their country; the citizens of a free state, instead of the slaves of a despotic monarch. They will no longer bear arms to gratify the ambition, or the caprice of a minister; they will no longer exert that impetuous and gallant spirit, for which they have ever been distinguished, in any cause unworthy of its efforts. The fire of valour, which they have too often employed for the purposes of destruction, will henceforth be directed to more generous ends. They will chuse another path to renown. Instead of attempting to take the citadel of glory by storm, they will prefer the fame of an honourable defence, and, renouncing the sanguinary laurel, strive, with more exalted enthusiasm, to obtain the civic wreath. Yes, the French nation will inviolably guard, will transmit to posterity the sacred rights of freedom. Future ages will celebrate, with grateful commemoration, the fourteenth of July; and strangers, when they visit France, will hasten with impatience to the Champ de Mars, filled with that enthusiasm which is awakened by the view of a place where any great scene has been acted. I think I hear them exclaim, "Here the Federation was held! here an assembled nation devoted themselves to freedom!" I fancy I see them pointing out the spot on which the altar of the country stood. I see them eagerly searching for the place where they have heard it recorded, that the National Assembly were seated! I think of these things, and then repeat to myself with transport, "*I* was a spectator of the Federation!"

But these meditations have led me to travel through the space of so many centuries, that it is really difficult to get back again to the present times. Did you expect that I should ever dip my pen in politics, who used to take so small an interest in public affairs, that I recollect a gentleman of my acquaintance surprized me not a little, by informing me of the war between the Turks and the Russians,[1] at a time when all the people of Europe, except myself, had been two years in possession of this intelligence?

---

1 The Russo-Turkish Wars, which had lasted intermittently since the seventeenth century, heated up again in 1787-91 and were not to end until 1878.

If, however, my love of the French revolution requires an apology, you shall receive one in a very short time; for I am going to Mons. du F——'s chateau, and will send you from thence the history of his misfortunes. They were the inflictions of tyranny, and you will rejoice with me that tyranny is no more.

Before I close my letter, I shall mention a singular privilege of the church of Rouen, which is the power of setting free a murderer every year on the day of Ascension. It seems that in the time of King Dagobert, who reigned in the sixth century, a horrible and unrelenting dragon desolated the country, sparing neither man nor beast. St. Romain, who was then Bishop of Rouen, asked for two criminals to assist him in an enterprize he had the courage to meditate against the dragon; and with these aides de camp he sallied forth, killed the monster, and delivered the country. In consequence of this miracle, Dagobert gave the successors of St. Romain the privilege of setting a murderer free every year on Ascension-day. The bones of St. Romain are carried by the criminal in a gilt box through the streets: the figure of a hideous animal representing the dragon, though it is suspected of slandering his countenance, accompanies these venerable bones, and has generally a young living wolf placed in its maw, except when it is jour maigre,[1] and then the dragon is provided with a large fish. The counsellors of the parliament, dressed in their scarlet robes, attend this procession to a church, where high mass is said; and, these ceremonies being performed, the criminal is set at liberty. But it is only when there are some strong alleviating circumstances in the case of the offender, that he is suffered in this manner to evade the punishment of his crimes.

Yesterday, in a little town called Sotte Ville, joined to Rouen by the bridge, a political dispute arose between the Curé and his parishioners. The enraged Curé exclaimed, "vous êtes une assemblée d'ânes."[2] To which one of the parishioners answered, with great calmness, "Oui Mons. le Curé, et vous en êtes le pasteur."[3]

---

1 Fast-day. [Williams's note]
2 You are an assembly of asses. [Williams's note]
3 Yes, sir, and you are our preacher. [Williams's note]

LETTER XV.

I HEARD La messe militaire,[1] on Sunday last, at a church where all the national guard of Rouen attended. The service began with the loudest thunder of drums and trumpets, and seemed more like a signal for battle than for devotion; but the music soon softened into the most soothing sounds, which flowed from the organ, clarinets, flutes, and hautboys; the priests chanted, and the people made responses. The wax tapers were lighted, holy water was sprinkled on the ground, incense was burnt at the altar, and the elevation of the host was announced by the sound of the drum; upon which the people knelt down, and the priest prostrated his face towards the earth. There is something affecting in the pomp and solemnity of these ceremonies. Indeed, the Roman Catholic worship, though a sad stumbling-block to reason, is striking to the imagination. I have more than once heard the service for the dead performed, and never can hear it without emotion; without feeling that in those melancholy separations, which bury every hope of the survivor in the relentless grave, the heart that can delude itself with the belief, that its prayers may avail any thing to the departed object of its affections, must find consolation in thus uniting a tribute of tenderness, with the performance of a religious duty.

We have been at several convents at Rouen. The first to which we went was a convent of Benedictine Nuns. When we had entered the gates we rang a bell, and a servant appeared, and desired us to go up stairs to the parloir. We opened a wrong door, and found, in a room grated across the middle with iron bars, a young man sitting on one side of the grate, and a young nun on the other. I could not help thinking that the heart of this young man was placed in a perilous situation; for where can a young woman appear so interesting, as when seen within that gloomy barrier, which death alone can remove? What is there, in all the ostentation of female dress, so likely to affect a man of sensibility, as that dismal habit which seems so much at variance with youth and beauty, and is worn as the melancholy symbol of an eternal renunciation of the world and all its pleasures? We made an apology to the nun for our intrusion, and she directed us to another apartment, where, a few minutes after we had seated ourselves on one side of the grate, La Depositaire

---

1 The military mass. [Williams's note]

entered on the other, and told us that the Abbess, whom we had desired to see, was not yet risen from dinner, and La Depositaire hoped we would wait a little. "Parce que," said she, "Madame l'Abbesse étoit obligée hier de se lever de table de bonne heure, et elle se trouvoit une peu incommodée."[1] You must observe that the Abbesse dined at three o'clock, and it was now past six. At length this lady, who was so fond of long dinners, appeared. She is a woman of fifty, but is still handsome; has a frank agreeable countenance, fine eyes, and had put on her veil in a very becoming manner. We wished to be admitted to the interior part of the convent, and with this view a French gentleman, who was of our party, "se mit à conter des histoires à Madame l'Abbesse."[2]

He told her that my sister and I, though English women, were Catholics, and wished to be received into the convent, and even, if it had been possible, to take the vows. The Abbess enquired if he was quite sure of our being Catholics; upon which the gentleman, a little puzzled what to answer, insinuated that Mons. du F——had probably the merit of our conversion. "But I have heard," said the Abbess, "from Madame——, that Mons. du F—— has become a protestant himself." Mons. du F——, who is truth itself, avowed his principles without hesitation; while the Abbess, turning to La Depositaire, exclaimed, "Mais comme Mons. est aimable! quel beaux sentiments! Ah Mons. vous êtes trop bon pour que Dieu vous laisse dans l'erreur."[3] "St. Augustin," continued she, "had once some doubts: I hope you will be a second St. Augustin: myself, and all my community, will pray for your conversion." La Depositaire, who was a tall thin old woman, with a sharp malignant countenance, added, casting a look on Mons. du F—— full of the contempt of superior knowledge, "It is not surprizing that a young man, after passing several years in England, that country of heretics, should find his faith somewhat shaken; but he only wants to be enlightened by Mons. le Curé de ——, who will immediately dissipate all his doubts."

From the Convent of Benedictines we went to that of the Carmelites, where religion, which was meant to be a source of

---

1 Because, said she, the Abbess was obliged to rise from table very soon yesterday, and found herself a little indisposed. [Williams's note]
2 Told a great many fables to the Abbess. [Williams's note]
3 How amiable he is! what noble sentiments! Ah, Sir, you are too good for God to leave you in error. [Williams's note]

happiness in this world, as well as in the next, wears an aspect of the most gloomy horror. When we entered the convent, it seemed the residence of silence and solitude: no voice was heard, no human creature appeared; and when we rang the bell, a person, whom we could not see, enquired, through a hole in the wall, what we wanted. On being informed that we wished to speak to the Superieure, putting her hand through the hole, she gave us a key, and desired us to unlock the door of the parloir. This we accordingly did; and in a few minutes the Superieure came to a thick double grate, with a curtain drawn at the inside, to prevent the possibility of being seen. Our French gentleman again talked of our desire to enter the convent, and begged to know the rules. A hollow voice answered, that the Carmelites rose at four in the morning in summer, and five in the winter:—"Obedient slumbers, that can wake and weep!"[1]—That they slept in their coffins, upon straw, and every morning dug a shovel-full of earth for their graves; that they walked to their devotional exercises upon their knees; that when any of their friends visited them, if they spoke, they were not suffered to be seen, or if they were seen, they were not suffered to speak; that with them it was toujours maigre,[2] and they only tasted food twice a day.

Our Frenchman said, "Il faut Madame que ses demoiselles réfléchissent, si cela leur convient."[3] The poor Carmelite agreed that the matter required some reflection, and we departed.

As we returned home meditating on the lot of a Carmelite, we met in the street three nuns walking in the habit of their order. Upon enquiry, we were told that they had been forced by their parents to take the veil, and, since the decree of the National Assembly giving them liberty,[4] they had obtained permission to pay a visit for three months to some friends who sympathized in their unhappiness, and were now on their journey.

---

1 Pope, *Eloisa to Abelard*, line 212. The line Williams cites here appears in a passage describing the peaceful pleasures of monastic life for those of "spotless mind" and "compos'd" desires.
2 Always a fast. [Williams's note]
3 These young ladies, Madam, must consider whether these regulations will suit them. [Williams's note]
4 The liberty granted to clerics in February 1790, when the National Assembly nullified existing monastic vows and forbade the taking of new ones. Once the vows were dissolved, monastics who were dissatisfied with clerical life were free to leave their convents and were awarded a pension.

The monks and nuns must in a short time decide whether they will finally leave their cloisters or not; and the religious houses which are vacated will be sold. In the department of Rouen a calculation has been made, that, after paying every monk seven hundred, and every nun five hundred livres a year, out of the revenues of the religious houses, the department will gain sixty thousand livres a year. The monks and nuns above sixty years of age, who chuse to leave their convents, will be allowed an annual pension of nine hundred livres.

A letter was read in the National Assembly, a few days ago, from a priest, intreating that the clergy might have permission to marry; a privilege which it is thought the Assembly will soon authorize. "On a bouleversé tout,"[1] said an old Curé, a fierce Aristocrate, with whom I was in company, "Et même on veut porter la profanation si loin que de marier les prêtres."[2] It is conjectured, however, that the younger part of the clergy think of this measure with less horror than the old Curé.

We arrived last night at Mons. du F——'s chateau, without having visited, during our stay at Rouen, the tomb of William the Conqueror,[3] who is buried at Caen, a town twelve leagues distant. But I have been too lately at the Champ de Mars, to travel twelve leagues in order to see the tomb of a tyrant.

Upon Mons. du F——'s arrival at the chateau, all his tenants, with their wives and daughters, came to pay their respects to Mon Seigneur, and were addressed by Mons. and Madame with those endearing epithets which give such a charm to the French language, and are so much more rejoicing to the heart than our formal appellations. Here a peasant girl is termed, by the lady of the chateau, "Ma bonne amie, Ma petite, Mon enfant;"[4] while those pretty monosyllables tu, ta, &c.[5] used only to the nearest relations, and to servants, impress the mind with the idea of that affectionate familiarity, which so gracefully softens the distance of situation, and

---

1 They have overturned every thing. [Williams's note]
2 And would even carry the profanation so far as to suffer the priests to marry. [Williams's note]
3 Guillaume Le Conquérant, Duke of Normandy (1028–87), who, after defeating the English forces at the Battle of Hastings in 1066, assumed the English throne.
4 My good friend, My little girl, My child. [Williams's note]
5 Thou, thy, &c. [Williams's note]

excites in the dependant, not presumption, but gratitude. "Et comment te porte tu, La Voie?"[1] said Mons. du F—— to one of his farmers —"Assez bien Mon Seigneur," replied he; "mais j'eus la fièvre à Pâques, à votre service."[2]

LETTER XVI.

I EMBRACE the first hours of leisure, which I have found since my arrival at the chateau, to send you the history of my friends.

Antoine Augustin Thomás du F——, eldest son of the Baron du F——, Counsellor of the Parliament of Normandy, was born on the fifteenth of July, 1750. His early years were embittered by the severity of his father, who was of a disposition that preferred the exercise of domestic tyranny to the blessings of social happiness, and chose rather to be dreaded than beloved. The endearing name of father conveyed no transport to *his* heart, which, being wrapt up in stern insensibility, was cold even to the common feelings of nature.

The Baron's austerity was not indeed confined to his son, but extended to all his dependants. Formed by nature for the support of the antient government of France, he maintained his aristocratic rights with unrelenting severity, ruled his feudal tenures with a rod of iron, and considered the lower order of people as a set of beings whose existence was tolerated merely for the use of the nobility. The poor, he believed, were only born for suffering; and he determined, as far as in him lay, not to deprive them of their natural inheritance. On the whole, if it were the great purpose of human life to be hated, perhaps no person ever attained that end more completely than the Baron du F——.

His son discovered early a taste for literature, and received an education suitable to his rank and fortune. As he advanced in life, the treatment he experienced from his father became more and more intolerable to him, as, far from inheriting the same character, he possessed the most amiable dispositions, and the most feeling heart.

---

1 And how do you do, La Voie? [Williams's note]
2 Pretty well, my Lord; but I had a fever last Easter, at your service. [Williams's note]

His mother, feeble alike in mind and body, submitted with the helplessness, and almost with the thoughtlessness of a child, to the imperious will of her husband. Their family was increased by two more sons, and two daughters; but these children, being several years younger than Mons. du F——, were not of an age to afford him the consolations of friendship; and the young man would have found his situation intolerable, but for the sympathy of a person, in whose society every evil was forgotten.

This person, his attachment to whom has tinctured the colour of his life, was the youngest of eight children, of a respectable family of Bourgeois at Rouen. There is great reason to believe that her father was descended from the younger branch of a noble family of the same name, and bearing the same arms. But, unhappily, some links were wanting in this chain of honourable parentage. The claim to nobility could not be traced to the entire satisfaction of the Baron; who, though he would have dispensed with any moral qualities in favour of rank, considered obscure birth as a radical stain, which could not be wiped off by all the virtues under heaven. He looked upon marriage as merely a convention of interest, and children as a property, of which it was reasonable for parents to make the most in their power.

The father of Mad^selle Monique C—— was a farmer, and died three months before the birth of this child; who, with seven other children, was educated with the utmost care by their mother, a woman of sense and virtue, beloved by all to whom she was known. It seemed as if this respectable woman had, after the death of her husband, only supported life for the sake of her infant family, from whom she was snatched by death, the moment her maternal cares became no longer necessary; her youngest daughter, Monique, having, at this period, just attained her twentieth year. Upon the death of her mother, Monique went to live with an aunt, with whom she remained only a very short time, being invited by Madame du F——, to whom she was well known, to come and live with her as an humble companion, to read to her when she was disposed to listen, and to enliven the sullen grandeur of the chateau, by her animating vivacity.

This young person had cultivated her excellent understanding by reading, and her heart stood in no need of cultivation. Mons. du F—— found in the charms of her conversation, and in the sympathy of her friendship, the most soothing consolation under the rigor of parental tyranny. Living several years beneath the same roof, he had constant opportunities of observing her disposition and character; and the passion with which she at length inspired him, was founded on the lasting basis of esteem.

If it was ever pardonable to deviate from that law, in the code of interest and etiquette, which forbids the heart to listen to its best emotions; which, stifling every generous sentiment of pure disinterested attachment, sacrifices love at the shrine of avarice or ambition; the virtues of Monique were such as might excuse this deviation. Yes, the character, the conduct of this amiable person, have nobly justified her lover's choice. How long might he have vainly sought, in the highest classes of society, a mind so elevated above the common mass!—a mind that, endowed with the most exquisite sensibility, has had sufficient firmness to sustain, with a calm and equal spirit, every transition of fortune; the most severe trials of adversity, and perhaps what is still more difficult to bear, the trial of high prosperity.

Mons. du F—— had been taught, by his early misfortunes, that domestic happiness was the first good of life. He had already found, by experience, the insufficiency of rank and fortune to confer enjoyment; and he determined to seek it in the bosom of conjugal felicity. He determined to pass his life with her whose society now seemed essential not only to his happiness, but to his very existence.

At the solemn hour of midnight, the young couple went to a church, where they were met by a priest whom Mons. du F—— had made the confident of his attachment, and by whom the marriage ceremony was performed.

Some time after, when the situation of his wife obliged Mons. du F—— to acknowledge their marriage to his mother, she assured her son that she would willingly consent to receive his wife as her daughter, but for the dread of his father's resentment. Madame du F——, with tears of regret, parted with Monique, whom she placed under the protection of her brothers: they conducted her to Caen, where she was soon after delivered of a son.

The Baron du F—— was absent while these things were passing: he had been suspected of being the author of a pamphlet written against the princes of the blood, and an order was issued to seize his papers, and conduct him to the Bastille; but he found means to escape into Holland, where he remained nearly two years. Having made his peace with the ministry, he prepared to come home; but before he returned, Mons. du F—— received intelligence that his father, irritated almost to madness by the information of his marriage, was making application for a lettre de cachet, in order to confine his daughter-in-law for the rest of her life; and had also obtained power to have his son seized and imprisoned. Upon this Mons. du F—— and his wife fled with precipitation to Geneva, leaving their infant at nurse near Caen. The Genevois seemed to think that the unfortunate situation of these strangers, gave them a claim to all the offices of friendship. After an interval of many years, I have never heard Mons. or Madame F—— recall the kindness they received from that amiable people, without tears of tenderness and gratitude.

Meanwhile the Baron, having discovered the place of his son's retreat, obtained, in the name of the King, permission from the cantons of Berne and Friburg to arrest them at Lausanne, where they had retired for some months. The wife of Le Seigneur Baillif secretly gave the young people notice of this design, and on the thirtieth of January, 1775, they had just time to make their escape, with only a few livres in their pockets, and the clothes in which they were dressed. Mons. du F——, upon his first going to Switzerland, had lent thirty louis to a friend in distress. He now, in this moment of necessity, desired to be repaid, and was promised the money within a month: mean time, he and his wife wandered from town to town, without finding any place where they could remain in security. They had spent all their small stock of money, and were almost without clothes: but at the expiration of the appointed time, the thirty louis were paid, and with this fund Mons. and Madame du F—— determined to take shelter in the only country which could afford them a safe asylum from persecution, and immediately set off for England, travelling through Germany, and part of Holland, to avoid passing through France.

They embarked at Rotterdam, and, after a long and gloomy passage, arrived late at night at London. A young man, who was their fellow passenger, had the charity to procure them a lodging in a garret, and directed them where to purchase a few ready-made clothes. When they had remained in this lodging the time necessary for becoming parishioners, their banns were published in the church of St. Anne, Westminster, where they were married by the Curate of the parish. They then went to the chapel of the French Ambassador, and were again married by his Chaplain; after which Mons. du F—— told me, "Les deux époux vinrent faire maigre chair à leur petite chambre."[1]

---

1 The new-married couple kept a fast in their little apartment. [Williams's note]

Mons. du F—— endeavoured to obtain a situation at a school, to teach the French language; but before such a situation could be found, his wife was delivered of a girl. Not having sufficient money to hire a nurse, he attended her himself. At this period they endured all the horrors of absolute want. Unknown and unpitied, without help or support, in a foreign country, and in the depth of a severe winter, they almost perished with cold and hunger. The unhappy mother lay stretched upon the same bed with her new-born infant, who in vain implored her succour, want of food having dried up that source of nourishment. The woman, at whose house they lodged, and whom they had for some weeks been unable to pay, after many threatenings, at length told them that they must depart the next morning. Madame du F—— was at this time scarcely able to walk across her chamber, and the ground was covered with snow. They had already exhausted every resource; they had sold their watches, their clothes, to satisfy the cravings of hunger; every mode of relief was fled—every avenue of hope was closed—and they determined to go with their infant to the sub-urbs of the town, and there, seated on a stone, wait with patience for the deliverance of death. With what anguish did this unfortu-nate couple prepare to leave their last miserable retreat! With how many bitter tears did they bathe that wretched infant, whom they could no longer save from perishing!

Oh, my dear, my ever beloved friends! when I recollect that I am not at this moment indulging the melancholy cast of my own disposition, by painting imaginary distress; when I recollect not only that these were real sufferings, but that they were sustained by *you*! my mind is overwhelmed with its own sensations.— The paper is blotted by my tears—and I can hold my pen no longer.

LETTER XVII.

—— "THE moral world,
Which though to us it seem perplex'd, moves on
In higher order; fitted, and impell'd,
By Wisdom's finest hand, and issuing all
In universal good."[1]

---

1 Thomson [Williams's note]. These lines are from James Thomson's *The Seasons: Winter*, 583-87.

Mons. and Madame du F—— were relieved from this extremity of distress at a moment so critical, and by means so unexpected, that it seemed the hand of Heaven visibly interposing in behalf of oppressed virtue. Early in the morning of that fatal day when they were to leave their last sad shelter, Mons. du F—— went out, and, in the utmost distraction of mind, wandered through some of the streets in the neighbourhood. He was stopped by a gentleman whom he had known at Geneva, and who told him that he was then in search of his lodging, having a letter to deliver to him from a Genevois clergyman. Mons. du F—— opened the letter, in which he was informed by his friend, that, fearing he might be involved in difficulties, he had transmitted ten guineas to a banker in London, and intreated Mons. du F—— would accept that small relief, which was all he could afford, as a testimony of friendship. Mons. du F—— flew to the banker's, received the money as the gift of Heaven, and then, hastening to his wife and child, bade them live a little longer.

A short time after, he obtained a situation as French usher[1] at a school; and Madame du F——, when she had a little recovered her strength, put out her infant to nurse, and procured the place of French teacher at a boarding-school. They were now enabled to support their child, and to repay the generous assistance of their kind friend at Geneva. At this period they heard of the death of their son, whom they had left at Caen.

Mons. and Madame du F—— passed two years in this situation, when they were again plunged into the deepest distress. A French jeweller was commissioned by the Baron du F——, to go to his son, and propose to him conditions of reconciliation. This man told Mons. du F—— that his father was just recovered from a severe and dangerous illness, and that his eldest daughter had lately died. These things, he said, had led him to reflect with some pain on the severity he had exercised towards his son; that the feelings of a parent were awakened in his bosom; and that if Mons. du F—— would throw himself at his father's feet, and ask forgiveness, he would not fail to obtain it, and would be allowed a pension, on which he might live with his wife in England. In confirmation of these assurances, this man produced several letters which he had received from the Baron to that effect; who, as a farther proof of his sincerity, had given this agent seven hundred pounds to put into the hands of Mons. du F—— for the support of his wife and child

---

1 An assistant teacher.

during his absence. The agent told him, that he had not been able to bring the money to England, but would immediately give him three drafts upon a merchant of reputation in London, with whom he had connections in business; the first draft payable in three months, the second in six, and the third in nine.

Mons. du F—— long deliberated upon these proposals. He knew too well the vindictive spirit of his father, not to feel some dread of putting himself into his power. But his agent continued to give him the most solemn assurances of safety; and Mons. du F—— thought it was not improbable that his sister's death might have softened the mind of his father. He reflected that his marriage had disappointed those ambitious hopes of a great alliance, which his father had fondly indulged, and to whom he owed at least the reparation of hastening to implore his forgiveness when he was willing to bestow it. What also weighed strongly on his mind was the consideration that the sum which his father had offered to deposit for the use of his wife, would, in case any sinister accident should befal him, afford a small provision for her and his infant.

The result of these deliberations was, that Mons. du F—— determined (and who can much blame his want of prudence?) he determined to confide in a father!—to trust in that instinctive affection, which, far from being connected with any peculiar sensibility of mind, it requires only to be a parent to feel—an affection, which, not confined to the human heart, softens the ferociousness of the tyger, and speaks with a voice that is heard amidst the howlings of the desart.

Mons. du F——, after the repeated promises of his father, almost considered that suspicion which still hung upon his mind, as a crime. But, lest it might be possible that this agent was commissioned to deceive him, he endeavoured to melt him into compassion for his situation. He went to the village where his child was at nurse, and, bringing her six miles in his arms, presented her to this man, telling him, that the fate of that poor infant rested upon his integrity. The man took the innocent creature in his arms, kissed her, and then, returning her to her father, renewed all his former assurances. Mons. du F—— listened and believed. Alas! how difficult is it for a good heart to suspect human nature of crimes which make one blush for the species! How hard is it for a mind glowing with benevolence, to believe that the bosom of another harbours the malignity of a demon!

Mons. du F—— now fixed the time for his departure with his father's agent, who was to accompany him to Normandy. Madame du F—— saw the preparations for his journey with anguish which she could ill conceal. But she felt that the delicacy of her situation forbad her interference. It was she who had made him an alien from his family, and an exile from his country. It was for her, that, renouncing rank, fortune, friends, and connections, all that is esteemed most valuable in life, he had suffered the last extremity of want, and now submitted to a state of drudgery and dependance. Would he not have a right to reproach her weakness, if she attempted to oppose his reconciliation with his father, and exerted that influence which she possessed over his mind, in order to detain him in a situation so remote from his former expectations? She was, therefore, sensible, that the duty, the gratitude she owed her husband, now required on her part the absolute sacrifice of her own feelings: she suffered without complaint, and endeavoured to resign herself to the will of Heaven.

The day before his departure, Mons. du F—— went to take leave of his little girl. At this moment a dark and melancholy presage seemed to agitate his mind. He pressed the child for a long while to his bosom, and bathed it with his tears. The nurse eagerly enquired what was the matter, and assured him that the child was perfectly well. Mons. du F—— had no power to reply: he continued clasping his infant in his arms, and at length, tearing himself from her in silence, he rushed out of the house.

When the morning of his departure came, Madame du F——, addressing herself to his fellow-traveller, said to him with a voice of supplication, "I entrust you, Sir, with my husband, with the father of my poor infant, our sole protector and support!—have compassion on the widow and the orphan!" The man, casting upon her a gloomy look, gave her a cold answer, which made her soul shrink within her. When Mons. du F—— got into the Brighthelmstone stage, he was unable to bid her farewell; but when the carriage drove off, he put his head out of the window, and continued looking after her, while she fixed her eyes on him, and might have repeated with Imogen,

"I would have broke mine eye-strings;
Crack'd them, but to look upon him; till the diminution
Of space had pointed him sharp as my needle;
Nay, followed him, till he had melted from
The smallness of a gnat to air; and then—
Then turn'd mine eye and wept!"[1]

---

1 Shakespeare, *Cymbeline* I.iii.17–22.

When the carriage was out of sight, she summoned all her strength, and walked with trembling steps to the school where she lived as a teacher. With much difficulty she reached the door; but her limbs could support her no longer, and she fell down senseless at the threshold. She was carried into the house, and restored to life and the sensations of misery.

LETTER XVIII.

MONS. du F—— arrived at his father's chateau in Normandy, in June 1778, and was received by Mons. le Baron, and all his family, with the most affectionate cordiality. In much exultation of mind, he dispatched a letter to Madame du F——, containing this agreeable intelligence; but his letter was far from producing in her mind the effect he desired. A deep melancholy had seized her thoughts, and her foreboding heart refused to sympathize in his joy. Short, indeed, was its duration. He had not been many days at the chateau, when he perceived, with surprize and consternation, that his steps were continually watched by two servants armed with fusees.[1]

His father now shewed him an arret,[2] which, on the fourth of June, 1776, he had obtained from the parliament of Rouen against his marriage. The Baron then ordered his son to accompany him to his house at Rouen, whither they went, attended by several servants. That evening, when the attendants withdrew after supper, the Baron, entirely throwing off the mask of civility and kindness, which he had worn in such opposition to his nature, reproached his son, in terms of the utmost bitterness, for his past conduct, inveighed against his marriage, and, after having exhausted every expression of rage and resentment, at length suffered him to retire to his own apartment.

There the unhappy Mons. du F——, absorbed in the most gloomy reflections, lamented in vain that fatal credulity which had led him to put himself into the power of his implacable father. At the hour of midnight his meditations were interrupted by the sound of feet approaching his chamber; and in a few moments the door was thrown open, and his father, attended by a servant armed,

---

1 Light muskets.
2 An authoritative sentence, legal decree, or legal judgment.

and two Cavaliers de Maréchaussée,[1] entered the room. Resistance and supplication were alike unavailing. Mons. du F——'s papers were seized; a few louis d'ors, which constituted all the money he possessed, were taken from him; and he was conducted in the dead of night, July the 7th, 1778, to St.Yon, a convent used as a place of confinement near Rouen, where he was thrown into a dungeon.

A week after, his father entered the dungeon. You will perhaps conclude that his hard heart felt at length the relentings of a parent. You will at least suppose, that his imagination being haunted, and his conscience tormented with the image of a son stretched on the floor of this subterraneous cell, he could support the idea no longer, and had hastened to give repose to his own mind by releasing his captive. Far different were the motives of his visit. He considered that such was his son's attachment to his wife, that, so long as he believed he had left her in possession of seven hundred pounds, he would find comfort from that consideration, even in the depth of his dungeon. His father, therefore, hastened to remove an error from the mind of his son, which left the measure of his woes unfilled. Nor did he chuse to yield to another the office of inflicting a pang sharper than captivity; but himself informed his son, that the merchant, who was to pay the seven hundred pounds to his wife, was declared a bankrupt.

A short time after, the Baron du F—— commenced a suit at law against that agent of iniquity whom he had employed to deceive his son, and who, practising a refinement of treachery of which the Baron was not aware, had kept the seven hundred pounds, with which he was intrusted, and given drafts upon a merchant who he knew would fail before the time of payment. Not being able to prosecute this affair without a power of attorney from his son, the Baron applied to him for that purpose. But Mons. du F——, being firmly resolved not to deprive his wife of the chance of recovering the money for herself and her child, could by no intreaties or menaces be led to comply. In vain his father, who had consented to allow him a few books, ordered him to be deprived of that resource, and that his confinement should be rendered still more rigorous; he continued inflexible.

Mons. du F—— remained in his prison without meeting with the smallest mark of sympathy from any one of his family, though his second brother, Mons. de B——, was now eighteen years of age;

---

1 Officers of justice. [Williams's note]

an age at which the sordid considerations of interest, how much soever they may affect our conduct at a more advanced period of life, can seldom stifle those warm and generous feelings which seem to belong to youth. It might have been expected that this young man would have abhorred the prospect of possessing a fortune which was the just inheritance of his brother, and which could only be obtained by detaining that brother in perpetual captivity. Even admitting that his inexorable father prohibited his visiting the prison of his brother, his heart should have told him, that disobedience, in this instance, would have been virtue: Or, was it not sufficient to remain a passive spectator of injustice, without becoming, as he afterwards did, the agent of cruelty inflicted on a brother?

Where are the words that can convey an adequate idea of the sufferings of Madame du F—— during this period? Three weeks after her husband's departure from England, she heard the general report of the town of Rouen, that the Baron du F—— had obtained a lettre de cachet against his son, and thrown him into prison. This was all she heard of her husband for the space of two years. Ignorant of the place of his confinement, uncertain if he still lived, perhaps her miseries were even more poignant than his. In the dismal solitude of a prison, his pains were alleviated by the soothing reflection that he suffered for her he loved; while that very idea was to her the most bitter aggravation of distress. Her days passed in anguish, which can only be conceived where it has been felt, and her nights were disturbed by the gloomy wanderings of fancy. Sometimes she saw him in her dreams chained to the floor of his dungeon, his bosom bathed in blood, and his countenance disfigured by death. Sometimes she saw him hastening towards her, when at the moment that he was going to embrace her, they were fiercely torn asunder. Madame du F—— was naturally of a delicate constitution, and grief of mind reduced her to such a deplorable state of weakness, that it was with infinite difficulty she performed the duties of her situation. For herself, she would have welcomed death with thankfulness; but she considered that her child now depended entirely on her labours for support: and this was a motive sufficiently powerful to prompt her to the careful preservation of her own life, though it had long become a burden. The child was three years old when her father left England; recollected him perfectly; and, whenever her mother went to visit her, used to call with eagerness for her papa. The enquiry, in the voice of her child, of, "When shall I see my dear, dear papa?" was heard by this unhappy mother with a degree of agony which it were vain indeed to describe.

LETTER XIX.

MONS. du F—— was repeatedly offered his liberty, but upon conditions which he abhorred. He was required for ever to renounce his wife; who, while she remained with her child in a distant country, was to receive from his father a small pension, as an equivalent for the pangs of disappointed affection, of disgrace and dishonour. With the indignation of offended virtue he spurned at these insulting propositions, and endeavoured to prepare his mind for the endurance of perpetual captivity.

Nor can imagination form an idea of a scene more dreadful than his prison, where he perceived with horror that the greatest number of those prisoners who had been many years in confinement, had an appearance of frenzy in their looks, which shewed that reason had been too weak for the long struggle with calamity, and had at last yielded to despair. In a cell adjoining Mons. du F——'s, was an old man who had been confined nearly forty years. His grey beard hung down to his waist, and, during the day, he was chained by his neck to the wall. He was never allowed to leave his cell, and never spoke; but Mons. du F—— used to hear the rattling of his chains.

The prisoners, a few excepted, were generally brought from their cells at the hour of noon, and dined together. But this gloomy repast was served in uninterrupted silence. They were not suffered to utter one word, and the penalty of transgressing this rule was a rigorous confinement of several weeks. As soon as this comfortless meal was finished, the prisoners were instantly obliged to return to their dungeons, in which they were locked up till the same hour the following day. Mons. du F——, in his damp and melancholy cell, passed two winters without fire, and suffered so severely from cold, that he was obliged to wrap himself up in the few clothes which covered his bed. Nor was he allowed any light, except that which during the short day beamed through the small grated window in the ceiling of his dungeon.

Is it not difficult to believe that these sufferings were inflicted by a father? A father! —— that name which I cannot trace without emotion; which conveys all the ideas of protection, of security, of tenderness;—that dear relation to which, in general, children owe their prosperity, their enjoyments, and even their virtues!—Alas, the unhappy Mons. du F—— owed nothing to *his* father, but that life, which from its earliest period his cruelty had embittered, and which he now condemned to languish in miseries that death only could heal.

A young gentleman, who was confined in a cell on one side of Mons. du F——'s, contrived to make a small hole through the wall; and these companions in misfortune, by placing themselves close to the hole, could converse together in whispers. But the Monks were not long in discovering this, and effectually deprived them of so great an indulgence, by removing them to distant cells. These unrelenting Monks, who performed with such fidelity their office of tormenting their fellow-creatures, who never relaxed in one article of persecution, and adhered with scrupulous rigour to the code of cruelty, were called, "Les Frères de la sainte Charité."[1] One among them deserved the appellation. This good old Monk used to visit the prisoners by stealth, and endeavour to administer comfort to their affliction. Often he repeated to Mons. du F——, "Mon chere frère, consolez vous; mettez votre confiance en Dieu, vos maux seront finis!"[2]

Mons. du F—— remained two years in prison without receiving any intelligence of his wife, on whose account he suffered the most distracting anxiety. He had reason to apprehend that her frame, which had already been enfeebled by her misfortunes, would sink beneath this additional load of misery, and that she would perhaps be rendered unable to procure that little pittance, which might preserve herself and her child from want. At length one of his fellow-prisoners, who was going to regain his liberty, took charge of a letter to Madame du F——, and flattered him with the hope of finding some means of transmitting to him an answer.

The letter paints so naturally the situation of his mind, that I have translated some extracts from it.

"My thoughts (he says) are unceasingly occupied about you, and my dear little girl. I am for ever recalling the blessed moments when I had the happiness of being near you, and at that recollection my tears refuse to be controuled. How could I consent to separate myself from what was most dear to me in the world? No motive less powerful than that of seeking your welfare, and that of my child, could have determined me—and alas! I have not accomplished this end. I know too well that you

---

1 The Brothers of the holy Charity. [Williams's note]
2 My dear brother, be comforted; place your confidence in God, your afflictions will have an end. [Williams's note]

have never received that sum of money which I thought I had secured for you, and for which I risked the first blessing of life. What fills my mind with the greatest horror, in the solitude of my prison, is the fear that you are suffering difficulties in a foreign country. Here I remain ignorant of your fate, and can only offer to Heaven the most ardent vows for your welfare.

"What joy would a letter from you give me! but I dare not flatter myself with the hope of such sweet consolation. All I can assure myself of is, that though separated, perhaps for ever, our souls are united by the most tender friendship and attachment. Perhaps I may not find it possible to write to you again for a long while: but be assured that no menaces, no sufferings, no dungeons shall ever shake my fidelity to you, and that I shall love you to the last hour of my existence. I find a consolation in the reflection that it is for you I suffer. If Providence ever permits us to meet again, that moment will efface the remembrance of all my calamities. Live, my dearest wife, in that hope. I conjure you preserve your life for my sake, and for the sake of our dear little girl! Embrace her tenderly for me, and desire her also to embrace you for her poor papa. I need not recommend my child to the care of so tender a mother; but I conjure you to inspire her mind with the deepest sense of religion. If she is born to inherit the misfortunes of her father, this will be her best source of consolation.

"Whatever offers may be made you by my father, I exhort you never have the weakness to listen to them, but preserve your rights, and those of my dear little girl, which, perhaps, may one day be of some value. If you are still at Mrs. D———'s boarding-school, tell her that I recommend my wife and child to her compassion.——— But what am I saying? I am ignorant if you are still with her, ignorant whether the dearest objects of my affection still live! But I trust that Providence has preserved you. Adieu! May God Almighty bless you, and my child! I never cease imploring him to have pity on the widow and the orphan in a land of strangers."

LETTER XX.

YOU, my dear friend, who have felt the tender attachments of love and friendship, and the painful anxieties which absence occasions, even amidst scenes of variety and pleasure; who understand the value at which tidings from those we love is computed in the arithmetic of the heart; who have heard with almost uncontroulable emotion the postman's rap at the door; have trembling seen the well-known hand which excited sensations that almost deprived you of power to break the seal which seemed the talisman of happiness: you can judge of the feelings of Mons. du F—— when he received, by means of the same friend who had conveyed his letter, an answer from his wife. But the person who brought the letter to his dungeon, dreading the risk of a discovery, insisted, that after having read it, he should return it to him immediately. Mons. du F—— pressed the letter to his heart, bathed it with his tears, and implored the indulgence of keeping it at least till the next morning. He was allowed to do so, and read it till every word was imprinted on his memory; and, after enjoying the sad luxury of holding it that night on his bosom, was forced the next morning to relinquish his treasure.

On the 10th of October, 1780, the Baron du F—— came to the convent, and ordered the monks to bring his son from his dungeon to the parloir, and leave them together. With the utmost reluctance Mons. du F—— obeyed this summons, having long lost all hope of softening the obdurate heart of his father. When the monks withdrew, the Baron began upbraiding him in the most bitter terms, for his obstinate resistance to his will, which, he informed him, had availed nothing, as he had gained his suit at law, and recovered the seven hundred pounds. Mons. du F—— replied, that the pain he felt from this intelligence would have been far more acute, had his wife been deprived, with his concurrence, of the money which was promised for her subsistence, and on the reliance of which promise he had been tempted to leave England. His father then enquired if he still persisted in his adherence to the disgraceful connection he had formed; to which his son answered, that not merely were his affections interested, but that his honour obliged him to maintain, with inviolable fidelity, a solemn and sacred engagement. The rage of the Baron, at these words, became unbounded. He stamped the ground with his feet; he aimed a stroke at his son, who, taking advantage of this moment of frenzy, determined to attempt his escape; and, rushing out of the apartment, and avoiding that side of the convent which the monks inhabited, he endeavoured to find his way to the garden, but missed the passage which led to it. He then flew up a staircase, from which he heard the voice of his father calling for assistance. Finding that all the doors which he passed were shut, he continued ascending till he reached the top of the building, where meeting with no other opening than a hole made in the sloping roof to let in light to a garret, he climbed up with much difficulty, and then putting his feet through the hole, and letting his body out by degrees, he supported himself for a moment on the roof, and deliberated on what he was about to do. But his mind was, at this crisis, wrought up to a pitch of desperation, which mocked the suggestions of fear. He quitted his hold, and, flinging himself from a height of nearly fifty feet, became insensible before he reached the ground, where he lay weltering in his blood, and to all appearance dead.

He had fallen on the high road leading from Rouen to Caen. Some people who were passing gathered round him, and one person having washed the blood from his face, instantly recognized his features, and exclaimed to the astonished croud, that he was the eldest son of the Baron du F——. Upon examining his body, it was found that he had broken his arm, his thigh, his ancle-bone, and his heel, besides having received many violent bruises. He still remained in a state of insensibility; and, while these charitable strangers were using their efforts to restore him to life, the monks hastened from their convent, snatched their victim from those good Samaritans who would have poured oil and wine into his wounds, and carried him to the infirmary of the convent, where he remained some weeks before he recovered his senses; after which he lay stretched upon a bed for three months, suffering agonies of pain.

His father, who had been the jailor, and almost the murderer of his son, heard of these sufferings without remorse, nor did he ever see him more. But, though he was sufficiently obdurate to bear unmoved the calamities he had inflicted on his child, though he could check the upbraidings of his own conscience, he could not silence the voice of public indignation. The report that Mons. du F—— had been found lying on the road bathed in blood, and had in that condition been dragged to the prison of St. Yon, was soon spread through the town of Rouen. Every one sympathized in the fate of this unfortunate young man, and execrated the tyranny of his unrelenting father.

The universal clamour reached the ear of his brother, Mons. de B——, who now, for the first time, out of respect to the public opinion, took a measure which his heart had never dictated during the long captivity of his brother, that of visiting him in prison. Mons. de B———'s design in these visits was merely to appease the public; for small indeed was the consolation they afforded to his brother. He did not come to bathe with his tears the bed where that unhappy young man lay stretched in pain and anguish; to lament the severity of his father; to offer him all the consolation of fraternal tenderness:—he came to warn him against indulging a hope of ever regaining his liberty—he came to pierce his soul with "hard unkindness' altered eye, which mocks the tear it forc'd to flow!"[1]

I will not attempt to describe the wretchedness of Madame du F———, when she heard the report of her husband's situation. Your heart will conceive what she suffered far better than I can relate it. Three months after his fall, Mons. du F——— contrived, through the assistance of the charitable old monk, to send her a few lines written with his left hand. "My fall" (he says) "has made my captivity known, and has led the whole town of Rouen to take an interest in my misfortunes. Perhaps I shall have reason to bless the accident, which may possibly prove the means of procuring me my liberty, and uniting me again to you!— In the mean time, I trust that Providence will watch with paternal goodness over the two objects of my most tender affection. Do not, my dearest wife, suffer the thoughts of my situation to prey too much upon your mind. My arm is almost well: my thigh and foot are not quite cured; but I am getting better.

"I could not suppress my tears on reading that part of your letter, wherein you tell me that my dear little girl often asks for her papa.— Kiss her for me a thousand times, and tell her that her papa is always thinking of her and her dear mama. I am well convinced that you will give her the best education your little pittance can afford. But above all, I beseech you, inspire her young mind with sentiments of piety: teach her to love her Creator: that is the most essential of all lessons. Adieu, dearest and most beloved of women!— Is there a period in reserve when we shall meet again? Oh how amply will that moment compensate for all our misfortunes!"

---

1 Lines 76-77 of Thomas Gray's "Ode On a Distant Prospect of Eton College" (written 1742, published 1747). Williams, who was undoubtedly quoting from memory, gives "which mocks" for Gray's "That mocks."

LETTER XXI.

AT length the Parliament of Rouen began to interest itself in the cause of Mons. du F——. The circumstances of his confinement were mentioned in that Assembly, and the President sent his Secretary to Mons. du F——'s prison, who had now quitted his bed, and was able to walk with the assistance of crutches. By the advice of the President, Mons. du F—— addressed some letters to the Parliament, representing his situation in the most pathetic terms, and imploring their interference in his behalf.

It is here necessary to mention, that Mons. de Bel B——, Procureur General de Rouen,[1] being intimately connected with the Baron du F——'s family, had ventured to demonstrate his friendship for the Baron, by confining his son nearly three years on his own authority, and without any lettre de cachet. And, though Mons. de Bel B—— well knew, that every species of oppression was connived at, under the shelter of lettres de cachet, he was sensible that it was only beneath their auspices that the exercise of tyranny was permitted; and in this particular instance, not having been cruel selon les règles,[2] he apprehended, that if ever Mons. du F—— regained his liberty, he might be made responsible for his conduct. He, therefore, exerted all his influence, and with too much success, to frustrate the benevolent intention of the President of the Parliament, respecting Mons. du F——. His letters were indeed read in that Assembly, and ordered to be registered, where they still remain a record of the pusillanimity of those men, who suffered the authority of Mons. de Bel B—— to overcome the voice of humanity; who acknowledged the atrocity of the Baron du F——'s conduct, and yet were deaf to the supplications of his son, while from the depth of his dungeon, he called upon them for protection and redress.

May the fate of the captive, in the land of France, no more hang suspended on the frail thread of the pity, or the caprice of individuals! May justice erect, on eternal foundations, her protecting sanctuary for the oppressed; and may humanity and mercy be the graceful decorations of her temple!

The Baron du F—— perceived that, notwithstanding his machinations had prevented the Parliament of Rouen from taking

---

1 Jean-Pierre-Prosper de Belbeuf was Procurer-General (i.e., Attorney General, Chief Prosecutor) to the Parlement of Normandie.
2 According to rules. [Williams's note]

any effectual measures toward liberating his son, it would be impossible to silence the murmurs of the public, while he remained confined at St.Yon. He determined, therefore, to remove him to some distant prison, where his name and family were unknown; and where, beyond the jurisdiction of the Parliament of Rouen, his groans might rise unpitied and unavenged. But the Baron, not daring, amidst the general clamour, to remove his son by force, endeavoured to draw him artfully into the snare he had prepared.

Mons. de B—— was sent to his brother's prison, where he represented to him, that, though he must not indulge the least hope of ever regaining his liberty, yet, if he would write a letter to Mons. M——, keeper of the seals, desiring to be removed to some other place, his confinement should be made far less rigorous. Mons. du F—— was now in a state of desperation, that rendered him almost careless of his fate. He perceived that the Parliament had renounced his cause. He saw no possibility of escape from St. Yon; and flattered himself, that in a place where he was less closely confined, it might perhaps be practicable; and therefore he consented to write the letter required, which Mons. de B—— conveyed in triumph to his father. There were, however, some expressions in the letter which the Baron disapproved, on which account he returned it, desiring that those expressions might be changed. But, during the interval of his brother's absence, Mons. du F—— had reflected on the rash imprudence of confiding in the promises of those by whom he had been so cruelly deceived. No sooner, therefore, did Mons. de B—— put the letter again into his hands, than he tore it into pieces, and peremptorily refused to write another.

Soon after this, Mons. du B——, the ambassador of the tyrant, again returned to his brother with fresh credentials, and declared to him, that if he would write to the keeper of the seals, desiring to be removed from St.Yon, he should, in one fortnight after his removal, be restored to liberty. Upon Mons. du F——'s asserting that he could no longer confide in the promises made him by his family, his brother, in a formal written engagement, to which he signed his name, gave him the most solemn assurance, that this promise should be fulfilled with fidelity. Mons. du F—— desired a few days for deliberation, and, during that interval, found means of consulting a magistrate of Rouen who was his friend, and who advised him to comply with the terms that were offered, after having caused several copies of the written engagement to be taken, and certified by such of the prisoners at St. Yon as were likely to regain their freedom; a precaution necessary, lest his own copy should be torn from his hands.

Thus, having neither trusted to the affection, the mercy, or the remorse of those within whose bosoms such sentiments were extinguished; having bargained, by a written agreement, with a father and a brother, for his release from the horrors of perpetual captivity, Mons. du F—— wrote the letter required.

Soon after, an order was sent from Versailles for his release from the prison of St. Yon, and with it a lettre de cachet, whereby he was exiled to Beauvais, with a command not to leave that town. Mons. de B——, acting as a Cavalier de la Maréchaussée,[1] conducted his brother to this place of exile, and there left him. A short time after, Mons. du F—— received an intimation, from that magistrate of Rouen who had interested himself in his misfortunes, that his father was on the point of obtaining another lettre de cachet, to remove him from Beauvais, to some prison in the south of France, where he might never more be heard of. This gentleman added, that Mons. du F—— had not one moment to lose, and advised him immediately to attempt his escape.

Early on the morning after he received this intelligence, Mons. du F——, who had the liberty to walk about the town, fled from Beauvais. The person who brought him the letter from the magistrate, waited for him at a little distance from the town, and accompanied him on his journey. When they reached Lisle in Flanders, not having a passport, they were obliged to wait from eleven o'clock at night till ten the next morning, before they could obtain permission from the Governor to proceed on their journey. Mons. du F—— concluded that he was pursued, and suffered the most dreadful apprehensions of being overtaken. His companion, with some address, at length obtained a passport, and attended him as far as Ostend. The wind proving contrary, he was detained two days in a state of the most distracting inquietude, and concealed himself on board the vessel in which he had taken his passage for England. At length the wind became favourable; the vessel sailed, and arrived late in the night at Margate. Mons. du F——, when he reached the English shore, knelt down, and, in a transport of joy, kissed the earth of that dear country which had twice proved his asylum.

---

1 An officer of justice. [Williams's note]

He then enquired when the stage-coach set off for London, and was told that it went at so early an hour the next morning, that he could not go till the day after, as he must wait till his portmanteau was examined by the custom-house officers, who were now in bed. The delay of a few hours in seeing his wife and child, after such an absence, after such sufferings, was not to be endured. In a violent agitation of mind, he snatched up his portmanteau, and was going to fling it into the sea, when he was prevented by the people near him, who said, that if he would pay the fees, his portmanteau should be sent after him. He eagerly complied with their demands, and set out for London. As he drew near, his anxiety, his impatience, his emotion increased. His present situation appeared to him like one of those delicious dreams, which sometimes visited the darkness of his dungeon, and for a while restored him in imagination, to those he loved. Scarcely could he persuade himself that he was beyond the reach of oppression; that he was in a land of freedom; that he was hastening every moment towards his wife and child. When he entered London, his sensations became almost too strong to bear. He was in the very same place which his wife and child inhabited—but were they yet alive? were they in health? had Heaven indeed reserved for him the transport of holding them once more to his bosom, of mixing his tears with theirs? When he knocked at the door of the house where he expected to hear of Madame du F——, he had scarcely power to articulate his enquiries after her and his child. He was told that they were in health, but that Madame du F——, being in a situation six miles from London, he could not see her till the next morning. Mons. du F—— had not been in a bed for several nights, and was almost overcome with agitation and fatigue. He, however, instantly set out on foot for the habitation of his wife, announced himself to the mistress of the family, and remained in another apartment, while she, after making Madame du F—— promise that she would listen to her with calmness, told her, that there was a probability of her husband's return to England. He heard the sobs, the exclamations, of his wife at this intelligence—he could restrain no longer—he rushed into the room—he flew into her arms—he continued pressing her in silence to his bosom. She was unable to shed a tear; and it was not till after he had long endeavoured to sooth her by his tenderness, and had talked to her of her child, that she obtained relief from weeping. She then, with the most violent emotion, again and again repeated the same enquiries, and was a considerable time before she recovered any degree of composure.

All the fortune Mons. du F—— possessed when he reached London, was one half guinea; but his wife had, during his absence, saved ten guineas out of her little salary. You will easily imagine how valuable this hoard became in her estimation, when she could apply it to the precious use of relieving the necessities of her husband. Mons. du F—— went to London the next day, and hired a little garret: there, with a few books, a rush-light, and some straw in which he wrapped his legs to supply the want of fire, he recollected not the splendour to which he had once been accustomed, but the dungeon from which he had escaped. He saw his wife and child once a week; and, in those solitary moments, when books failed to sooth his thoughts, he anticipated the hour in which he should again meet the objects most dear to his heart, and passed the intervals of time in philosophic resignation. His clothes being too shabby to admit of his appearing in the day, he issued from his little shed when it was dark, and endeavoured to warm himself by the exercise of walking.

Unfortunately he caught the small-pox, and his disorder rose to such a height, that his life was despaired of. In his delirium, he used to recapitulate the sad story of his misfortunes; and when he saw any person near his bed-side, would call out, with the utmost vehemence, "Qu'on fasse sortir touts les François!"[1] After having been for some days in the most imminent danger, Mons. du F—— recovered from this disease.

LETTER XXII.

SIX months after Mons. du F——'s return to England, his family found themselves compelled to silence the public clamours, by allowing him a small annual pension. Upon this, Madame du F—— quitted her place, and came to live with her husband and her child in an obscure lodging. Their little income received some addition by means of teaching the French language in a few private families.

A young lady, who came to pay me a visit at London in 1785, desired to take some lessons in French, and Madame du F—— was recommended to us for that purpose. We soon perceived in her conversation every mark of a cultivated mind, and of an amiable

---

1 Make all the French go out. [Williams's note]

disposition. She at length told us the history of her misfortunes, with the pathetic eloquence of her own charming language; and, after having heard that recital, it required but common humanity, to treat her with the respect due to the unhappy, and to feel for her sorrows that sympathy to which they had such claim. How much has the sensibility of Mons. and Madame du F—— over-rated those proofs of esteem and friendship which we were enabled to shew them in their adversity!—But I must not anticipate.

On the seventh of October, 1787, the Baron died, leaving, besides Mons. du F——, two other sons, and a daughter.

I must here mention, that at the time when Mons. du F—— was confined to his bed in the prison of St. Yon, from the consequences of his fall, his father, in order to avoid the clamours at Rouen, went for some weeks to Paris. He there made a will, disinheriting his eldest son. By the old laws of France, however, a father could not punish his son more than once for the same offence. Nor was there any thing in so mild a clause that could much encourage disobedience; since this single punishment, of which the mercy of the law was careful to avoid repetition, might be extended to residence for life in a dungeon. Such was evidently the intention of the Baron du F——: and, though his son, disappointing this intention, had escaped with only three years of captivity, and some broken limbs, the benignant law above-mentioned interposed to prevent farther punishment, and left the Baron without any legal right to deprive Mons. du F—— of his inheritance. His brothers, being sensible of this, wrote to inform him of his father's death, and recal him to France. He refused to go while the lettre de cachet remained in force against him. The Baron having left all his papers sealed up, which his younger sons could not open but in the presence of their brother, they obtained the revocation of the lettre de cachet, and sent it to Mons. du F——, who immediately set off for France.

The Baron's estate amounted to about four thousand pounds a year. Willing to avoid a tedious litigation with his brothers, Mons. du F—— consented to divide with them this property. But he soon found reason to repent of his imprudent generosity; those very brothers, on whom he had bestowed an equal share of his fortune, refusing to concur with him in his application to the parliament of Rouen for the revocation of the arret against his marriage. Mons. du F——, surprised and shocked at their refusal, began to entertain some apprehensions of his personal safety; and dreading that, supported by the authority of his mother, another lettre de cachet might be obtained against him, he hastened back to England. Nor was it till after he had received assurances from several of the magistrates of Rouen, that they would be responsible for the safety of his person, that he again ventured to return to France, accompanied by Madame and Mademoiselle du F——, in order to obtain the revocation of the arret. On their arrival at Rouen, finding that the parliament was exiled, and that the business could not be prosecuted at that time, they again came back to pass the winter in England.

At this period his mother died; and in the following summer Mons. and Madame du F—— arrived in France, at the great epocha of French liberty, on the 15th of July, 1789, the very day after that on which the Bastille was taken. It was then that Mons. du F—— felt himself in security on his native shore.—It was then that his domestic comforts were no longer embittered with the dread of being torn from his family by a separation more terrible than death itself.—It was then that he no more feared that his repose at night would be broken by the entrance of ruffians prepared to drag him to dungeons, the darkness of which was never visited by the blessed beams of day!

He immediately took possession of his chateau, and only waits for the appointment of the new judges, to solicit the revocation of the arret against his marriage, and to secure the inheritance of his estate to Mademoiselle du F——, his only daughter, who is now fifteen years of age, and is that very child who was born in the bosom of adversity, and whose infancy was exposed to all the miseries of want. May she never know the afflictions of her parents, but may she inherit their virtues!

Under the antient government of France, there might have been some doubt of Mons. du F——'s obtaining the revocation of the arret against his marriage. Beneath the iron hand of despotism, justice and virtue might have been overthrown. But happier omens belong to the new constitution of France. The judges will commence their high office with that dignity becoming so important a trust, by cancelling an act of the most flagrant oppression. They will confirm that solemn, that sacred engagement which Mons. and Madame du F—— have three times vowed at the altar of God!—which has been sanctioned by laws human and divine—which has been ratified in earth and in heaven!

No sooner had Mons. and Madame du F—— taken possession of their property, than they seemed eager to convince us, how little this change of fortune was capable of obliterating, for one moment, the remembrance of the friends of their adversity. With all the earnestness of affection, they invited us to France, and appeared to think their prosperity incomplete, and their happiness imperfect, till we accepted the invitation. You will believe that we are not insensible witnesses of the delightful change in their fortune. We have the joy of seeing them, not only possessing all the comforts of affluence, but universal respect and esteem.

Mons. du F—— endeavours to banish misery from his possessions. His tenants consider him as a father, and, "when the eye sees him it blesses him." I said to one of the peasants whom I met in my walk yesterday, "Je suis charmée de voir que Mons. est si bien aimé ici."—"Oh pour ça, oui Madame, et à bonne raison, car il ne nous fait que du bien!"[1]

Such is the history of Mons. du F——. Has it not the air of a romance? and are you not glad that the denouement is happy?— Does not the old Baron die exactly in the right place; at the very page one would chuse?—Or, if I sometimes wish that he had lived a little longer, it is only from that desire of retribution, which, in cases of injustice and oppression, it is so natural to feel.—It is only because the knowledge of the overthrow of the antient government would have been a sufficient punishment to him for all his cruelty. He would have sickened at the sight of general happiness. The idea of liberty being extended to the lower ranks, while, at the same time, tyranny was deprived of its privileges, he would have found insupportable; and would have abhorred a country, which could no longer boast of a Bastille; a country where iron cages were broken down, where dungeons were thrown open, and where justice was henceforth to shed a clear and steady light, without one dark shade of relief from lettres de cachet.

But peace be to his ashes! If the recollection of his evil deeds excites my indignation, it is far otherwise with Mons. and Madame du F——. Never did I hear their lips utter an expression of resentment, or disrespect, towards his memory; and never did I, with that warmth which belongs to my friendship for them, involuntarily pass a censure on his conduct, without being made sensible, by their behaviour, that I had done wrong.

Adieu!

---

1 I am happy to see that Monsieur is so much beloved.—Oh, yes, Madam, and well he may, he does us nothing but good. [Williams's note]

LETTER XXIII.

I Am glad you think that a friend's having been persecuted, imprisoned, maimed, and almost murdered under the antient government of France, is a good excuse for loving the revolution. What, indeed, but friendship, could have led my attention from the annals of imagination to the records of politics; from the poetry to the prose of human life? In vain might Aristocrates have explained to me the rights of kings, and Democrates have descanted on the rights of the people. How many fine-spun threads of reasoning would my wandering thoughts have broken; and how difficult should I have found it to arrange arguments and inferences in the cells of my brain! But however dull the faculties of my head, I can assure you, that when a proposition is addressed to my heart, I have some quickness of perception. I can then decide, in one moment, points upon which philosophers and legislators have differed in all ages: nor could I be more convinced of the truth of any demonstration in Euclid, than I am, that, that system of politics must be the best, by which those I love are made happy.

Mons. du F——'s chateau is near the little town of Forges,[1] celebrated for its mineral waters, and much resorted to in summer on that account. We went to the fountain on pretence of drinking the waters, but in reality to see the company. The first morning we made our appearance, the ladies presented us with nosegays of fine spreading purple heath, which they called Bouquets à la fontaine.[2]

I was told, before I left England, that I should find that French liberty had destroyed French urbanity. But every thing I have seen and heard, since my arrival in France, has contradicted this assertion, and led me to believe that the French will carefully preserve, from the wreck of their monarchical government, the old charter they have so long held of superiority in politeness. I am persuaded the most determined Democrates of the nation, whatever other privileges they may chuse to exercise, will always suffer the privilege of being rude to lie dormant.

In every country it is social pleasure that sheds the most delicious flowers which grow on the path of life; but in France she covers the

---

1 Near the northwest coast of France, some forty kilometers northeast of Rouen.
2 Nosegays of the fountain. [Williams's note]

whole way with roses, and the traveller can scarcely mark its ruggedness. Happy are a people, so fond of talking as the French, in possessing a language modelled to all the charming purposes of conversation. Their turn of expression is a dress that hangs so gracefully on gay ideas, that you are apt to suppose that wit, a quality parsimoniously distributed in other countries, is in France as common as the gift of speech. Perhaps that brilliant phraseology, which dazzles a foreigner, may be familiar and common to a French ear: but how much ingenuity must we allow to a people, who have formed a language, of which the common-place phrases give you the idea of wit!

You, who are a reader of Madame Brulart's works, will know, that I am here on a sort of classic ground. The Abbaye de Bobec is but a few miles distant from this chateau, and I walk every day in the forest where Michel and Jaqueline[1] erected their little hut; which you may remember, having unfortunately built too low to admit of their standing upright, they comforted themselves with the reflection, "Qu'on ne peut pas penser à tout;"[2] and, when they were once seated on their dwelling, in which it was a vain attempt to stand, expatiated on the comforts of being "chez soi."[3] Upon enquiry, I have heard that poor Jaqueline, three years after the happy change in her fortune, was killed by a stroke of lightning, and that Michel (as he was bound to do, being the hero of a romance) died of grief.

The Abbé de Bobec has much reputation in this part of the country for wisdom; but a French gentleman, who dined with him yesterday, told me this morning, "il m'a donné une indigestion de bon sens."[4] This is something in the style of a young Frenchman, who went to visit an acquaintance of his at Rotterdam, and has ever since called that worthy gentleman, "La raison continue (comme on dit la fièvre continue) avec des redoublemens."[5]

An alarm has been spread, but without any foundation, that the Austrian troops were marching to invade France. It puts me in mind of the old trick of the Roman patricians, who, whenever the plebians grew refractory, called out, that the Equi and the Volsci were coming: the Equi and the Volsci, however, never came.

---

1 Stéphanie-Félicité de Genlis (Madame Sillery) published a story titled "Michel et Jacqueline" in the early 1780s.
2 One cannot think of every thing. [Williams's note]
3 At home. [Williams's note]
4 He gave me an indigestion of good sense. [Williams's note]
5 Reasoning continued, as you would speak of a fever with fresh paroxysms. [Williams's note]

LETTER XXIV.

WE have had a fête at the chateau, on the day of St. Augustin,[1] who is Mons. du F——'s patron; and, though Mons. is become a protestant, I hope he will always show this mark of respect to his old friend St. Augustin. Indeed I am persuaded that Luther and Calvin, if they had been of our party, would have reconciled their minds to these charming rites of superstition.

The ceremonies began with a discharge of fusées, after which Mademoiselle du F—— entered the saloon, where a great croud were assembled, with a crown of flowers in her hand, and addressed her father in these words:—"Mon très cher papa, pourrois-je profiter d'un moment plus favorable pour vous souhaiter une bonne fête, que celui où nos bons, et *vrais amis* sont ici rassemblés, et s'unissent à moi pour célébrer cet heureux jour? C'est dans vos biens cher papa, c'est dans votre chateau que la Divine Providence nous réunit, pour chanter vos vertus, et ce courage héroïque qui vous a fait supporter tous vos *Malheurs*. L'orage est passé, jouissez maintenant cher papa du bonheur que vous meritez si bien-de l'estime que vous vous êtes acquis dans tous les cœurs sensibles. Que votre chère enfant contribue à votre félicité, que l'Eternel daigne exaucer les vœux que je lui addresse pour la conservation et le bonheur d'une tendre père, à qui j'offre mes homages, ma reconnoissance, et les sentimens d'un cœur qui vous est tout dévoué."[2]

She then placed the crown of flowers upon his head, and he embraced her tenderly. A number of ladies advanced, presented him with nosegays, and were embraced in their turn.

We had seen, while we were at Paris, a charming little piece performed at the Theatre de Monsieur, called "La Fédération, ou La

---

1 The feast of St. Augustine was celebrated on August 28.

2 "My dearest papa, can I chuse a more favourable moment to wish you an agreeable fête than this, when our best, our faithful friends are here assembled, and join with me in celebrating this happy day? It is in the midst of your possessions, my dear papa, it is in your chateau, that Divine Providence has re-united us, to declare your virtues, and the heroic fortitude with which you have supported your misfortunes. The storm is past, and you can now, my dear papa, enjoy the happiness you so well deserve, and the esteem of every amiable mind. May your child contribute to your felicity! May the Supreme Being hear the prayers which I address to him for the preservation of a tender father, to whom I offer my duty, my gratitude, and the best affections of my heart!" [Williams's note]

Famille Patriotique." Madame du F—— sent for a copy of this piece, and it was now performed by the company assembled at the chateau. The tenants, with their wives and daughters, formed the most considerable part of the audience, and I believe no play, in antient or modern times, was ever acted with more applause. My sister took a part in the performance, which I declined doing, till I recollected that one of the principal characters was a statue; upon which, I consented to perform le beau rôle de la statue.[1] And, in the last scene, I, being the representative of Liberty, appeared with all her usual attributes, and guarding the consecrated banners of the nation, which were placed on an altar, on which was inscribed, in transparent letters, "A la Liberté, 14 Juillet, 1789."[2] One of the performers, pointing to the statue, says "Chaque peuple à décoré cette idole de quelques attributs qui lui sont particuliers.—Ce bonnet sur-tout est devenu un emblème éloquent.—Ne pourrions-nous pas en ajouter d'autres qui deviendront peut-êtres aussi célèbres?"[3] He then unfolds a scarf of national ribband, which had been placed at the foot of the altar, and adds, "Cette noble écharpe!—Ces couleurs si bien assorties ne sont-elles pas dignes de figurer aussi parmi les attributs de la Liberté?"[4] The scarf was thrown over my shoulder, and the piece concluded with Le Carillon national:[5] after a grand chorus of ça ira,[6] the performers ranged themselves in order, and ça ira was danced. Ça ira hung on every lip, ça ira glowed on every countenance! Thus do the French, lest they should be tempted, by pleasure, to forget one moment the cause of liberty, bind it to their remembrance in the hour of festivity, with fillets and scarfs of national ribband; connect it with the sound of the viol and the harp, and appoint it not merely to regulate the great movements of government, but to mold the figure of the dance. When the cotillon was finished, some beautiful fireworks were played off, and we then went to supper. "Vous êtes bien

---

1 The fine part of the statue. [Williams's note]
2 To Liberty, July 14th, 1789. [Williams's note]
3 Every nation had decorated this idol with some peculiar attributes.—This cap has been long one of her most eloquent emblems.—Can we not add some others, which may, perhaps, become no less celebrated? [Williams's note]
4 That noble scarf!—are not its auspicious colours worthy of appearing amongst the attributes of Liberty? [Williams's note]
5 The national bells. [Williams's note]
6 It will go on. [Williams's note]

placée Mons."[1] said madame du F—— to a young Frenchman, who was seated between my sister and me at table. "Madame," answered he, in a stile truly French, "me voila heureux pour la première fois, à vingt trois ans."[2]

After supper we returned to the saloon, where the gentlemen danced with the peasant girls, and the ladies with the peasants. A more joyous scene, or a set of happier countenances, my eyes never beheld. When I recollected the former situation of my friends, the spectacle before me seemed an enchanting vision: I could not forbear, the whole evening, comparing the past with the present, and, while I meant to be exceedingly merry, I felt that tears, which would not be suppressed, were gushing from my eyes—but they were tears of luxury.

LETTER XXV.

A DECREE has passed in the National Assembly, instituting rewards for literary merit. The proposal met with great opposition from one of the members, I do not wish to remember his name, who said the state stood in need of husbandmen, not poets; as if the state would be encumbered by having both. This gentleman thinks, that, provided wheat and oats flourish, the culture of *mind* may be dispensed with; and that, if the spade and harrow are sharpened, the quill of genius may be stripped of all its feathers. Mais, vive l'Assemblée Nationale![3]—they have determined never to abolish the *nobility* of the muses, or deprive the fine arts *de leurs droits honorifiques.*[4]

Apropos of poets.—The French have conquered many old prejudices, but their prejudice against Shakespeare still exists. They well know, that though in England it is our policy, or our pleasure, to have an opposition on every other subject, we have not one dissenting voice about Shakespeare; and therefore they allow that he may, perhaps, deserve to be the idol of the British nation, a sort of household god whom we delight to honour; but they have gods of

---

1 You are well placed, Sir. [Williams's note]
2 I am made happy, Madam, for the first time, at three and twenty years of age. [Williams's note]
3 Long live the National Assembly. [Williams's note]
4 Of their honorary rights. [Williams's note]

their own to whom they pay homage, and have little idea that Shakespeare was not only the glory of England, but of human nature. It would be a hopeless attempt to convince them, that the genius of their boasted Corneille[1] has something of the proud and affected greatness of Lewis the Fourteenth, while that of Shakespeare has more affinity to the noble dignified simplicity of Henry the Fourth. They repeat, till you are weary of the remark, that French tragedies are regular dramas, while Shakespeare's plays are monsters. This reminds me of Boileau's answer to an author who had brought him a play to read, of which Boileau disapproved.[2] Sir, exclaimed the enraged author, I defy malice to say that my piece transgresses any one of the rules. "Why, Sir," replied Boileau, "it transgresses the first rule of all, that of keeping the reader awake."

The young gentleman who, as I mentioned to you, was confined at St. Yon, in the cell adjoining Mons. du F——'s, and with whom he used to converse in whispers through a hole in the wall, is come to pay a visit at the chateau. This young man went very early into the army: but, at the age of twenty, his father being at St. Domingo, and his mother considering her son as a spy upon her conduct, which was such as shrunk from inspection, obtained a lettre de cachet against him, and he was confined three years at St. Yon. He has told me, that, after the first year, he lost all hope of ever regaining his liberty. A morbid melancholy seized his mind; he lay stretched on the same bed for two years; and sometimes refused to taste food for several days together. When his father, at his return from St. Domingo, came to liberate him, he was so feeble that he was unable to walk.

His father again left France, and the brother of this young man has suffered a fate even more severe than himself. At the age of fifteen, he was guilty of some indiscretions, which incurred the resentment of his unrelenting mother, and another lettre de cachet was obtained.—"Is there any cause in nature that makes these hard

---

1 Pierre Corneille (1606-84), a major dramatist credited for establishing the genre of French classical tragedy, is best-known for the tetralogy comprising *Le Cid* (1637), *Horace* (1640), *Cinna* (1643), and *Polyeucte* (1643).

2 Nicolas Boileau (1636-1711), an important poet and literary theorist, was widely known for his advocacy of classical standards in contemporary literature. His major works include *L'Art poétique* (1674) and the satiric *Le Lutrin* (1674-83), which strongly influenced Pope's *The Rape of the Lock*.

hearts?"[1]—He was confined ten years, and only released when all the prisons were thrown open, by order of the National Assembly. But for this unhappy young man their mercy came too late—His reason was gone for ever! and he was led out of his prison, at the age of five and twenty, a maniac. When the sensibility with which his brother relates these family misfortunes melts us into tears, we are told, que la tristesse, est la maladie du charbon Anglois,[2] and will never be tolerated in France.

You will not be surprized to hear that Mons. du F—— has, with great complacency, relinquished his title; and that, being a ci-devant[3] captive, as well as a ci-devant Baron, he feels that the enjoyment of personal security, the sweetness of domestic comfort, in short, that the common rights of man are of more value than he ever found the rights of nobility in the solitude of his dungeon. He is ready to acknowledge, that confinement in a subterraneous cell, a fall from a height of fifty feet, and the fracture of his limbs, are things which even the title of Baron can scarcely counterbalance; and he therefore drinks a libation, every day after dinner, à la santé de l'Assemblée Nationale,[4] though they have deprived him of the soothing epithet of Mon-Seigneur. We, however, shall soon cease to pledge him in this toast. The day of our departure draws near. We must leave the charming society at the chateau—we must leave the peasants dance under the shade of the old elms, while the setting sun pours streams of liquid gold through the foliage—we must leave Le maitre de violon, qui se ride en riant, avec sa malheureuse figure.[5]—All this must we leave!—To-morrow is the last day of our residence at the chateau. What a desolate word is that monosyllable of last—how sad, how emphatical its meaning!— There is something in it which gives the most indifferent things an interest in our affections.—I am sure I could write a volume with this little word for my text; but I may as well explain myself in one line— I am sorry to leave France!

---

1 Shakespeare, King Lear, III.vi. 75-76.
2 Melancholy is the disease of English coal fires. [Williams's note]
3 Former.
4 To the health of the National Assembly. [Williams's note]
5 The player on the violin, who, with his miserable figure, has become wrinkled from laughing. [Williams's note]

LETTER XXVI.

London.

WE left France early in September, that we might avoid the equinoctial gales; but were so unfortunate as to meet, in our passage from Dieppe to Brighton, with a very violent storm. We were two days and two nights at sea, and beat four and twenty hours off the coast of Brighton; and it would be difficult for you, who have formed your calculations of time on dry land, to guess what is the length of four and twenty hours in a storm at sea. At last, with great difficulty, we landed on the beach, where we found several of our friends and acquaintance, who, supposing that we might be among the passengers, sympathised with our danger, and were anxious for our preservation.

Before the storm became so serious as to exclude every idea but that of preparing to die with composure, I could not help being diverted with the comments on French customs, and French politics, which passed in the cabin. "Ah," says one man to his companion, "one had need to go to France, to know how to like old England when one gets back again."— "For my part," rejoined another, "I've never been able to get drunk once the whole time I was in France—not a drop of porter to be had—and as for their victuals, they call a bit of meat of a pound and a half, a fine piece of roast beef."— "And pray," added he, turning to one of the sailors, "What do you think of their National Assembly?"— "Why," says the sailor, "if I ben't mistaken, the National Assembly has got some points from the wind."

I own it has surprized me not a little, since I came to London, to find that most of my acquaintance are of the same opinion with the sailor. Every visitor brings me intelligence from France full of dismay and horror. I hear of nothing but crimes, assassinations, torture, and death. I am told that every day witnesses a conspiracy; that every town is the scene of a massacre; that every street is blackened with a gallows, and every highway deluged with blood. I hear these things, and repeat to myself, Is this the picture of France? Are these the images of that universal joy, which called tears into my eyes, and made my heart throb with sympathy?—To me, the land which these mighty magicians have suddenly covered with darkness, where, waving their evil wand, they have reared the dismal scaffold, have clotted the knife of the assassin with gore, have called forth the shriek of despair, and the agony of torture; to me, this land of desolation appeared drest in additional beauty beneath the genial smile of liberty. The woods seemed to cast a more refreshing shade, and the lawns to wear a brighter verdure, while the carols of freedom burst from the cottage of the peasant, and the voice of joy resounded on the hill, and in the valley.

Must I be told that my mind is perverted, that I am become dead to all sensations of sympathy, because I do not weep with those who have lost a part of their superfluities, rather than rejoice that the oppressed are protected, that the wronged are redressed, that the captive is set at liberty, and that the poor have bread? Did the universal parent of the human race, implant the feelings of pity in the heart, that they should be confined to the artificial wants of vanity, the ideal deprivations of greatness; that they should be fixed beneath the dome of the palace, or locked within the gate of the chateau; without extending one commiserating sigh to the wretched hamlet, as if its famished inhabitants, though not ennobled by *man*, did not bear, at least, the ensigns of nobility stamped on our nature by God?

Must I hear the charming societies, in which I found all the elegant graces of the most polished manners, all the amiable urbanity of liberal and cultivated minds, compared with the most rude, ferocious, and barbarous levellers that ever existed? Really, some of my English acquaintance, whatever objections they may have to republican principles, do, in their discussions of French politics, adopt a most free and republican style of censure. Nothing can be more democratical than their mode of expression, or display a more levelling spirit, than their unqualified contempt of *all* the leaders of the revolution.

It is not my intention to shiver lances, in every society I enter, in the cause of the National Assembly. Yet I cannot help remarking, that, since that Assembly does not presume to set itself up as an example to this country, we seem to have very little right to be furiously angry, because they think proper to try another system of government themselves. Why should they not be suffered to make an experiment in politics? I have always been told, that the improvement of every science depends upon experiment. But I now hear that, instead of their new attempt to form the great machine of society upon a simple principle of general amity upon the FEDERATION of its members, they ought to have repaired the feudal wheels and springs, by which their ancestors directed its movements. Yet if mankind had always observed this retrograde motion, it would surely have led them to few acquisitions in virtue, or in knowledge; and we might even have been worshipping the idols of paganism at this moment. To forbid, under the pains and penalties of reproach, all attempts of the human mind to advance to greater perfection, seems to be proscribing every art and science. And we cannot much wonder that the French, having received so small a legacy of public happiness from their forefathers, and being sensible of the poverty of their own patrimony, should try new methods of transmitting a richer inheritance to their posterity.

Perhaps the improvements which mankind may be capable of making in the art of politics, may have some resemblance to those they have made in the art of navigation. Perhaps our political plans may hitherto have been somewhat like those ill-constructed misshapen vessels, which, unfit to combat with the winds and waves, were only used by the antients to convey the warriors of one country to despoil and ravage another neighbouring state; which only served to produce an intercourse of hostility, a communication of injury, an exchange of rapine and devastation.—But it may possibly be within the compass of human ability to form a system of politics, which, like a modern ship of discovery, built upon principles that defy the opposition of the tempestuous elements ("and passions are the elements of life"—)[1] instead of yielding to their fury makes them subservient to its purpose, and sailing sublimely over the untracked ocean, unites those together whom nature seemed for ever to have separated, and throws a line of connection across the divided world.

One cause of the general dislike in which the French revolution is held in this country, is the exaggerated stories which are carefully circulated by such of the aristocrates as have taken refuge in England. They are not all, however, persons of this description. There is now a young gentleman in London, nephew to the Bishop de Sens, who has lost his fortune, his rank, all his high expectations, and yet who has the generosity to applaud the revolution, and the magnanimity to reconcile himself to personal calamities, from the consideration of general good; and who is "faithful found" to his country, "among the faithless."[2] I hope this amiable young Frenchman will live to witness, and to share the honours,

---

1 Pope, *An Essay on Man*, I.162.
2 Cf. Milton, *Paradise Lost*: "So spake the Seraph *Abdiel* faithful found, / Among the faithless" (V.896-97).

the prosperity of that regenerated country; and I also hope that the National Assembly of France will answer the objections of its adversaries in the manner most becoming its own dignity, by forming such a constitution as will render the French nation virtuous, flourishing, and happy.

FINIS.

Appendix A: Excerpts From Later Volumes of Williams's Letters from France

[After the success of the 1790 *Letters Written in France*, which went through several editions, Williams and her new publisher G. G. and J. Robinson brought out seven more volumes of letters between 1792 and 1796. Later organized into two series, each containing four volumes, these letters continue the narrative of the Revolution through the overthrow of the monarchy, the September Massacres, the executions of Louis XVI and Marie Antoinette, the Reign of Terror, the fall of Robespierre, and the beginnings of the Directory. Throughout, Williams attempts to keep alive—both for herself and for her audience—faith that the founding values of the Revolution would eventually triumph. We present below excerpts from each of the volumes that succeeded the 1790 *Letters Written in France*, which together present one of the most powerful eyewitness accounts ever rendered of the key events in the French Revolution.]

1. Letters from France: Containing Many New Anecdotes (1792)

[Published in London in 1792, Williams's *Letters from France: Containing Many New Anecdotes Relative to the French Revolution, and the Present State of French Manners* continues the ebullient tone of the first volume. In twenty four undated letters to the same unnamed correspondent addressed in Volume 1, Williams describes, with great enthusiasm and optimism, her personal travels and experiences in France from September 1791 through the early months of 1792.

Although this second volume hints that the Revolution has not led to perfect harmony in France, Williams consistently searches for a benign interpretation of what she sees. In the fifteenth letter, for instance, she argues that even though high sugar prices have sparked street riots in Paris, the Parisians have so much respect for the National Guard that there is no danger of any significant disorder. The final letter begins with Williams lamenting the French declaration of war against Austria and military defeat at Tournai, but it ends with her assurances that France will be victorious and that liberty will spread across all of Europe.

[handwritten margin notes: "important", "great optimism of Frances success"]

Most of this volume is occupied with pleasant anecdotes, beginning with a description of the celebrations in Rouen that were
sparked by the King's acceptance of the Constitution, an event that
takes place only days after Williams's return to France from England and that harks back to her account of the Fête de la Fédération in Volume 1. As she does also in that earlier volume with the
story of the du Fossé family, Williams here demonstrates the benefits of the Revolution by relating a tale about which she herself
comments, "Perhaps a novel-writer ... might almost spin a volume
from these materials" (156).]

THE STORY OF AUGUSTE AND MADELAINE, FROM *LETTER XXI*

... A young Frenchman [Auguste], whose usual residence was at
Paris, having travelled as far as Toulouse the year before the revolution, was invited by a party of his friends to accompany them to
Bareges, where some of them were going in pursuit of amusement,
and others in search of health from the medicinal springs which
rise so plentifully, both in hot and cold streams, among the Pyre-
nean mountains....

Among a number of persons of rank and fortune, there was
however one family at Bareges in a different situation. This family consisted of an elderly infirm French officer, who had been
long afflicted with the palsy, and his daughter, a young woman
about nineteen years of age. Their appearance and mode of living seemed to indicate, that, though in search of relief this old
officer had journeyed to Bareges, he had in so doing far exceed-
ed the bounds of economy which his circumstances prescribed,
and was forced to deny himself every accomodation his infirmi-
ties could spare. He lived in the most retired manner, in the
worst lodging at Bareges; and, while the other ladies were
dressed in a style of expensive variety and profusion, his daughter wore only a plain linen gown, which, though always perfectly clean, was coarse; and her dark hair was left unpowdered and
without any ornament whatever. Fortunately for Madelaine
however (for that was her name), her person was calculated to
make her coarse gown appear to the best advantage; and though
she was not very beautiful, her countenance had an expression
of sweetness which answered the end of beauty by exciting love
and admiration....

One evening, when Auguste was walking in the town of Bareges with some ladies, he saw Madelaine at a little distance assisting with great difficulty to support her father, who appeared to be seized with a fit. Auguste darted like an arrow towards the spot, and held up the officer till he found himself somewhat recovered; and then Auguste, with a sort of gentle violence, obliged Madelaine, who was pale and trembling, to let go her father's arm, and suffer him to assist the servant in leading him home, which was but a few steps farther. Auguste entered the house, where he remained till the old officer was a little revived; and, after prevailing upon Madelaine to take a few hartshorn drops, he retired.

The next morning he felt that common civility required he should pay the old officer a visit, and learn how he had passed the night. It happened that Madelaine had the very same idea. "Surely," thought she, "it will be very strange if this young man, who was so kind, so careful of my father, and who made me take some hartshorn drops, should neglect to call and enquire after us." This idea had come across her mind several times; and she was meditating upon it at her father's bedside, when Auguste was announced.

The old officer, who had all the finished politeness of his country and his profession, received him in the most courteous manner; and, though he spoke with some difficulty, yet he was profuse in acknowledgments for the service Auguste had rendered him. Madelaine's thanks were few and simply expressed; but the tone in which they were uttered was such that Auguste felt he could have sacrificed his life to have deserved them.

The old officer still continued sick, and therefore Auguste still considered it as an indispensible mark of attention to go every day, and learn the state of his health. He also began to feel that these visits became every day more necessary to his own happiness. That happiness was indeed embittered by many painful reflections. He well knew that to obtain his father the Count de ———'s consent to marry Madelaine, was as impossible as it was for himself to conquer the passion she had inspired. He knew exactly the order in which his father's enquiries would run on this subject. He was aware that there were two interrogatories to be answered. The first was—"How many thousand livres has she a year?" And the second—"Is she noble?" And nothing could be more embarassing than that the enquiry concerning fortune would, he was sure, come first; since that was the only article which could not be answered in a satisfactory manner; for to Madelaine's family no objection could have been made. By the way, though the former nobility of France would not absolutely contaminate the pure streams of noble blood by an union with the daughter of a *roturier*, they had always sufficient generosity to abate some generations of nobility in favour of a proper equivalent in wealth.

Auguste, while he was convinced of the impossibility of obtaining his father's consent to his marriage, did not pay Madelaine one visit the less from that consideration; and when the usual hour of his visit arrived, he often suddenly broke a chain of admirable reasoning on the imprudence of his attachment, in order to hasten to the dwelling of her he loved. In a short time he ceased all kind of reasoning on the subject, and abandoned his heart without reserve to the most violent and unconquerable passion....

... In a few weeks the old officer felt that his dying hour was near. Auguste knelt with Madelaine at his bedside—her voice was suffocated by tears; and Auguste had scarcely power to articulate in broken accents that he would devote his life to the happiness of Madelaine. The old officer fixed his eyes with a look of tender anxiety upon his daughter, and soon after expired. Madelaine mourned for her father with uncontrouled affliction, nor could all the attentions of her lover dispel that anguish with which her affectionate heart lamented the loss of her parent.

The winter being far advanced, she proposed to defer her journey to the distant province where she and her father had lived, until spring; and to place herself in the mean time in a convent not far from Bareges. Auguste exerted all the eloquence of love to induce her to consent immediately to a private marriage. She hesitated at this proposal; and while they were conversing together on the subject, the door of the room in which they were sitting was suddenly thrown open, and Auguste saw his father the Count de —— enter. He had heard of the attachment which detained his son at Bareges, and had hastened to tear him from the spot before it was too late. He upbraided his son with great bitterness, and began also to upbraid Madelaine: but there was something in her looks, her silence, and her tears, which stifled the terms of haughty reproach in which he was prepared to address her; and ordering his son to leave the room, he desired to speak to her alone. After explaining to her the absolute impossibility of her being ever united to his son, and his determination to disinherit him, and leave his whole fortune to his second son, if Auguste should persist in his attachment to her—after endeavouring to awaken her pride and her generosity, he desired to know where she proposed going. She told him her intention of placing herself immediately in the convent of ———. He approved of this design, and left her to go to his son. No sooner was the door of the room shut, than Madelaine gave way to those tears which she had scarcely been able to restrain while the Count was speaking. She had never felt so sensibly her orphan condition as at this moment; and the dear remembrance of her fond father was mingled with the agony of disappointed love.

Meantime the Count de ——— declared to his son, that his only chance of ever obtaining his mistress depended on his absolute unconditional submission to his commands, and that he must instantly attend him to Paris. Auguste eagerly enquired what was to become of Madelaine; and his father told him that she had determined to take refuge in the convent of ———. Auguste absolutely refused to depart till he was allowed an interview with Madelaine. The Count was obliged to consent; but before he suffered them to meet, he obtained a promise from Madelaine not to mention to her lover any particulars of the conversation which had passed between her and the Count....

She set out early the next morning for the convent of ———; but not till after she had sat for some time weeping in the chair which Auguste used to occupy.

Madelaine passed the remaining part of the winter in the convent of ———, during which period she received frequent letters from Auguste; and when spring arrived he conjured her, instead of removing to her own province, to remain a little longer in her present situation; and flattered her with hopes of being able ere long to fulfil those engagements upon which all his happiness depended.

In the summer of this year an event took place which will render that summer for ever memorable. The French nation, too enlightened to bear any longer those monstrous oppressions which ignorance of its just rights alone had tolerated, shook off its fetters, and the revolution was accomplished.

Madelaine was a firm friend to the revolution, which she was told had made every Frenchman free. "And if every Frenchman is free," thought Madelaine, "surely every Frenchman may marry the woman he loves." It appeared to Madelaine, that, putting all political considerations, points upon which she had not much meditated, out of the question, obtaining liberty of choice in marriage was alone well worth the trouble of a revolution; and she was as warm a patriot from this single idea, as if she had studied the declaration of rights made by the Constituent Assembly, in all its extent and consequences.

The Count de ——, who was informed of the correspondence between the two lovers, and who saw little hopes of his son's subduing a passion which this intercourse of letters served to cherish, contrived means to have Auguste's letters intercepted at the convent. In vain Madelaine enquired with all the anxiety of tenderness for letters. In vain she counted the hours till the return of the post-days. Post after post arrived, and brought no tidings of Auguste. Three months passed in the cruel torments of anxiety and suspense, and were at length succeeded by despair. Madelaine believed she was forgotten—forgotten by Auguste!—She consulted her own heart, and it seemed to her impossible; yet, after a silence of three months, she could doubt no longer....

The little pittance which Madelaine, after paying her father's debts, had left for her own support, was insufficient to defray her expenses as a pensioner in the convent. She had already, by her sweetness and gentleness, gained the affections of some of the nuns, to whom she was also attached, and who incessantly conjured her to take the veil. "And why," she sometimes exclaimed, "why should I hesitate any longer in so doing? Since Auguste is lost, what have I to regret in renouncing the world? What sacrifice do I make? what happiness do I resign?"....

Madelaine at length determined to join the holy sisterhood of the convent. The white veil for her novitiate was prepared. The day was fixed, when, prostrate with her face towards the earth, and with flowers scattered over her, and a part of her long tresses cut off, she was to enter upon that solemn trial prepatory to her eternal renunciation of the world—of Auguste!

A few days before that which was appointed for the ceremony, Madelaine was called to the parlour, where she found her lover, with some of the municipal officers of the town, wearing their national scarfs....

One of the municipal officers then informed her, that they had received the day before a decree of the National Assembly, forbidding any nuns to be professed. He added, that the municipality had already given information of this new law to the abbess, who had consented to allow Madelaine to leave the convent immediately. As he pronounced these last words, Madelaine looked at her lover. Auguste hastened to explain to her that his uncle, who loved him and pitied his sufferings, had at length made a will, leaving him his fortune upon condition that his father consented to his marriage with Madelaine.

When her lover and the municipal officers departed, Madelaine retired to her apartment, to give way to those delicious tears which were poured from a heart overflowing with wonder, thankfulness, and joy.... "I always loved the revolution," thought Madelaine, as she laid aside the white gown in which she was to be married the next morning; "and this last decree is surely of all others the best and wisest—but if it had come too late!"—At this idea Madelaine took up the veil for her novitiate, which lay upon her table, and bathed it with a flood of tears.

The next morning Auguste and Madelaine were married in the parish church of ——, and immediately after the ceremony set out for Paris, where they now live, and are, I am told, two of the happiest people and the best patriots in France. (pp. 156–82)

2. Letters from France: Containing ... Interesting and Original Information, vol. I (1793)

[Williams's third volume, *Letters from France: Containing a Great Variety of Interesting and Original Information Concerning the Most Important Events that Have Lately Occurred in that Country, and Particularly Respecting the Campaign of 1792* was published in 1793 along with Volume 4, completing the first series of letters. Williams returned to Paris in early August of 1792 and witnessed the storming of the Tuileries Palace on 10 August and the overthrow of the monarchy, which culminated in the execution of King Louis XVI on 21 January of the following year. On 22 September, the Legislative Assembly proclaimed France a republic. Already at war with Austria and Prussia, France declared war on England and Holland in February 1793, and on Spain in March. France's military campaign suffered a serious setback when Dumouriez, chief commander of the Northern troops (or Army of the North), defected to the Austrians on 5 April 1793, further threatening the tenuous political and military stability of France.

Volume 3 contains seven letters and an Appendix, though Williams herself wrote only the first letter, dated 25 January 1793, four days after the execution of Louis XVI. Here she briefly outlines events from the overthrow of the monarchy on 10 August 1792 to the massacres on 2 September of over 1,000 political prisoners of the Republic, reviling the massacres, the Paris Commune, and especially the unholy triumvirate of Maximilien Robespierre (her chief villain), Georges Danton, and Jean-Paul Marat, and their disruption of "Bastille day ideals." Nonetheless, Williams steadfastly claims that the anarchy in France is only temporary and that the true ideals of the revolution will not die.]

In the Advertisement to Volume 3, Williams notes that Letters 2-6 (which occupy most of the book) are written by "another hand," subsequently identified by scholars as her life partner John Hurford Stone (1763-1818; see Introduction, pp. 22-24). Stone writes from the cities of St. Menehould, Clermont, Varennes, Verdun, and Reims during the Austrian/Prussian campaigns of October and November 1792. Ardently supporting Revolutionary ideals, he pursues the camp of French general Charles Dumouriez, sketching the history of the campaigns and focusing on the engagements between Dumourier and the Duke of Brunswick. The Appendix to Volume 3 contains correspondence of General Dumouriez.]

THE SEPTEMBER MASSACRES IN RETROSPECT, FROM *LETTER I*

PARIS, *January* 25, 1793.

DEAR SIR,

THE event which has this week taken place in Paris, will no doubt furnish you with ample matter for speculation. Imagination contemplates with an overwhelming emotion that extraordinary vicissitude of fortune which conducted Louis the Sixteenth from the radiant palace of Versailles, to the gloomy tower of the Temple— from the first throne of Europe, to the scaffold and the block— while the feelings of the heart, which run a faster pace than the reasonings of the head, reject for a while all calculation of general good or evil, and melt in mournful sympathy over "greatness fallen from its high estate." But, when we consider the importance which this event may have in its consequences, not only to this country, but to all Europe, we lose sight of the individual sufferer, to meditate upon the destiny of mankind....

That conflict which after the King's acceptance of the new constitution existed in this country between the executive and legislative powers, between the court and the people, has since the tenth of August been succeeded by a conflict far more terrible; a conflict between freedom and anarchy, knowledge and ignorance, virtue and vice. While the real patriots of France, in their different conflicts with the ancient despotism, risked their lives, and shed their blood, and by their desperate valour confirmed the liberty of their country, a set of men, who exposed not their persons to the smallest danger in the enterprise, contrived, without peril or exertion, to seize upon a considerable portion of power; and never surely in the annals of tyranny have we heard of power more shamefully abused. Those demagogues, known by the appellation of the "Commune provisoire de Paris" [Provisional Government of Paris], have, during the short period of their usurpation, committed more crimes than despotism itself would have achieved in ages. The crimes of tyrants, by exciting our abhorrence, serve to promote the cause of freedom.... Surrounding nations, who might perhaps have been animated by the example of a country which has long served as a model to the rest of Europe, have heard of the second of September, and have shrunk back into the torpor of slavery. They have beheld, in the room of the pure and sublime worship of liberty, the grim idol of anarchy set up, and have seen her altar smeared with sanguinary rites. They have beheld the inhuman judges of that night wearing the municipal scarf which their polluting touch profaned, surrounded by men armed with pikes and sabres dropping with blood—while a number of blazing torches threw their glaring light on the ferocious visages of those execrable judges, who, mixing their voices with the shrieks of the dying, passed sentence with a savage mockery of justice, on victims devoted to their rage. They have beheld infernal executioners of that night, with their arms bared for the purposes of murder, dragging forth those victims to modes of death at which nature shudders.—— Ah! ye slaughtered heroes of the immortal 14th of July, was it for this ye overthrew the towers of the Bastile, and burst open its gloomy dungeons?—was it for this, ye generous patriots, that with heroic contempt of life ye shed your blood to give liberty and happiness to your enslaved country?—Ah! had ye foreseen that the fanatics of liberty, fierce as the fanatics of superstition, would have their day of St. Bartholomew, would not your victorious arms have been unnerved? Would not the sacred glow of freedom have been frozen in your veins? Ah! what is become of the delightful visions which elevated the enthusiastic heart? —What is become of the transport which beat high in every bosom, when an assembled million of the human race vowed on the altar of their country, in the name of the represented nation, inviolable fraternity and union—an eternal federation? This was indeed the golden age of the revolution.—But it is past!—the enchanting spell is broken, and the fair scenes of beauty and of order, through which imagination wandered, are transformed into the desolation of the wilderness, and clouded by the darkness of the tempest. If the genius of Liberty—profaned Liberty! does not arise in his might, and crush those violators of freedom, whose crimes have almost broken the heart of humanity, the inhabitants of Paris may indeed "wish for the wings of the dove, that they may fly away and be at rest—for there is violence and strife in the city."

At the head of this band of conspirators is Robespierre—gloomy and saturnine in his disposition, with a countenance of such dark aspect as seems the index of no ordinary guilt—fanatical and exaggerated in his avowed principles of liberty, possessing that species of eloquence which gives him power over the passions, and that cool determined temper which regulates the most ferocious designs with the most calm and temperate prudence. His crimes do not appear to be the result of passion, but of some deep and extraordinary malignity, and he seems formed to subvert and to destroy. "One, next to him in power, and next in crime," is Danton, who, though not inferior to his associate in vice, and superior in ability, having less self-command, is consequently less dangerous.—This man, at the period of the massacres, was Minister of Justice, and, being conjured to exert his authority in putting a stop to those horrors, coolly answered, "Quand le peuple ont exercé *leurs* droits, je reprendrai les *miennes*" ["When the people have exerted *their* rights, I will resume *mine*"].

Marat, though sometimes spoken of as one of the leaders of this faction, is in reality only one of its instruments ...

This triumvirate, resembling the celebrated triumvirate of Rome in every thing that bears the marks of baseness and of crimes, had associated in their guilt a number of lesser chiefs, who in their turn had enlisted others as instruments of the same horrid purpose.... But was it likely, you will ask, that the extirpation of priests, of the imprisoned agents of the aristocracy, and proscribed conspirators, could lead to the furtherance of their views? How, by making themselves the executors of such summary justice, could they arrive at the accomplishment of their wishes? Those victims alone would certainly have proved insufficient to the accomplishment of their designs, and there is no doubt that the proscription extended to the most distinguished members of the Assembly, and to the most virtuous and respectable men of the executive council. But these statesmen of the Commune felt that to strike at once those men, whom the people had been accustomed to consider as their firmest friends, would be too daring and desperate an act. A general insurrection of the mob, therefore, seemed to them the best mode of eventually accomplishing their purpose. And as no mob sufficiently great was to be procured by their own means, they contrived to make the Assembly itself ignorantly acquiesce in their diabolical projects. On the day, therefore, when these massacres began, the Commune appeared at the bar, and informed the Assembly, that at two o'clock they should order the alarm guns to fire, and the tocsin to sound, that the people summoned into the Champ de Mars might from thence march directly to meet the approaching enemy, who were coming with hasty steps to Paris, after having cut off the four thousand men sent to the relief of Verdun.—This was a falsehood, contrived and calculated, as they hoped, to accomplish their purpose: but though the people were much agitated, they were not sufficiently wound up for such an enterprise. Instead therefore of meeting in immense crowds in the Champ de Mars, where these assassins would have more readily found the means of urging them to any crime, they met peaceably in their different sections to consult on the best measures for the public safety, totally ignorant at the moment what horrid deeds were about to be transacted. Finding, therefore, that the people were not to be made the instruments, they were forced to make use of the means which they had previously concerted. The priests confined in the Carmes, under pretence of waiting some opportunity for banishment according to a decree of the Assembly, fell the first victims.—The prisoners in the Abbaye were the next, who had been sent thither since the 10th of August by warrants from their murderers: the other prisons were visited successively, where this work of death, for the executioners were very few, lasted two days, and at the prison of La Force extended to four. One is tempted to enquire with Lear, "Is there any cause in nature that makes these hard hearts?" Various conjectures have been formed respecting the number put to death in those four days—they have been lessened or exaggerated according to the political opinions of the relater. Lists of all the prisoners at that time confined are now printed by authority; and the amount is stated at one thousand and eighty-eight, including the felons, who formed nearly half the number....

Such were the immediate evils of the second of September: their consequences will probably extend far beyond the limits of that country which was the theatre of this inhuman violence. The inhabitants of Paris must bear, through every succeeding age, the recorded disgrace of having remained in a state of stupified astonishment and terror, while no more than fifty hired assassins imprinted an indelible stain upon the country. But the bitter punishment of having incurred that disgrace, is, perhaps, all which this country has to fear. Anarchy cannot be lasting. The evils it may produce will be but the evils of this day and of to-morrow—Those disorders which may for awhile convulse the infant republic, will cease with the lives of their perpetrators, who can assassinate individuals, but cannot assassinate opinions which appear to be widely diffused. Yet these are considerations which may lead us to fear, that, if the evils of anarchy will be temporary, they will also be terrible. It is well known that all the legislative assembly did, was to undo what the constituent assembly had done. Convinced, from the conduct of the court, that the liberty of France could only be preserved by the terrible means of another revolution, the second legislature, not deeming the national guard sufficient for this purpose, armed every man in Paris, and consequently placed a formidable power in the hands of that swarm of idle and profligate persons which infest great capitals, and who, having nothing to lose, feel that "havock, and spoil and ruin are their gain." Such persons are, under an established government, checked in their outrages on society, by the terror of punishment; but in the crisis of a revolution they become the dangerous instruments of party rage and faction. They may still commit enormities, of which the bourgeois of Paris, who appear since the second of September to be sunk in a state of complete stupefaction, may remain pusillanimous witnesses; but which may provoke the indignation of the other departments of the kingdom, where, in general, the love of liberty is connected with the utmost horror of anarchy. Hence civil commotions may arise. Upon the whole, the French revolution is still in its progress, and who can decide how its last page will finish?

The surrounding nations of Europe, after contemplating the savage spectacle which the second of September presented, will perhaps feel, that despotism, armed with its arbitrary impositions, its gloomy towers, and its solitary dungeons, is not more hideous than anarchy. Despotism may be compared to a stream, which, supplied from a casual spring, or unequal source, leaves, for the most part, the region through which it passes parched and desolate; yet, sometimes shedding partial moisture, cheers the eye with a spot of scanty verdure. But anarchy is the impetuous torrent that sweeps over the land with irresistible violence, and involves every object in one wide mass of ruin. (pp. 1-20)

3. Letters from France: Containing ... Interesting and Original Information, vol. II (1793)

[Published in 1793, the fourth and final volume in the first series of *Letters from France* shares the subtitle of the third volume, with which it was published, *Containing a Great Variety of Interesting and Original Information Concerning the Most Important Events that have Lately Occurred in that Country, and Particularly Respecting the Campaign of 1792.* It consists of five letters written between February and May of 1793; the final letter was authored by Williams's friend Thomas Christie.

In the first letter of this volume, Williams describes the trial, conviction, and execution of Louis XVI. The second and third letters include an extended discussion on the wars with Austria, Prussia, and the Dutch Republic; the impact of Dumouriez's defection and treason; and the growing political instability of the National Convention and the corruption of the founding principles of the Revolution. Letters IV and V focus attention on English misconceptions of the French Revolution, offering an extended critique and analysis of the British press and the pamphlet wars. Most notably, Edmund Burke's counter-revolutionary *Reflections on the Revolution in France* is blamed for contributing to the downfall of the French monarchy and the execution of Louis XVI. In an effort to clarify for British readers the importance of the French Revolution, Christie distinguishes its value as a transformational set of ideas, rights, and principles of government, from other so-called revolutions in which the "contest ... is about *masters*, but the *system* continues the same." In spite of the growing threat of anarchy in France, the volume concludes with the characteristic hope that freedom and liberty will eventually triumph over corruption and tyranny.]

THE EXECUTION OF LOUIS XVI, FROM *LETTER* 1

Paris, Feb. 10, 1793.
The calmness which Lewis the sixteenth displayed on this great trial of human fortitude, is attributed not only to the support his mind received from religious faith, but also to the hope which it is said he cherished, even till his last moment, that the people, whom he meant to address from the scaffold, would demand that his life might be spared. And his confessor, from motives of compassion,

had encouraged him in this hope. After ascending the scaffold with a firm step, twice the unhappy monarch attempted to speak, and twice Santerre prevented him from being heard, by ordering the drums to beat immediately. Alas! had he been permitted to speak, poor was his chance of exciting commiseration! Those who pitied his calamities had carefully shunned that fatal spot; and those who most immediately surrounded him only waited till the stroke was given, in order to dip their pikes and their handkerchiefs in his blood!

Setting aside all considerations of the former elevated rank, or the peculiar misfortunes of the sufferer, to refuse the privilege of utterance to one whose lips are the next moment to be closed in death—has in it something so repugnant to all the feelings of our nature, that it seems a degree of severity which could only have been practiced by that man who had remained passive when the cry of humanity called upon him to act, and who was prompted to action at the very moment when the same sentiment urged him to desist. It is, however, asserted by many persons, that Santerre, in having hindered the king from being heard, only performed his duty, and perhaps prevented the most terrible mischiefs. The utmost precaution had indeed been used to avoid any disorder, or the possibility of impeding the execution of the sentence. Every section of Paris was under arms: a third part of the citizens of each section were appointed to guard that section to which they belonged; a third part to form the escort of the king, and a third part to patrol the streets. Forty pieces of cannon were brought to the place of execution! and the fathers, the sons, and brothers of those who fell on the 10th of August had been assiduously select-ed to surround the scaffold! It was also understood, that orders had been issued, that any person who cried *grace*, should be instantly put to death. Notwithstanding these precautions, an address from the king might have produced a popular movement in his favour....

Had the king been able to excite the pity of any part of that armed multitude which filled the vast Place de la Revolution, a profusion of blood might have been spilt—A civil war might have spread desolation through the city of Paris; but the life of the king would have been no less sacrificed—and instead of receiving death at one stroke, he would probably have fallen pierced by a thousand wounds. Two persons who were on the scaffold assert, that the unhappy monarch, finding the hope he had cherished, of awaken-ing the compassion of the people, frustrated by the impossibility of his being heard, as a last resource, declared that he had secrets to reveal of importance to the safety of the state, and desired he might be led to the National Convention. Some of the guards who heard this declaration, cried, "Yes, let him go to the Convention!"—Others said "No."—Had the king been conducted to the Convention, it is easy to imagine the effect which would have been produced on the minds of the people, by the sight of their former monarch led through the streets of Paris, with his hands bound, his neck bare, his hair already cut off at the foot of the scaffold in preparation for the fatal stroke—with no other covering than his shirt. At that sight the enraged populace would have melted into tenderness, and the Parisian women, among whom were numbers who passed the day in tears of unavailing regret, would have rushed between the monarch and his guards, and have attempted his rescue, even with the risk of life. Santerre, who foresaw these consequences, who perceived the danger of this rising dispute among the guards, called to the executioner to do his office.—Then it was that despair seized upon the mind of the unfortunate monarch—his countenance assumed a look of horror—twice with agony he repeated, "Je suis perdu! je suis perdu!" ["I am undone! I am undone!"] His confessor mean time called to him from the foot of the scaffold, "Louis, fils de St. Louis, montez au ciel" ["Son of St. Louis, ascend to heaven!"]; and in one moment he was delivered from the evils of mortality.

The executioner held up the bleeding head, and the guards cried "Vive la Republique!" Some dipt their handkerchiefs in the blood—but the greater number, chilled with horror at what had passed, desired the commandant would lead them instantly from the spot. The hair was sold in separate tresses at the foot of the scaffold; and, as if every incident of this tragedy had been intended to display the strange vicissitudes of human fortune, as if every scene were meant "to point a moral," the body was conveyed in a cart to the parish church of St. Madelaine, and laid among the bodies of those who had been crushed to death on the Place de Louis XV, when Louis the sixteenth was married, and of those who had fallen before the chateau of the Thuilleries on the 10th of August.

The grave was filled with quick lime, and a guard placed over it till the corpse was consumed. The ground was then carefully levelled with the surrounding earth, and no trace or vestige remains of that spot to which, shrouded by the doubtful gloom of twilight, ancient loyalty might have repaired, and poured a tear, or superstition breathed its ritual for the departed spirit. (pp. 33-39)

I am ready to own, that there were in that revolution several circumstances calculated to shock Mr. Burke's early prejudices; and I am far from accusing him of having no motive to write against it, but that of reconciling himself to the court: for he had always seen government through the spectacles of old establishments, and not as it is in itself, or as ought to be founded in the nature of man, and in the principles of eternal reason. But while I make this concession, which candour obliges me to do, I must at the same time declare, that I cannot give him all the credit that some do for his predictions respecting the French revolution; for many of them have not been verified, and he that makes a number of bold guesses, will always succeed in some of them. Those that have taken place, have generally arisen from other causes than those supposed by Mr. Burke; and I may add, as to the rest, that the judicious friends of the French revolution foresaw as well as he did, and feared, the evils he predicted; but as they believed there was a possibility that they might not happen, they were glad to see a trial made for the instruction of the human race. For instance, in treating of military juries, and other novelties, proposed in France, Mr. Christie declined vindicating them, and represented them only as bold experiments, worthy of being made, to ascertain how far we could go in extending liberty and equal laws to all the classes of society. It is taking a safe side, in all cases, to prophesy the failure of great undertakings, for few of them succeed, compared to those that fail. There were, I dare say, many narrow-minded, splenetic, or selfish men, who predicted the ruin of those heroic spirits, who first projected a voyage round the world, and perhaps reproached their undertaking as a mad attempt, which would end in their own destruction and that of the seamen they carried with them. It is easy to argue in this way; but generous minds hope the best, and see with pleasure the commencement of enterprises, that promise to improve the condition of humanity; rejoice in their progress, and mourn at their fall.

But there is another reproach of more importance to be made to Mr. Burke: it is, that, in all probability, his predictions, and those of the writers who followed him on the same side in France, were in a great measure the causes of the evils they foretold. Mr. Burke predicted the death of Louis the sixteenth, at a time when not a human being in France had such an idea in his mind; and the eloquent and specious description he gave of the imaginary disgrace and distress of royalty, most certainly had a considerable effect on the mind of that unfortunate prince, and still more on that of the queen, and the persons of her court. We all know that the king had no reason to be discontented with his situation as it was determined by the Constituent Assembly; but we also know, that nothing is so easy for an able man, as to render a weak man discontented with his condition, by persuading him that he is ill-treated, and painting to him delusive pictures of advantages that he ought to enjoy, or of inconveniences that he ought not to suffer. But for Mr. Burke, and his associates in France, it is highly probable Louis the sixteenth might now have been reigning peaceably on his throne. I do not mean to accuse their intentions; but I am warranted to say, that their writings contributed at once to render the court discontented with the revolution, and the nation suspicious of the court. Of consequence, they had a great share in producing the calamities of the monarch and his unfortunate family. (pp. 214-18)

saying it was as much the fault of the noble as the peasants.

THE FATE OF THE FRENCH REVOLUTION, FROM LETTER V

Revolutions exhibit man acting on a great scale: hence they produce great virtues, and at the same time great vices. Three years of confusion form a vast period in the life of an individual; but they make only a point in the *life of a nation*. They make, indeed, almost an imperceptible point, if that nation is considered as a part of the great whole, and as affecting, by its conduct, the future fate of Europe, and of the world. The revolutions of all other nations, our own and that of America excepted, have done nothing for mankind. What signifies it to the world who is despot in Turkey; who vanquishes or is vanquished in Persia; who is Pope of Rome? The contest then is about the *masters*, but the *system* continues the same. In France, the contest has been about *principles*, and these the most important, the most sacred, the most essential to the happiness of man. Let France be arraigned before the tribunal of the human race—she must plead guilty to many charges—but she will still appear a meritorious criminal. For who before her declared aloud, in the name of twenty-five millions of men, to attending Europe, those truths which lay concealed in the works of a few philosophers? Who, before her, dared to combat *all* errors, and, braving every prejudice, through good report and evil report, published the complete manifesto of the neglected rights of human kind!!

But I must conclude. What I have already written, or may far- /
ther write, will, I am persuaded, find favour with you, and with a
few more of the well-informed and reflecting: but I do not expect
that such ideas will meet with general approbation, at this moment
of agitation and prejudice. For my part, I am prepared for censure;
but I entreat you to witness, that I appeal from the public judgment
of 1792, to that of 1799.... I will add, that certain persons will do
well to be moderate in their triumph at this moment, lest their sentiments and declarations should be recorded and produced at a
time when they may be less suitable than they are just now.

Whether France will finally be able to extricate herself from an
intestine, as well as external war, which now assail her at once—
whether she will be able to support her republic; or, fatigued with
anarchy, repose herself in limited monarchy; or finally, overwhelmed by her foes, be forced to accept that constitution which
they choose to give her, are points that surpass my powers to
decide. Were I to conjecture, I would say, that she will succeed in
maintaining her own freedom, but not in communicating it to her
neighbors. But should she even be overpowered by her enemies,
and should continental despots wish to load her with the most
galling chains, I cannot forget, Madam, that Britain is concerned in
this transaction! And this recollection cheers my mind; for a free
and generous people cannot condemn twenty-five millions of men
to be slaves! No: the severest sentence that England can suffer to be
pronounced, even on her rival, would be, "Let France be delivered
from the dominion of a ferocious mob—let her be delivered from
anarchy, and restored to reason and lawful sway!" Thus, terminate
how it will, I trust the French revolution will promote the good of
France, and this prospect consoles me amidst the present evils.

The French revolution began in wisdom; but what wise men
begin well, fools often by their interference spoil at the end. The
French legislators borrowed from ignorance only the strength of its
arm; they certainly never intended to make use of its disordered
head. One revolution therefore sufficed all wise men; but the court
forced a second one, and then all was confounded. The people
were called upon to judge, when they had no means of judging.
They had already *acted*, and their honest energy ought then to have
ceased. Deprived of the means of obtaining knowledge, by the
degradation into which the ancient system of civil polity had
placed them, they ought not to have been placed in the rank of
political judges.

It is much too rash to conclude, that the cause of France is lost—

the probability is still in its favour; and were it otherwise, Madam, I should say, "Victrix causa diis placuit, sed victa Catoni" ["The victorious cause pleased the gods, but Cato was for the vanquished"]. Mean must be his mind, and low his thoughts, who can regret having espoused such a cause, or wish that he had taken the side of corrupt politicians, instead of that of a people struggling for freedom, the first gift of Heaven....

When I said that the French revolution began in wisdom, I admitted that it came afterwards into the hands of fools. But the *foundation was laid in wisdom*. I must entreat you to mark that circumstance; for if even the superstructure should fall, the foundation would remain. The BASTILLE, though honoured by Mr. Burke with the title of the *king's castle* (a shocking satire on every humane and just prince), will never be rebuilt in France; and the declaration of the rights of man will remain eternal, as the truths it contains. In the early ages of the world, the revolutions of states, and the incursions of barbarians, often overwhelmed knowledge, and occasioned *the loss of principles*: but since the invention of printing has diffused science over Europe, and accumulated the means of extending and preserving truth, PRINCIPLES can no more be lost. Like vigorous seeds committed to the bosom of the fertile earth, accidental circumstances may prevent their vegetation for a time, but they will remain alive, and ready to spring up at the first favourable moment.... (pp. 263-70)

4. Letters Containing a Sketch of the Politics of France [May 1793-July 1794], vol. I (1795)

[*Letters Containing a Sketch of the Politics of France, from the Thirty-first of May 1793, till the Twenty-eighth of July 1794, and of the Scenes which have Passed in the Prisons of Paris* was published in London in 1795, the first of a two-volume set. Written in Switzerland and Paris, the nine letters and three appendices of this first volume of the second series of *Letters* describe the political turmoil in France at a time that includes Williams's incarceration as a foreign subversive under Robespierre's Reign of Terror. Williams comments on such events as the assassination of Marat and the trials and executions of Charlotte Corday (Marat's assassin) and Marie Antoinette. She also includes other stories of everyday people who were caught in the web of suspicion plaguing France during this phase of the Revolution. Among her heroes are a brave young man who took his brother's place at the guillotine and women such as

Madame Roland who serenely faced execution or committed suicide out of sympathy for revolutionary ideals.

The appendices contain transcriptions of three important revolutionary documents: a letter signed by seventy-three deputies protesting the infringements of civil liberties during the terror (dated 6th June, 2nd year of the French Republic [1794]), a manifesto proposing a march on Paris to restore order (dated 12th June, 1793), and a transcript of Madame Roland's defense, protesting her innocence and that of her husband. Despite the climate of political violence and recrimination, Williams retains an optimistic faith in the ideals of the Revolution. As this volume closes, Robespierre has been executed and Williams is again in Paris, where the Terror now "seems like one of those frightful dreams which presents to the disturbed spirit phantoms of undescribable horror, and 'deeds without a name'; awakened from which, we hail with rapture the cheering beams of the morning, and anticipate the meridian lustre of the day."]

THE ASSASSINATION OF MARAT AND THE EXECUTION
OF CHARLOTTE CORDAY, FROM *LETTER V*

An event also happened at this period, which, from the calumnies to which it gave rise, and the consequences it produced, proved fatal to the arrested deputies. This was the assassination of Marat. In the first dawn of the conspiracy Marat became a principal instrument in the hands of the traitors, who found him well fitted for their purposes; and being saved from the punishment which usually follows personal insult by the contempt which the deformity and diminutiveness of his person excited, he became the habitual retailer of all the falsehoods and calumnies which were invented by his party against every man of influence or reputation.... His rage for denunciation was so great that he became the dupe of the idle; and his daily paper contains the names of great criminals who existed only in the imagination of those who imposed on his credulous malignity.

After this first preacher of blood had performed the part allotted to him in the plan of evil, he was confined to his chamber by a lingering disease to which he was subject, and of which he would probably soon have died. But he was assassinated in his bath by a young woman who had travelled with this intention from Caen in Normandy. Charlotte Anne Marie Corday was a native of St. Saturnin in the department of the Orne. She appears to have lived in a state of literary retirement with her father, and by the study of antient and modern historians to have imbibed a strong attachment to liberty. She had been accustomed to assimilate certain periods of antient history with the events that were passing before her, and was probably excited by the examples of antiquity to the commission of a deed, which she believed with fond enthusiasm would deliver and save her country.

Being at Caen when the citizens of the department were enrolling themselves to march to the relief of the convention, the animation with which she saw them devoting their lives to their country, led her to execute, without delay, the project she had formed. Under pretence of going home, she came to Paris, and the third day after her arrival obtained admission to Marat. She had invented a story to deceive him; and when he promised her that all the promoters of the insurrection in the departments should be sent to the guillotine, she drew out a knife which she had purchased for the occasion, and plunged it into his breast.

She was immediately apprehended, and conducted to the Abbaye prison, from which she was transferred to the Conciergerie, and brought before the revolutionary tribunal.

She acknowledged the deed, and justified it by asserting that it was a duty she owed her country and mankind to rid the world of a monster whose sanguinary doctrines were framed to involve the country in anarchy and civil war, and asserted her right to put Marat to death as a convict already condemned by the public opinion. She trusted that her example would inspire the people with that energy which had been at all times the distinguished characteristic of republicans; and which she defined to be that devotedness to our country which renders life of little comparative estimation.

Her deportment during the trial was modest and dignified. There was so engaging a softness in her countenance, that it was difficult to conceive how she could have armed herself with sufficient intrepidity to execute the deed. Her answers to the interrogatories of the court were full of point and energy. She sometimes surprised the audience by her wit, and excited their admiration by her eloquence. Her face sometimes beamed with sublimity, and was sometimes covered with smiles.... She retired while the jury deliberated on their verdict; and when she again entered the tribunal there was a majestic solemnity in her demeanour which perfectly became her situation. She heard her sentence with attention and composure; and after conversing for a few minutes with her counsel and a friend of mine who had sat near her during the trial, and whom she requested to discharge some trifling debts she had incurred in the prison, she left the court with the same serenity, and prepared herself for the last scene.

... it is difficult to conceive the kind of heroism which she displayed in the way to execution. The women who were called furies of the guillotine, and who had assembled to insult her on leaving the prison, were awed into silence by her demeanour, while some of the spectators uncovered their heads before her, and others gave loud tokens of applause. There was such an air of chastened exultation thrown over her countenance, that she inspired sentiments of love rather than sensations of pity. She ascended the scaffold with undaunted firmness, and, knowing that she had only to die, was resolved to die with dignity. She had learned from her jailor the mode of punishment, but was not instructed in the detail; and when the executioner attempted to tie her feet to the plank, she resisted, from an apprehension that he had been ordered to insult her; but on his explaining himself she submitted with a smile. When he took off her handkerchief, the moment before she bent under the fatal stroke, she blushed deeply; and her head, which was held up to the multitude the moment after, exhibited this last impression of offended modesty. (pp. 126-35)

THE TRIAL AND EXECUTION OF MARIE ANTOINETTE,
FROM *LETTER VI*

For a long time the Jacobins had demanded the trial of Marie Antoinette, whose existence they declared endangered that of the republic. She was accordingly arraigned for having committed a series of crimes, which in the language of the indictment comprehended not merely counter-revolutionary projects, but all the enormities of the Messalinas, Brunehauts, Fredegondes, and Medicis. A curious account of the evidence in support of these charges, and the effect which her behaviour produced upon Robespierre, is given by Vilate, a young man of the revolutionary tribunal. The scene passed during the trial, at a tavern near the Tuilleries, where he was invited to dine with Robespierre, Barrere, and St. Just. "Seated around the table," he says, "in a close and retired room, they asked me to give them some leading features of the evidence on the trial of the Austrian. I did not forget that expostulation of insulted nature when, Hebert accusing Antoinette of having committed the most shocking crime, she turned with dignity towards the audience, and said, "I appeal to the conscience and feelings of every mother present, to declare if there be one amongst them who does not shudder at the idea of such horrors." Robespierre, struck with this answer as by an electrical stroke, broke his plate with his fork. "That blockhead Hebert!" cried he, "as if it were not enough that she was really a Messalina, he must make her an Agrippina also, and furnish her with the triumph of exciting the sympathy of the public in her last moments."

Marie Antoinette made no defence, and called no witnesses, alleging that no positive fact had been produced against her. She had preserved an uniform behaviour during the whole of her trial, except when a starting tear accompanied her answer to Hebert. She was condemned about four in the morning, and heard her sentence with composure. But her firmness forsook her in the way from the court to her dungeon—she burst into tears; when, as if ashamed of this weakness, she observed to her guards, that though she wept at that moment, they should see her go to the scaffold without shedding a tear.

In her way to execution, where she was taken after the accus-tomed manner in a cart, with her hands tied behind her, she paid little attention to the priest who attended her, and still less to the surrounding multitude. Her eyes, though bent on vacancy, did not conceal the emotion that was labouring at her heart—her cheeks were sometimes in a singular manner streaked with red, and some-times overspread with deadly paleness; but her general look was that of indignant sorrow. She reached the place of execution about noon; and when she turned her eyes towards the gardens and the palace, she became visibly agitated. She ascended the scaffold with precipitation, and her head was in a moment held up to the peo-ple by the executioner. (pp. 153-56)

5. Letters Containing a Sketch of the Politics of France [May 1793-July 1794], vol. II (1795)

[Williams's sixth volume of *Letters* appeared as the second of the two-volume *Letters Containing a Sketch of the Politics of France, from the Thirty-first of May 1793, till the Twenty-eighth of July 1794, and of the Scenes which have Passed in the Prisons of Paris* (1795) and contains seven letters and three appendices. In this volume, she continues to denounce the violent and bloody turn the Revolution took during the Reign of Terror and laments the loss of the noble idealism that characterized the early phase of the Revolution. In the first two letters, she describes the trials and executions of Hébert, Danton, Desmoulins, and others, and remarks upon the irony of the Revolution turning on its own champions. Her third letter recounts the despotic acts of Robespierre and contrasts the forced expressions of enthusiasm required of the participants of the Festival of the Supreme Being with the sincerity and gaiety of the crowds who attended the first annual federation several years earlier. Details of her confinement in the Hôtel Talaru as a political prisoner are featured in the fourth letter, while her fifth letter provides narrative commentary on the rebellion of Lyons and its fall. In Letter Six, she contemplates the schism between juring and non-juring priests and denounces the desecration of the church by devotees of the Temple of Reason. She reflects upon the injustice of war in her final letter and accuses Robespierre's regime of purposely losing battles in the war with the royalists in order to sustain public support for themselves and contempt for the Girondins. As always, she concludes this volume optimistically, claiming that though the Revolution has passed through a dark period, ultimately it will succeed in returning to the values upheld in 1790 and will overcome tyranny of every kind. The three appendices contain, respectively, a comparison of the despots of the Revolution with the emperors of Rome; letters written by Custine, a condemned man, to his wife shortly before his execution; and Madame Roland's account of Servan's and Dumourier's part in the downfall of the monarchy and the Church.]

THE FESTIVAL OF THE SUPREME BEING, FROM *LETTER III*

But let us leave martyrs of liberty; and return to the polluted festival instituted by a tyrant. David, ever ready to fulfill the mandates of his master Robespierre, steps forth, marshals the procession, and, like the herald in Othello, "orders every man to put himself into triumph."

At this spot, by David's command, the mothers are to embrace their daughters—at that, the fathers are to clasp their sons—here, the old are to bless the young, and there, the young are to kneel to the old—upon this boulevard the people are to sing—upon that, they must dance—at noon they must listen in silence, and at sun-set they must rend the air with acclamations.

Ah, what was then become of those civic festivals which hailed the first glories of the revolution! What was become of that sublime federation of an assembled nation which had nobly shaken off its ignominious fetters, and exulted in its new-born freedom! What was become of those moments when no emotions were pre-ordained, no feelings measured out, no acclamations decreed; but when every bosom beat high with admiration, when every heart throbbed with enthusiastic transport, when every eye melted into tears, and the vault of heaven resounded the bursts of unpremeditated applause!

But let us not even now despair of the cause of liberty. Let us not abandon a fair and noble region filled with objects which excite the thrill of tenderness or the glow of admiration, because along the path which France has chosen serpents have lurked beneath the buds of roses, and beasts of prey have issued from the lofty woods: let us discover, if we can, a less tremendous road, but let us not renounce the land of promise....

From this profusion of gay objects, which in happier moments would have excited delightful sensations, the drooping soul now turned distasteful. The scent of carnage seemed mingled with these lavish sweets; the glowing festoons appeared tinged with blood; and in the back ground of this festive scenery the guillotine arose before the disturbed imagination. I thought of that passage in Mr. Burke's book, "In the groves of *their* academy, at the end of every vista I see the gallows!" Ah Liberty! best friend of mankind, why have sanguinary monsters profaned thy name, and fulfilled this gloomy prediction!—— (pp. 86–90)

THERMIDOR, FROM *LETTER III*

What most occupied the minds of the prisoners at this period was contriving the means of escaping from their tyrants by a voluntary death, which was now become difficult, since they had been stripped of every instrument which could have served that purpose. Such was the situation of these unhappy victims of tyranny, when on the night of the 9th of Thermidor the tocsin sounded, and the city was called to arms. Many circumstances which I shall afterwards relate, led the prisoners to believe that these sounds were the signal of a general massacre. But the tocsin now rung the joyful, the triumphant peal of liberty. Before I give you a detail of the scenes which passed on the 9th of Thermidor, I must trace the political events which led to that memorable epocha, and rescued France from a state which was the astonishment and shame of human nature; from a state more terrible than all which the most cunning tyrant could have inflicted upon slaves whom he had previously disarmed. And all this was suffered by a nation which called itself free, which had taken up arms to assert its freedom, and gained the most glorious victories in its defence. France, covered with all the laurels of heroic valour, and the terror of combined Europe, held out her neck to vulgar assassins and executioners, instead of crumbling them into dust.—Such are the strange contradictions of human nature! The effects resulting from the terrible impulse of revolutionary government upon the moral world, may perhaps be compared to those produced upon the natural scene by the tremendous tempests which sometimes sweep along the western islands; when the mingled elements rush forth in irresistible fury, when the deluging waters bear away vegetation, trees, and rocks, and the shrieking whirlwinds shake the dwellings of man to their foundations.—The storm is past—the enormous vapours have rolled away—a soft light hovers on the horizon, and we are now left at leisure to sigh over the ruins that surround us, and lament the victims laid prostrate by the blast. But let us hope that this stormy revolution will at least produce some portion of felicity to succeeding generations, who have not, like us, felt the tumultuous horrors of this convulsion of the passions, who will owe their happiness to the struggles of a race that is passed away, and whom they have never known; while we, who have been spectators of the cruel conflict—we, who have lost the friends we loved and honoured, are often unable, amidst the tears we shed over their tombs, to consider "all partial evil as universal good." (pp. 115-17)

THE STAIN OF THE TERROR, FROM *LETTER VII*

In the first days of the revolution, when liberty and philosophy went hand in hand together, what a moral revolution was instantly effected throughout Europe, by the sublime and immortal principles which this great change seemed about to introduce into government! But what eternal regrets must the lovers of Liberty feel, that her cause should have fallen into the hands of monsters ignorant of her charms, by whom she has been transformed into a Fury, who, brandishing her snaky whips and torches, has enlarged the limits of wickedness, and driven us back into regions of guilt hitherto unknown!

So unexampled are the crimes which have been committed, that it will require stronger evidence than the historian is commonly bound to produce, to persuade future generations of their reality. Alas! but a faint outline has been drawn of this terrifying picture, over which the friend of liberty would, if it were possible, like the recording angel, drop a tear, that might blot it out for ever.—"If some sweet oblivious antidote" could drive from my brain the remembrance of these things, and from my heart the feelings that oppress it, as well as from the knowledge of the world, I should be tempted to snatch from the enemies of Liberty the triumph they assume from this mournful history. But these horrors must stain the page of the revolution for ever. The bloody characters must remain indelible on the wall, a dreadful, but instructive lesson to future ages, and to those countries which are destined to labour through revolutions, and who will learn, while they contemplate this terrific chart, how to avoid the rocks on which Liberty has been nearly wrecked.

Dreadful indeed has been the crisis we have passed! yet it is some consolation, amidst this mighty mass of evil, that France is at length beginning to learn wisdom from the things she has suffered. France no longer looks around to find apologies for the crimes that have been committed: she herself holds up the criminals to the world. She boasts not of her victories over Europe armed against her rights; but she triumphs in the conquests she has made over herself. It is some relief, while I am struggling through the gloomy history of these horrors, that I see again the dawn of that glorious light which will chase them away. The last stroke has been given to that vile and degrading system, which ignoble usurpers had framed: we may now approach the altar of Liberty with confidence and hope; the hideous spectres that haunted it have fled for ever; and its incense in future will rise grateful to heaven, and spread fragrance over a regenerated land. (pp. 211-14)

6. Letters Containing a Sketch of the Scenes ... during the Tyranny of Robespierre (1795)

[In the seven long letters comprising *Letters Containing a Sketch of the Scenes which Passed in Various Departments of France during the Tyranny of Robespierre, and of the Events which Took Place in Paris on the 28th of July 1794* (1795), Williams repeats the euphoric pattern of her 1790 *Letters Written in France* by welcoming the return of justice and humanity to France after the "gloomy terror of despair." Here, as after the destruction of the Bastille, those who were imprisoned are made heroes, and "tears of compassion" are shed for the victims of tyranny. Williams thus sets up the end of the Terror as the rebirth of sympathy, plenty, and joy.

Williams describes the devastations of city and countryside from war, hunger, and the horrors wrought by the tribunals, recording political struggles among the revolutionaries, including the execution of Danton in April 1794, and documenting the oppressions of the Terror and the strategies and subterfuges by which people survived it. She recounts the story of her own eviction from France after the April 1794 exile of foreigners and offers a romantic narrative about Monsieur de M——, an enlightened patriot not unlike Monsieur du Fossé, whose wrongful persecution by the revolutionary government leads to tragedy for himself and his loved ones. While vividly representing the Terror as a "savage" scene "where all is wildly horrible, and every figure on the canvas is a murderer," Williams also portrays this phase of the Revolution as an aberration in which a few men became "monsters" through "the possession of power, or the grovelling passion of fear." Above all, she attributes the grim events to the hypocrisy and cunning of Robespierre. An appendix carries a personal account from a diplomat who had been imprisoned and includes a portrait of Jean-Paul Marat's "quackery." Now that the fall of Robespierre has "stopped the torrent of human blood," Williams believes, "the clouds of doubt, mistrust, and apprehension [have] vanished" despite grief for the victims, and "the clear sunshine of joy beam[s] upon every heart." Rather than losing faith in the Revolution, Williams implies, the French people have moved forward to create a new constitution that will strengthen the ship of state.]

THE END OF THE TERROR, FROM *LETTER I*

Paris.

MY DEAR SIR,

My pen, wearied of tracing successive pictures of human crimes and human calamity, pursues its task with reluctance; while my heart springs forward to that fairer epocha which now beams upon the friends of liberty—that epocha when the French republic has cast aside her dismal shroud, stained with the blood of the patriot, and bathed with the tears of the mourner; and presents the blessed images of justice and humanity healing the deep wounds of her afflicted bosom: when the laws of mercy are but the echo of the public opinion, of that loud cry for the triumph of innocence, of that horror of tyranny, which hangs upon every lip, and thrills at every heart. The generous affections, the tender sympathies so long repressed by the congealing stupefaction of terror, burst forth with uncontrolable energy; and the enthusiasm of humanity has taken [the] place of the gloomy terror of despair, as suddenly as, when the massy ice dissolves in the regions of the north, summer awakens her clear rills, her fresh foliate and her luxuriant flowers. Not to have suffered persecution during the tyranny of Robespierre, is now to be disgraced; and it is expected of all those who have escaped that they should assign some good reason, or offer some satisfactory apology for their suspicious exemption from imprisonment.... The tide of sympathy and compassion has indeed run so high, that it has been observed to produce a sort of affectation of complaint in ordinary minds; and as it was said in the departments after the taking of the Bastille, that every Parisian who came into the country, declared himself one of the conquerors, and most of them had even seized De Launy by the shoulder, so at present if we were to lend our belief to all those who tell us they were on the fatal list destined for the guillotine on the 11th of Thermidor, the day after Robespierre's execution, we must suppose that his appointed hecatomb for that day consisted, instead of his ordinary sacrifice, of half Paris at least. But after all the cruelties that have passed, how soothing is the moment when pity becomes the fashion, and when tyranny is so execrated that to have been its victim is glory! The tears of compassion now flow even for those objects whom once to commiserate was death....

Paris once more reassumes a gay aspect, the poor again have bread, and the rich again display the appendages of wealth. The processions of death which once darkened the streets, are now succeeded by carriages elegant in simplicity, though not decorated with the blazonry of arms, or the lace of liveries. The cheerfulness habitual to parisian physiognomy, again lights up its reviving look; and the quick step, the joyous smile, the smart repartee, the airy gesture, have succeeded the dismal reserve, and the trembling circumspection which so ill suited the national character. With the careless simplicity of children who after the rigours of school hasten to their sports; the Parisians, shaking off the hideous remembrance of the past, fly to the scenes of pleasure....

In the mean time literature and the arts, covered with sack-cloth and ashes during the reign of our jacobin vandals, again revive, the national library offers every other day its treasures of literature to the public, and its long galleries and ample tables are filled with persons of both sexes, who, amidst the silence which is there observed, enjoy the charms of meditation, or the pleasure of study.

The noble gallery of the national museum filled with the master-pieces of art, is crowded three times a decade [i.e., a ten-day period] with citizens of all classes, the poor as well as the rich; who cannot fail to humanize their souls, as well as improve their taste by such contemplation. (pp. 1-10)

ON FRANCE AND ENGLAND, FROM *LETTER III*

It had generally been understood, that the present war was the war only of the English minister; and that the people of England, though well wishers to the cause of freedom, were not sufficiently powerful to counteract the designs of the administration. As long as this opinion of the apathy of the English prevailed, we had lived in tolerable security; for it was difficult to persuade the French, notwithstanding the experience they had of the late war, that a free people would twice waste its treasure and its strength, in so short a period, against nations struggling into freedom. The treason of Toulon, however, awakened the French from their dream of the *bonhommie* of the British nation towards them; and nothing was now talked of but the cowardly and ferocious English, and marching to Carthage.

In this language more was meant than was obvious to a common observer; for it was the business of the committee of government to work up the people to a strong degree of national hatred, in order to carry into effect a plan of invasion which they were meditating, although its impracticability had been demonstrated by those with whom they advised.... In the mean time the crimes of the English government were the standing order of the day at the jacobins; and had it not been for the spur given to malignity by these declamatory harangues, nothing could have been more amusing than their style.

One of the most distinguished of these performers in politics was the tragedian of Lyons. "We are now entering," says Collot, "into the conscience of Pitt, into that volcano which vomits forth every crime. We have traversed this mortiferous and pestilential lava; let us now march up to the crater, I mean the English government. If this government was not inherently bad, Pitt could not have found the means of being so abominable. I would not put this government into competition with that of France. This would be comparing the excess of every vice, with the assemblage of every virtue; a government," adds this orator, just returned from Lyons reeking with the blood of thousands of innocent victims, "such as Heaven ought to have given to all nature; while the other is vicious, wanting all the virtues which we esteem, and filled with every thing that is held in abhorrence amongst us." ...

The jacobins were astonished that so well-informed a nation as the English should be reduced to so pitiable a condition as that of being ruled by monsters and volcanos; and this wonder grew till Robespierre, who had hitherto kept silence except when a member became ultra-revolutionary, told them they were all in the wrong. "It is to no purpose," says he, "to talk to the English about their government, or attempt to make them better; for you are all very much deceived if you think that either the morals or understanding of the English nation are to be compared with the French. They are two hundred years behind you, and hate you with a very constant and perfect hatred. If therefore you wish to inform them, you must accommodate yourselves to their incapacity, and adapt your language to their comprehension." (pp. 52-58)

ROBESPIERRE V. DANTON, FROM *LETTER IV*

Robespierre feared, that the same means which he, with the aid of the commune of Paris, had employed against the Gironde, might be again put in practice to overthrow himself; and as he saw that the commune aspired to independence, and had already given signs of an ambitious spirit, he dreaded lest some rival might start up, who, with more generosity and larger promises, might push him from his seat. This rival he saw in the person of Danton, who, with greater talents than Robespierre, and with a mind somewhat less atrocious, had from natural indolence neglected to cultivate that sort of popularity which would soon have raised him to be the chief of this cabal. Of this party were Camille Desmoulins, the author of the libel against the Gironde, ... Fabre d'Eglantine, who was an intriguer, with more address and less honesty than Camille; La Croix, who was a wretch covered with crimes.... These men had only hinted disapprobation at the excess of the tyranny which was then exercised. But Robespierre collected the whispers of the party before any plan was actually arranged, and declared loudly, though mysteriously, both in the convention and at the jacobins', that the republic was in danger from the combinations of seditious and perverse men; whom he represented as new men, patriots of yesterday, who were eager to lay hold of the pillars of the revolution, and, by climbing to the height of the mountain, precipitate those who had hitherto sat there with so much success....The party of Danton had lost much of its influence with the people by the indolence of the chief, and the rapacity of the subalterns; while Robespierre had neglected no means to obtain that dominion on which he had perseveringly bent his mind. Under Robespierre's banner the great majority of the committee had enlisted; but his sworn and sacred allies were St. Just and Couthon, whose souls were of adamantine temper. Barrere had not yet taken all his degrees in atrocity, being only their lacquey, and having nothing very original in wickedness, except the phraseology he made use of in its justification.

Robespierre now thought that it was necessary to his safety to be disencumbered of the faction of the commune, and the faction of Danton. It was not difficult to bring a thousand charges against them, of which one alone before the great tribunal of national justice would have been sufficient to have directed the sword of national vengeance; but as the accusers could proffer none of those charges without criminating themselves, they had recourse to the expedient of their being accomplices of the faction de l'étranger [of foreigners], which was a most inexhaustible source for the fabrication of all indictments and bills for conspiracies. When the committee of public safety had marked their victims, it was necessary to inform the convention, that they were going to prepare the sacrifice; not that they feared any opposition or remonstrance, but for the sake of regularity. The convention, therefore, was instructed by St. Just, that a conspiracy was framed by foreigners, who were about to commit a number of horrible things, starve, plunder, and murder the good people of the republic; that this faction had already overthrown religion and morality, and was about to form a new sect of immorality, and the love of sensual enjoyments, from which innocence and virtue had every thing to dread; that the great directors of these machinations of the English court, were foreigners then at Paris, who had corrupted the agents of government; and that it was necessary they should all be punished together.

The convention was seized with horror at hearing those things, and ... decreed ... that whoever, by any act whatever, should attempt to degrade, destroy, or put obstacles in the way of the national convention, should be punished with death.

The faction of Hebert, Chaumette, and Danton, were led successively to the guillotine. (pp. 70-76)

PUBLIC DISCOURSE DURING THE TERROR, FROM *LETTER VI*

Nothing perhaps contributed to mislead the people of Europe so much, with respect to the state of the French nation at this period, as the intelligence which was conveyed to them by the public papers. It required a more intimate knowledge of French affairs than foreigners in general could find the means of obtaining, to reconcile the intelligence given in those newspapers with the atrocities which they heard were committed. While pillage and murder, under the name of confiscation and punishment, blackened every part of the republic; the papers presented us with the most elegant and philosophical reports on agriculture, literature, and the fine arts. But for the long catalogue of victims which closed the evening paper, we might ... have fancied that the reign of philosophy had begun, and that, where there was apparently so earnest a desire to civilize and succour mankind, there could not be so monstrous an assemblage of treason, atrocity, and carnage.

Most of these interesting and instructive reports, which tended to soften the hideousness of the general outline, were made by men who had not the means or the courage to stem the torrent, who sighed in secret over its ravages, and employed their moments in doing something which might tend to rescue their country from the barbarism into which it was hastening. I particularly allude to the reports of Gregoire on the improvement of the language, on the public libraries, and on the establishment of national gardens throughout the republic....

While Robespierre behind the scenes was issuing daily mandates for murder, we see him on the stage the herald of mercy and of peace—we see him affecting to pour the balm of consolation into the wounds which he was himself inflicting; and, like the unrelenting inquisitor, recommending to mercy the wretch whom he was delivering to torture. "Consult," says this finished actor, "only the good of the country, and the interests of mankind. Every institution, every doctrine which consoles and elevates the mind, should be cherished; reject all those which tend to degrade and corrupt it. Re-animate, exalt every generous sentiment, every sublime moral idea, which your enemies have sought to obliterate; draw together by the charm of friendship, and the ties of virtue, those men whom they have attempted to separate....

However well Robespierre performed the hypocrite, he had not sufficient address to preserve the character; for humanity, and misfortune, and glory, and friendship, enlightening and consoling the world; and all the mockery and show of the festival, with all the hopes and expectations of the unfortunate prisoners, vanished into thin air. The festival [of the Supreme Being] ... took place on the 20th of Prairial; and on the 22d the law for condemnation, without witness or defence, passed the convention, and the work of death went on with redoubled speed.

Had the tyrants who were thus successful in their usurpation, after crushing their immediate rivals, established a more humane system of government, of which they would have been the protectors, the world might still have remained ignorant at least of the excess of their crimes; and might have attributed their severity to the perilous circumstances in which they were placed, by the coalesced powers without, and the intrigues of the royal and aristocratical party within. In this case, none of those atrocious acts which the fall of Robespierre has unveiled would have been known, and what is now the subject of general horror would have been regarded only as necessary evil.

The historian, therefore, who should have taken the public acts, or the papers relating the transactions of the day, as the basis of his information, would have deceived himself and posterity. And even now the task will be difficult to transmit with accuracy and impartiality the history of that extraordinary epocha; which furnishes a most awful and stupendous monument of all that is sublime, and base; of all that is most virtuous, and most vile; of all that can excite mankind to the daring and heroic act, and of all that can make man with unutterable horror fly from man as from a pestilence. (pp. 137-48)

FRANCE AFTER THERMIDOR, FROM *LETTER VII*

Upon the fall of Robespierre, the terrible spell which bound the land of France was broken; the shrieking whirlwinds, the black precipices, the bottomless gulphs, suddenly vanished; and reviving nature covered the wastes with flowers, and the rocks with verdure.

All the fountains of public prosperity and public happiness were indeed poisoned by that malignant genius, and therefore the streams have since occasionally run bitter; but the waters are regaining their purity, are returning to their natural channels, and are no longer disturbed and sullied in their course....

The eventful scenes of the last winter will lead us to the present moment at which revolutionary government ceases, and a new constitution is presented to the people of France. The vessel of the state, built with toil and trouble, and cemented with blood, will soon be launched. We have yet seen nothing but disjointed planks, and heard only the discordant turbulence of the hammer and the anvil. The fabric is at length erected; and it now remains to be tried, if it be framed of materials sufficiently firm and durable to defy the shock of the conflicting elements, and float majestically down the stream of time. (pp. 190-92)

7. Letters Containing a Sketch of the Politics of France [July 1794-1795] (1796)

[The eighth and final volume of Williams's history is titled *Letters Containing a Sketch of the Politics of France, from the Twenty-eighth of July 1794, to the Establishment of the Constitution in 1795, and of the Scenes which have Passed in the Prisons of Paris* (1796). In nine letters, Williams covers the events occurring between the fall of Robespierre and the beginning of the Directory. Much of this volume is devoted to cataloging Robespierre's abuses of power. The chief enemy of the Revolution throughout Williams's *Letters*, Robespierre ("the great conspirator against the liberty of France") and his regime get the same treatment here that Williams gave to the *ancien régime* in her first volume. But the British also receive their share of criticism in Williams's powerful jeremiad against the slave-trade.

Williams depicts France after Thermidor as both joyful and vengeful, undergoing fierce internal conflicts between the remaining Jacobins on the one hand and the royalists on the other, while also attempting to settle accounts with Robespierre's surviving deputies. Although the new constitution promises future stability, the "pure" thread of the Revolution seems lost politically. For Williams, it is kept alive solely by the army, which racks up victory after victory because—in her view—the soldiers are fighting for the principles of the Revolution's early days. Williams would eventually come to regret her faith in the French army, but we are left at the close of the *Letters* with a profound understanding of why the stage was so well prepared for Napoleon to be seen as a political savior.]

THE NATIONAL CONVENTION AFTER ROBESPIERRE, FROM *LETTER I*

In the sketch I have sent you of revolutionary government in France, too long have I been compelled to wound your feelings by the tale of successive calamities; too long have I been forced to dwell on images of dismay.... But let me now attempt to communicate at least a portion of that exulting gladness with which I turn from the crimes of tyrants, to recount the triumphs of liberty; to trace humanity pouring balm into the wounds of the oppressed, and justice stretching forth her arm to shield the innocent, and strike the guilty—...

Although the great conspirator against the liberty of France had fallen, the colossal spectre of tyranny rising from his tomb still hovered round the national convention. Those deputies who had composed part of the two committees of government, who had of late excited Robespierre's jealous fears, and who, having been marked as the objects of his immediate vengeance, had themselves contributed to overthrow that sanguinary usurper, were the very men who had been the sharers in his crimes....

The convention, which had been long divided into two distinct classes, those who ruled without opposition, and those who obeyed without murmur, were too much habituated to the extremes of tyranny and servitude, to lay aside at the first moment the one, or shake off the chains of the other; and the committees of government considered themselves as the lawful successors of Robespierre. (pp. 1-5)

THE REVOLUTIONARY TRIBUNAL, FROM *LETTER III*

THE revolutionary tribunal, which, from its institution, and the horrible assassinations which it had been the instrument of committing, will remain for ever a striking monument of the perversion that tyrants can make of law and justice, now became the instrument of national vengeance in the punishment of those who have been the immediate actors in those judicial murders. The president of this institution had suffered with Robespierre on the 10th Thermidor; and the public accuser, Fouquier Tainville [sic], had been left since that period, during eight months, to feel in the gloom of a prison a thousand deaths in the rendings of that remorse which could not but gnaw his conscious soul. This wretch, who had scattered death around him, who had rioted in the tears of the innocent, and feasted his heart on the despair of the victims whom a breath from his polluted lips sent every day to the scaffold, was now condemned to feel the pangs he had inflicted, and to implore in vain the mercy he had denied.

With this grand inquisitor were arraigned more than thirty persons, who had been judges or jurymen of the tribunal under the administration of the decemvirs.... in reading these letters your heart has already formed their indictment, and will rejoice that retributive justice is about to stretch forth its too long retarded arm, and avenge humanity for a series of unexampled crimes....

The trial of these judges and jurymen had been wisely protracted; it was expedient to have their long catalog of atrocities unfolded in all their minute horrors; to make the people feel what tyranny they had suffered, and from what evils they had escaped. For though every person had some private history of cruelty to recount, some friend or relation who had suffered unjustly to lament; yet the great mass of guilt was unperceived till the evidence was combined and collected....

I went to the revolutionary tribunal on the day when the public accuser recapitulated the charges, after the examination of the witnesses was finished. I felt an emotion of the deepest horror on entering that hall, where so many persons who were dear to me had undergone the mockery of a trial, and from whence they had been dragged to death. A thousand tender and cruel remembrances pressed upon my heart; I looked eagerly towards the benches where my friends had once been placed, and saw those very seats now occupied by their murderers. I gazed with a gloomy kind of curiousity upon the countenances of those assassins, which I expected to find impressed with the savage character of their souls: but in this I was deceived; I saw faces that indicated no marks of villany, and some that bore the traces of the better feelings of our nature, and bespoke minds that only extraordinary circumstances and temptation had rendered wicked. (pp. 40-45)

JOY AT THERMIDOR, FROM *LETTER IV*

Dr. Warton observes, in his Essay on the Genius of Pope, that no story which has been invented is so pathetic as what has really happened. This observation may be peculiarly applied to the period of the revolutionary government in this country; the pencil of fiction has no colouring more gloomy than that which truth then presented, and the stories of romance offer no stronger conflicts of the passions, no incidents more affecting, or sorrows more acute, than what happened, and what has been suffered, during the tyranny of Robespierre.

You may therefore easily imagine how many scenes of domestic felicity the revolution of the 10th of Thermidor produced; how many families, bereaved of all they loved, of all that gave existence value, and pining with incurable anguish, were suddenly restored to transports so unhoped that they seemed like some dream of blessedness shedding its dear illusions over the darkness of despair. (pp. 52-53)

THE NEW CONSTITUTION AND THE BRITISH SLAVE TRADE, FROM *LETTER VII*

Thus finished the three years' session of this memorable assembly, forming an æra the most eventful in the history of mankind. This assembly was replaced by the new legislature, which consisted of two distinct houses, under the names of the Council of Five Hundred, and the Council of the Elders, composed of two thirds of the late Convention, and of the other third named by the people.

The first act of the councils was the formation of the executive power, under the title of the Directory; and the new machine of government was put into action. The void left by the kingdom of France, which the orator told us was struck out of the chart of Europe, though every power during this interval of annihilation has feelingly experienced the effects of its invisible hand, is now filled up by a powerful and triumphant republic.

I cannot conclude this sketch of revolutionary government without observing, that we should beware of the injustice of accusing the French people of those crimes of which they are the mourners, and of which they only have been the victims. They, who have seen their fields ravaged, their vineyards stained with blood, their cities reduced to ashes; they, who have lost their fathers, their husbands, their children, their friends; they, who, far from throwing a veil over the atrocities they abhor, have proclaimed, have published them to the world—to charge that people with the enormities under which they have groaned, would be indeed to arraign the oppressed for the guilt of the oppressor. With equal candour might the English be stigmatized as a barbarous nation, because Clive has famished Asiatic provinces, or because, on the coast of Africa, the slave-merchant traffics in blood; while all in the British parliament who are distinguished for genius or worth, all whose names are pronounced with honour and respect, have passed the sentence of condemnation on that detestable commerce, and, laying aside their political divisions on other points, here form *but one party, the party of humanity*. But why is humanity forced to proceed with tardy and incumbered steps? why is she thus impeded in her progress? Ah, let us, till the slave-trade no longer stains the British name, be more gentle in our censures of other nations! I know not how that partial morality can be justified, which measures right and wrong by geographical divisions; and, while it pours forth the bitterness of declamation against human crimes in France, sanctions them in Africa. I have related to you, with the detestation I have felt, the evils of that tyranny which assumed the name of revolutionary government; but the faithful historian of a slave-ship would perhaps admit, that there are horrors beyond the drowning scenes of Carrier, or the guillotines of Robespierre. The wretched African, torn for ever from all he loved, and condemned to miseries which can only terminate in death, would perhaps, while chained beneath those decks where the air he breathes is contagion, and where he struggles with convulsive agony, smile at the approach of the axe which would relieve intolerable torments, or the opening planks which would bury him with his oppressors beneath the billows of the ocean. With all the feelings of an Englishwoman at my heart, a heart that glows for the real honour of my country, I pour the fervent wish that she may speedily wipe away this foul reproach; and that, while her sources of commercial wealth flow in lavish abundance from every quarter of the globe, she may reject with indignant scorn that execrable traffic of which humanity is the barter.

Upon the whole, the cause of liberty is not the less sacred, nor her charms less divine, because sanguinary monsters and sordid savages have defiled her temple, and insulted her votaries. Like Midas, their uncouth ears have been deaf to her sweet sounds; and we ought not to wonder, that by such judges the coarse dialect of jacobinical jargon, like the unharmonious gratings of Marsyas's reeds, was preferred to the heavenly breathings of Apollo's lute.

But those barbarous triumphs are past, and anarchy and vandalism can return no more. The new constitution, like the spear of Romulus thrown with a strong hand, will fix itself in the earth, so that no human force can root it up, and will become, like the budding wood, the object of a people's veneration. (pp. 174-79)

THE FRENCH ARMY, FROM *LETTER IX*

The horrors which desolated the interior part of France had too long formed a melancholy contrast with the resplendent glories that hung around its frontiers; and the honour of the French name, sinking beneath the obloquy with which it was loaded by the crimes of its domestic tyrants, was only sustained by the astonishing achievements of the French armies. They alone remained pure and unsullied by the contagious guilt which overspread their country. They alone appear to have been the true representatives of the French nation, and every family in France could boast of having a deputy upon the frontier. It was the duty of the French soldiers not to deliberate upon internal commotions, but to repulse the hostile invader: and Europe, which has been the theatre of their exploits, has been awed by their overwhelming greatness. (pp. 206-07)

Appendix B: Selected Poetry by Williams

[Williams was a poet of radical sensibility who often attempted in her poetry to align the reader's sympathies with those who were socially oppressed. She came to public notice at an early age with the publication in 1782 of *Edwin and Eltruda*, a sentimental romance, followed in 1784 by *Peru: A Poem in Six Cantos*, which attacks the tragic results of European imperialism in South America. In 1786, her two-volume *Poems* (published by T. Cadell) garnered over 1,500 subscribers and became immensely popular, inspiring among others Anna Seward and William Wordsworth (see Appendix E), and leading to a second and enlarged edition in 1791.

In addition to "To Sensibility," a poem published in *Poems* (1786) that articulates the affective dynamics crucial to so much of Williams's work, we reproduce three poems that illustrate her social and political agendas. *A Poem on the Bill Lately Passed for Regulating the Slave Trade* was written just after the passage of the 1788 bill, introduced into Parliament by Sir William Dolben, limiting the number of slaves that could be transported in one shipload from Africa to the British West Indies, a small but significant step in ameliorating the conditions of the slave trade. It was published in 1788 by T. Cadell. "The Bastille, A Vision" first appeared in the second volume of Williams's two-volume *Julia, a Novel; Interspersed with Some Poetical Pieces* (published by Cadell in 1790) and was written in full sympathy with the Revolution before her first trip to France. *A Farewell, for Two Years, to England. A Poem* (published by Cadell in 1791), marked the occasion of Williams's second departure from England; it continues her critique of the British slave trade and reaffirms her commitment to the "change sublime in Gallia's state."

We reproduce here the first published editions of all four poems. In *Poems* (1786), the poem now referred to as "To Sensibility" is titled "Sensibility" at the beginning of the text, but "To Sensibility" in the running heads.]

1. "To Sensibility"

In *Sensibility*'s lov'd praise
  I tune my trembling reed;
And seek to deck her shrine with bays,
  On which my heart must bleed!

No cold exemption from her pain   5
  I ever wish'd to know;
Cheer'd with her transport, I sustain
  Without complaint her woe.

Above whate'er content can give,
  Above the charm of ease,   10
The restless hopes, and fears that live
  With her, have power to please.

Where but for her, were Friendship's power
  To heal the wounded heart,
To shorten sorrow's ling'ring hour,   15
  And bid its gloom depart?

'Tis she that lights the melting eye
  With looks to anguish dear;
She knows the price of ev'ry sigh,
  The value of a tear.   20

She prompts the tender marks of love
  Which words can scarce express;
The heart alone their force can prove,
  And feel how much they bless.

Of every finer bliss the source!   25
  'Tis she on love bestows
The softer grace, the boundless force
  Confiding passion knows;

When to another, the fond breast
  Each thought for ever gives;   30
When on another, leans for rest,
  And in another lives!

Quick, as the trembling metal flies,
   When heat or cold impels,
Her anxious heart to joy can rise,   35
   Or sink where anguish dwells!

Yet tho' her soul must griefs sustain
   Which she alone, can know;
And feel that keener sense of pain
   Which sharpens every woe;   40

Tho' she the mourner's grief to calm,
   Still shares each pang they feel,
And, like the tree distilling balm,
   Bleeds, others wounds to heal;

While she, whose bosom fondly true,   45
   Has never wish'd to range;
One alter'd look will trembling view,
   And scarce can bear the change,

Tho' she, if death the bands should tear,
   She vainly thought secure;   50
Thro' life must languish in despair
   That never hopes a cure;

Tho' wounded by some vulgar mind,
   Unconscious of the deed,
Who never seeks those wounds to bind   55
   But wonders why they bleed;—

She oft will heave a secret sigh,
   Will shed a lonely tear,
O'er feelings nature wrought so high,
   And gave on terms so dear;   60

Yet who would hard INDIFFERENCE choose,
   Whose breast no tears can steep?
Who, for her apathy, would lose
   The sacred power to weep?

Tho' in a thousand objects, pain,   65
    And pleasure tremble nigh,
Those objects strive to reach, in vain,
    The circle of her eye.

Cold, as the fabled god appears
    To the poor suppliant's grief,   70
Who bathes the marble form in tears,
    And vainly hopes relief.

Ah *Greville!* why the gifts refuse
    To souls like thine allied?
No more thy nature seem to lose   75
    No more thy softness hide.

No more invoke the playful sprite
    To chill, with magic spell,
The tender feelings of delight,
    And anguish sung so well;   80

That envied ease thy heart would prove
    Were sure too dearly bought
With friendship, sympathy, and love,
    And every finer thought.

2. *A Poem on the Bill Lately Passed for Regulating the Slave Trade*

THE QUALITY OF MERCY IS NOT STRAIN'D;
IT DROPPETH, AS THE GENTLE RAIN FROM HEAV'N
UPON THE PLACE BENEATH. IT IS TWICE BLESS'D;
IT BLESSETH HIM THAT GIVES, AND HIM THAT TAKES.
                                        SHAKESPEARE.

THE hollow winds of Night, no more
In wild, unequal cadence pour
On musing Fancy's wakeful ear,
The groan of agony severe
From yon dark vessel, which contains   5
The wretch new bound in hopeless chains;
Whose soul with keener anguish bleeds,

As AFRIC'S less'ning shore recedes—
No more where Ocean's unseen bound
Leaves a drear world of waters round,   10
Between the howling gust, shall rise
The stifled Captive's latest sighs—;
No more shall suffocating death
Seize the pent victim's sinking breath;
The pang of that convulsive hour   15
Reproaching Man's insatiate power;
Man! who to AFRIC'S shore has past
Relentless, as the annual blast
That sweeps the Western Isles, and flings
Destruction from its furious wings—   20
And Woman, she, too weak to bear
The galling chain, the tainted air;
Of mind too feeble to sustain
The vast, accumulated pain;
No more, in desperation wild,   25
Shall madly strain her gasping child;
With all the mother at her soul,
With eyes where tears have ceas'd to roll,
Shall catch the livid infant's breath;
Then sink in agonizing death.   30
       BRITAIN! the noble, blest decree
That sooths despair, is fram'd by Thee!
Thy powerful arm has interpos'd,
And *one* dire scene for ever clos'd;
Its horror shall no more belong   35
To that foul drama, deep with wrong.
Oh, first of EUROPE'S polish'd lands,
To ease the Captive's iron bands!
Long as thy glorious annals shine,
This proud distinction shall be thine: 40
Not first alone when Valour leads,
To rush on Danger's noblest deeds;
When Mercy calls thee to explore
A gloomy path, untrod before,
Thy ardent spirit springs to heal,   45
And, greatly gen'rous, dares to feel!—
Valour is like the meteor's light,
Whose partial flash leaves deeper night;
While Mercy, like the lunar ray,
Gilds the thick shade with softer day.   50

FOR this, in Fame's immortal shrine,
A double wreathe, O PITT, is thine!
For this! while distant ages hear
With Admiration's sacred tear,
Of powers, whose energy sublime   55
Disdain'd to borrow force from Time,
With no gradations mark'd their flight,
But rose, at once, to Glory's height;
The deeds of Mercy, that embrace
A distant sphere, an alien-race,   60
Shall Virtue's lips record, and claim
The fairest honors of thy name!
'Tis ever Nature's gen'rous view;
Great minds, should noble ends pursue;
As the clear sun-beam, when most bright,   65
Warms, in proportion to its light.—
And RICHMOND, he! who, high in birth,
Adds the unfading rays of worth;
Who stoops, from scenes in radiance drest,
To ease the mourner's aching breast;   70
The tale of private woe to hear,
And wipe the friendless orphan's tear!—
His bosom for the Captive bleeds,
He, Guardian of the injur'd! pleads
With all the force that Genius gives,   75
And warmth that but with Virtue lives;
For Virtue, with divine controul,
Collects the various powers of soul;
And lends, from her unsullied source,
The gems of thought their purest force.   80
    OH blest decree! whose lustre seems
Like the sweet Morn's reviving beams,
That chase the hideous forms of night,
And promise day more richly bright;
Great deed! that met consenting minds   85
In all, but those whom Av'rice binds;
Who creep in Interest's crooked ways,
Nor ever pass her narrow maze;
Or those, whom hard Indiff'rence steels
To every pang another feels.   90
For *Them* has Fortune, round their bowers,
Twin'd (partial nymph!) her lavish flowers;

For *Them*, from unsunn'd caves, she brings
Her summer ice; for *Them*, she springs
To climes, where hotter suns produce   95
The richer fruits delicious juice:
While *They*, whom wasted blessings tire,
Nor leave *one* want, to feed desire;
With cool, insulting ease, demand
Why for yon hopeless, Captive Band,   100
Is ask'd, to mitigate despair,
The mercy of the common air?
The boon of larger space to breathe,
While coop'd that hollow deck beneath?
A lengthen'd plank, on which to throw   105
Their shackled limbs, while fiercely glow
The beams direct, that on each head
The fury of contagion shed?—
And dare presumptuous, guilty man,
Load with offence his fleeting span?   110
Deform Creation with the gloom
Of crimes, that blot its cheerful bloom;
Darken a work so perfect made,
And cast the Universe in shade!—
Alas, to Afric's fetter'd race   115
Creation wears no form of grace!
To Them, Earth's pleasant vales are found
A blasted waste, a sterile bound;
Where the poor wand'rer must sustain
The load of unremitted pain!   120
A region, in whose ample scope
His eye discerns no gleam of hope;
Where Thought no kind asylum knows,
On which its anguish may repose,
But Death, that to the ravag'd breast   125
Comes not in shapes of terror drest,
Points to green hills where Freedom roves,
And minds renew their former loves;
Or, low'ring in the troubled air,
Hangs the fierce spectre of Despair,   130
Whose soul abhors the gift of life,
Who steadfast grasps the reeking knife,
Bids the charg'd heart in torrents bleed,
And smiles in frenzy, at the deed.

So, when rude winds the sailor urge   135
On polar seas, near Earth's last verge;
Long with the blast he struggles hard,
To save his bark, in ice imbarr'd;
But finds at length o'ercome with pain,
The conflict with his fate is vain;   140
Then heaves no more the useless groan,
But hardens like the wave to stone.
     YE noble minds! who o'er a sky
Where clouds are roll'd, and tempests fly,
Have bid the lambent lustre play   145
Of *one* pure, lovely, azure ray;
Oh, far diffuse its op'ning bloom,
And the wide hemisphere illume!
Ye, who *one* bitter drop have drain'd
From Slav'ry's cup, with horror stain'd;   150
Oh, let no fatal dregs be found,
But dash her chalice on the ground:
Oh, while she links her impious chain,
And calculates the price of pain;
Weighs Agony in sordid scales,   155
And marks if Death, or Life prevails;
In one short moment, seals the doom
Of years, which anguish shall consume;
Decides how near the mangling scourge
May to the grave its victim urge,   160
Yet for awhile, with prudent care
The half-worn wretch, if useful, spare;
And speculates with skill refin'd,
How deep a wound will stab the mind;
How far the spirit can endure   165
Calamity, that hopes no cure;—
Ye! who can selfish cares forego,
To pity those which others know;
As Light, that from its centre strays,
To glad all Nature with its rays;   170
Oh! ease the pangs ye stoop to share,
And rescue millions from despair!—
For you, while Morn in graces gay,
Wakes the fresh bloom of op'ning Day;
Gilds with her purple light your dome,   175
Renewing all the joys of home;

Of home! dear scene, whose ties can bind
With sacred force the human mind;
That feels each little absence pain,
And lives but to return again;   180
To that lov'd spot, however far,
Points, like the needle to its star;
That native shed which first we knew,
Where first the sweet affections grew;
Alike the willing heart can draw,   185
If fram'd of marble, or of straw;
Whether the voice of pleasure calls,
And gladness echoes thro' its walls;
Or, to its hallow'd roof we fly,
With those we love to pour the sigh;   190
The load of mingled pain to bear,
And soften every pang we share!—
Ah, think how desolate *His* state,
How *He* the chearful light must hate,
Whom, sever'd from his native soil,   195
The Morning wakes to fruitless toil;
To labours, hope shall never chear,
Or fond domestic joy endear;
Poor wretch! on whose despairing eyes
His cherish'd home shall never rise!   200
Condemn'd, severe extreme, to live
When all is fled that life can give!—
And ah! the blessings valued most
By human minds, are blessings lost!
Unlike the objects of the eye,   205
Enlarging, as we bring them nigh,
Our joys, at distance strike the breast,
And seem diminish'd when possest.
    Who, from his far-divided shore,
The half-expiring Captive bore?   210
Those, whom the traffic of their race
Has robb'd of every human grace;
Whose harden'd souls no more retain
Impressions Nature stamp'd in vain;
All that distinguishes their *kind*,   215
For ever blotted from their mind;
As streams, that once the landscape gave
Reflected on the trembling wave,

Their substance change, when lock'd in frost,
And rest, in dead contraction lost;— 220
Who view unmov'd, the look, that tells
The pang that in the bosom dwells;
Heed not the nerves that terror shakes,
The heart convulsive anguish breaks;
The shriek that would their crimes upbraid, 225
But deem despair a part of trade.—
Such only, for detested gain,
The barb'rous commerce would maintain.
The gen'rous sailor, he, who dares
All forms of danger, while he bears 230
The BRITISH Flag o'er untrack'd seas,
And spreads it on the polar breeze;
He, who in Glory's high career,
Finds agony, and death are dear;
To whose protecting arm we owe 235
Each blessing that the happy know;
Whatever charms the soften'd heart,
Each cultur'd grace, each finer art,
E'en thine, most lovely of the train!
Sweet Poetry! thy heav'n-taught strain— 240
His breast, where nobler passions burn,
In honest poverty, would spurn
The wealth, Oppression can bestow,
And scorn to wound a fetter'd foe.
True courage in the unconquer'd soul 245
Yields to Compassion's mild controul;
As, the resisting frame of steel
The magnet's secret force can feel.
    WHEN borne at length to Western Lands,
Chain'd on the beach the Captive stands, 250
Where Man, dire merchandize! is sold,
And barter'd life is paid for gold;
In mute affliction, see him try
To read his new possessor's eye;
If one blest glance of mercy there, 255
One half-form'd tear may check despair!—
Ah, if that eye with sorrow sees
His languid look, his quiv'ring knees,
Those limbs, which scarce their load sustain,
That form, consum'd in wasting pain; 260

Such sorrow melts his ruthless eye
Who sees the lamb, he doom'd to die,
In pining sickness yield his life,
And thus elude the sharpen'd knife.—
Or, if where savage habit steels   265
The vulgar mind, one bosom feels
The sacred claim of helpless woe—
If Pity in that soil can grow;
Pity! whose tender impulse darts
With keenest force on nobler hearts;   270
As flames that purest essence boast,
Rise highest when they tremble most.—
Yet *why* on one poor chance must rest
The int'rests of a kindred breast?
Humanity's devoted cause   275
Recline on Humour's wayward laws?
To Passion's rules must Justice bend,
And life upon Caprice depend?—
          AH ye, who one fix'd purpose own,
Whose untir'd aim is *Self* alone;   280
Who think in gold the essence lies
From which extracted bliss shall rise;
To whose dull sense, no charm appears
In social smiles, or social tears;
As mists that o'er the landscape sail,   285
Its beauteous variations veil;
Or, if in some relenting hour,
When Nature re-assumes her power,
Your alms to Penury ye lend,
Or serve, for once, a suff'ring friend;   290
Whom no weak impulse e'er betray'd
To give that friend incautious aid;
Who with exact precision, pause
At that nice point which Int'rest draws;
Your watchful footsteps never found   295
To stray beyond that guarded bound;—
Does fleeting Life proportion bear
To all the wealth ye heap with care?
When soon your days in measur'd flight
Shall sink in Death's terrific night;   300
Then seize the moments in your power,
To Mercy consecrate the hour!

Risque something in her cause at last,
And thus atone for all the past;
Break the hard fetters of the Slave;   305
And learn the luxury to save!—
Does Avarice, your god, delight
With agony to feast his sight?
Does he require that victims slain,
And human blood, his altars stain?   310
Ah, not alone of power possest
To check each *virtue* of the breast;
As when the numbing frosts arise,
The charm of vegetation dies;
His sway the harden'd bosom leads   315
To Cruelty's remorseless deeds;
Like the blue lightning when it springs
With fury on its livid wings,
Darts to its goal with baleful force,
Nor heeds that ruin marks its course.—   320
　　　OH Eloquence, prevailing art!
Whose force can chain the list'ning heart;
The throb of Sympathy inspire,
And kindle every great desire;
With magic energy controul   325
And reign the sov'reign of the soul!
That dreams while all its passions swell,
Its shares the power it feels so well;
As visual objects seem possest
Of those clear hues by light imprest;   330
Oh, skill'd in every grace to charm,
To soften, to appal, to warm;
Fill with thy noblest rage the breast,
Bid on those lips thy spirit rest,
That shall, in BRITAIN'S Senate, trace   335
The wrongs of AFRIC'S Captive Race!—
But Fancy o'er the tale of woe
In vain one heighten'd tint would throw;
For ah, the Truth, is all we guess
Of anguish in its last excess: 340
Fancy may dress in deeper shade
The storm that hangs along the glade,
Spreads o'er the ruffled stream its wing,
And chills awhile the flowers of Spring:

But, where the wintry tempests sweep   345
In madness, o'er the darken'd deep;
Where the wild surge, the raging wave,
Point to the hopeless wretch a grave;
And Death surrounds the threat'ning shore—
Can Fancy add one horror more?   350
        LOV'D BRITAIN! whose protecting hand
Stretch'd o'er the Globe, on AFRIC'S strand
The honour'd base of Freedom lays,
Soon, soon the finish'd fabric raise!
And when surrounding realms would frame,   355
Touch'd with a spark of gen'rous flame,
Some pure, ennobling, great design,
Some lofty act, almost divine;
Which Earth may hail with rapture high,
And Heav'n may view with fav'ring eye;   360
Teach them to make all Nature free,
And shine by emulating Thee!—

THE END.

3. "The Bastille, A Vision"

[In the second volume of *Julia* (pp. 218-23), Mr. F—— reads a poem about the Bastille to Julia and her friend Charlotte. The poem was sent to him by "a friend lately arrived from France, and who, for some supposed offence against the state, had been immured several years in the Bastille, but was at length liberated by the interference of a person in power. The horrors of his solitary dungeon were one night cheered by the following prophetic dream" (II, 217).]

THE BASTILLE, A VISION.

I. 1.

"DREAR cell! along whose lonely bounds,
"Unvisited by light,
"Chill silence dwells with night,

"Save when the clanging fetter sounds!
"Abyss, where mercy never came,   5
"Nor hope, the wretch can find;
"Where long inaction wastes the frame,
"And half annihilates the mind!

I. 2.

"Stretch'd helpless in this living tomb,
"Oh haste, congenial death!   10
" Seize, seize this ling'ring breath,
"And shroud me in unconscious gloom—
"Britain! thy exil'd son no more
"Thy blissful vales shall see;
"Why did I leave thy hallow'd shore,   15
"Distinguish'd land, where all are free?"

I. 3.

Bastille! within thy hideous pile,
Which stains of blood defile.—
Thus rose the captive's sighs,
Till slumber seal'd his weeping eyes—   20
Terrific visions hover near!
He sees an awful form appear!
Who drags his step to deeper cells,
Where stranger wilder horror dwells.

II. 1.

"Oh, tear me from these haunted walls,   25
"Or those fierce shapes controul!
"Lest madness seize my soul—
"That pond'rous mask of iron[1] falls,
"I see!"——"Rash mortal, ha! beware,
"Nor breathe that hidden name!   30
"Should those dire accents wound the air,
"Know death shall lock thy stiff'ning frame."

---

1 Alluding to the prisoner who has excited so many conjectures in Europe.
   [Williams's note]

II. 2.

"Hark! that loud bell which sullen tolls!
"It wakes a shriek of woe.
"From yawning depths below;   35
"Shrill through this hollow vault it rolls!"
"A deed was done in this black cell,
"Unfit for mortal ear!
"A deed was done, when toll'd that knell,
"No human heart could live and hear!   40

II. 3.

"Rouze thee from thy numbing trance,
"Near yon thick gloom advance;
"The solid cloud has shook;
"Arm all thy soul with strength to look.—
"Enough! thy starting locks have rose,   45
"Thy limbs have fail'd, thy blood has froze:
"On scenes so foul, with mad affright,
"I fix no more thy fasten'd sight."

III. 1.

"Those troubled phantoms melt away!
"I lose the sense of care—   50
"I feel the vital air—
"I see, I *see* the light of day!—
"Visions of bliss! eternal powers!
"What force has shook those hated walls?
"What arm has rent those threat'ning towers?   55
"It falls—the guilty fabric falls!"

III. 2.

"Now, favour'd mortal, now behold!
"To soothe thy captive state,
"I ope the book of fate,
"Mark what its registers unfold!   60
"Where this dark pile in chaos lies,
"With nature's execrations hurl'd,
"Shall Freedom's sacred temple rise,
"And charm an emulating world!

III. 3.

"'Tis her awak'ning voice commands   65
"Those firm, those patriot bands,
"Arm'd to avenge her cause,
"And guard her violated laws!—
"Did ever earth a scene display
"More glorious to the eye of day,   70
"Than millions with according mind,
"Who claim the rights of human kind?

IV. 1.

"Does the fam'd Roman page sublime,
"An hour more bright unroll,
"To animate the soul,   75
"Than this, lov'd theme of future time?—
"Posterity, with rev'rence meet,
"The consecrated act shall hear;
"Age shall the glowing tale repeat,
"And youth shall drop the burning tear!   80

IV. 2.

"The peasant, while he fondly sees
"His infants round the hearth,
"Pursue their simple mirth,
"Or emulously climb his knees,
"No more bewails their future lot,   85
"By tyranny's stern rod opprest;
"While Freedom guards his straw-roof'd cot,
"And all his useful toils are blest.

IV. 3.

"Philosophy! oh, share the meed
"Of Freedom's noblest deed!   90
"'Tis thine each truth to scan,
"Guardian of bliss, and friend of man!
"'Tis thine all human wrongs to heal,
"'Tis thine to love all nature's weal;
"To give each gen'rous purpose birth,   95
"And renovate the gladden'd earth."

4. *A Farewell, for Two Years, to England. A Poem.*

SWEET Spring! while others hail thy op'ning flowers,
The first young hope of Summer's blushing hours;
Me they remind, that when her ardent ray
Shall reach the summit of our lengthen'd day,
Then, ALBION! far from Thee, my cherish'd home,   5
To foreign climes my pensive steps must roam;
And twice shall Spring, dispelling Winter's gloom,
Shed o'er thy lovely vales her vernal bloom;
Twice shall thy village-maids, with chaplets gay,
And simple carols, hail returning May;   10
And twice shall Autumn, o'er thy cultur'd plain,
Pour the rich treasures of his yellow grain;
Twice shall thy happy peasants bear along
The lavish store, and wake the harvest-song;
Ere from the bounded deep my searching eye,   15
Ah! land belov'd, shall thy white cliffs descry.—
Where the slow Loire, on borders ever gay,
Delights to linger, in his sunny way,
Oft, while I seem to count, with musing glance,
The murm'ring waves that near his brink advance,   20
My wand'ring thoughts shall seek the grassy side,
Parental Thames! where rolls thy ample tide;
Where, on thy willow'd bank, methinks, appears
Engrav'd the record of my passing years;
Ah! not like thine, their course is gently led,   25
By zephyrs fann'd, thro' paths with verdure spread;
They flow, as urg'd by storms the mountain rill
Falls o'er the fragments of the rocky hill.
    My native scenes! can aught in time, or space,
From this fond heart your lov'd remembrance chase?   30
Link'd to that heart by ties for ever dear,
By Joy's light smile, and Sorrow's tender tear;
By all that ere my anxious hopes employ'd,
By all my soul has suffer'd, or enjoy'd!
Still blended with those well-known scenes, arise   35
The varying images the past supplies;
The childish sports that fond attention drew,
And charm'd my vacant heart when life was new;
The harmless mirth, the sadness robb'd of power
To cast its shade beyond the present hour—   40

And that dear hope which sooth'd my youthful breast,
And show'd the op'ning world in beauty drest;
That hope which seem'd with bright unfolding rays
(Ah, vainly seem'd!) to gild my future days;
That hope which, early wrapp'd in lasting gloom,   45
Sunk in the cold inexorable tomb!—
And Friendship, ever powerful to controul
The keen emotions of the wounded soul,
To lift the suff'ring spirit from despair,
And bid it feel that life deserves a care.   50
Still each impression that my heart retains
Is link'd, dear Land! to thee by lasting chains.
        She too, sweet soother of my lonely hours!
Who gilds my thorny path with fancy's flowers,
The Muse, who early taught my willing heart   55
To feel with transport her prevailing art;
Who deign'd before my infant eyes to spread
Those dazzling visions she alone can shed;
She, who will still be found where'er I stray,
The lov'd companion of my distant way;   60
'Midst foreign sounds, her voice, that charms my ear,
Breath'd in my native tongue, I still shall hear;
'Midst foreign sounds, endear'd will flow the song
Whose tones, my ALBION, will to thee belong!
        And when with wonder thrill'd, with mind elate,   65
I mark the change sublime in GALLIA'S state!
Where new-born Freedom treads the banks of Seine,
Hope in her eye, and Virtue in her train!
Pours day upon the dungeon's central gloom,
And leads the captive from his living tomb;   70
Tears the sharp iron from his loaded breast,
And bids the renovated land be blest—
My thoughts shall fondly turn to that lov'd Isle,
Where Freedom long has shed her genial smile.
Less safe in other lands the triple wall,   75
And massy portal, of the Gothic hall,
Than in that favour'd Isle the straw-built thatch,
Where Freedom sits, and guards the simple latch.
        Yet, ALBION! while my heart to thee shall spring,
To thee its first, its best affections bring;   80
Yet, when I hear exulting millions pour
The shout of triumph on the GALLIC shore;

Not without sympathy my pensive mind
The bounds of human bliss enlarg'd, shall find;
Not without sympathy my glowing breast   85
Shall hear, on any shore, of millions blest!
Scorning those narrow souls, whate'er their clime,
Who meanly think that sympathy a crime;
Who, if one wish for human good expand
Beyond the limits of their native land,   90
And from the worst of ills would others free,
Deem that warm wish, my Country! guilt to thee.
Ah! why those blessings to one spot confine,
Which, when diffus'd, will not the less be thine?
Ah! why repine if far those blessings spread   95
For which so oft thy gen'rous sons have bled?
Shall ALBION mark with scorn the lofty thought,
The love of Liberty, herself has taught?
Shall *her* brave sons, in this enlighten'd age,
Assume the bigot-frown of papal rage,   100
Nor tolerate the vow to Freedom paid,
If diff'ring from the ritual *they* have made?
Freedom! who oft on ALBION'S fost'ring breast
Has found *her* friends in stars and ermine drest,
Allows that some among her chosen race   105
Should there the claim to partial honours trace,
And in the long-reflected lustre shine
That beams thro' Ancestry's ennobled line;
While she, with guardian wing, can well secure
From each proud wrong the undistinguish'd poor.   110
On GALLIA'S coast, where oft the robe of state
Was trail'd by those whom Freedom's soul must hate;
Where, like a comet, rank appear'd to glow
With dangerous blaze, that threaten'd all below;
There Freedom now, with gladden'd eye, beholds   115
The simple vest that shows in equal folds.
    And tho' on Seine's fair banks a transient storm
Flung o'er the darken'd wave its angry form;
That purifying tempest now has past,
No more the trembling waters feel the blast;   120
The bord'ring images, confus'dly trac'd
Along the ruffled stream, to order haste;
The vernal day-spring bursts the partial gloom,
And all the landscape glows with fresher bloom.

When, far around that bright'ning scene, I view   125
Objects of gen'ral bliss, to GALLIA new;
Then, ALBION! shall my soul reflect with pride
Thou wert her leading star, her honour'd guide;
That, long in slav'ry sunk, when taught by thee,
She broke her fetters, and has dar'd be free;   130
In new-born majesty she seems to rise,
While sudden from the land oppression flies.
So, at the solemn hour of Nature's birth,
When brooding darkness veil'd the beauteous earth,
Heaven's awful mandate pierc'd the solid night,   135
"Let there be light," it said, "and there was light!"
    Ah! when shall Reason's intellectual ray
Shed o'er the moral world a more perfect day?
When shall that gloomy world appear no more
A waste, where desolating tempests roar?   140
Where savage Discord howls in threat'ning form,
And wild Ambition leads the mad'ning storm;
Where hideous Carnage marks his dang'rous way,
And where the screaming vulture scents his prey?—
Ah! come, blest Concord! chase, with smile serene,   145
The hostile passions from the human scene!
May Glory's lofty path be found afar
From agonizing groans and crimson war;
And may the ardent mind, that seeks renown,
Claim, not the martial, but the civic crown!   150
While pure Benevolence, with happier views
Of bright success, the gen'ral good pursues;
Ah! why, my Country! with indignant pain,
Why in thy senate did she plead in vain?
Ah! why in vain enforce the Captives' cause,   155
And urge Humanity's eternal laws?
With fruitless zeal the tale of horror trace,
And ask redress for AFRIC'S injur'd race?
Unhappy race! ah! what to them avail'd,
That touching eloquence, whose efforts fail'd?   160
Tho' in the senate Mercy found combin'd
All who possess the noblest pow'rs of mind,
On other themes, pre-eminently bright,
They shine, like single stars, with sep'rate light;
Here, only *here*, with intermingled rays,   165
In one resplendent constellation blaze;

Yes, Captive race! if all the force display'd
By glowing Genius, in Compassion's aid,
When, with that energy she boasts alone,
She made your wrongs, your ling'ring tortures known;   170
Bade full in view the bloody visions roll,
Shook the firm nerves, and froze the shudd'ring soul!—
As when the sun, in piercing radiance bright,
Dispelling the low mists of doubtful light,
Its lustre on some hideous object throws,   175
And all its hateful horror clearly shows—
If Genius could in Mercy's cause prevail,
When Interest presses the opposing scale,
How swift had BRITONS torn your galling chain,
And from their country wip'd its foulest stain!—   180
But oh, since mis'ry, in its last excess,
In vain from BRITISH honour hopes redress;
May other Lands the bright example show,
May other regions lessen human woe!
Yes, GALLIA, haste! tho' Britain's sons decline   185
The glorious power to save, that power is thine;
Haste! since, while BRITAIN courts that dear-bought gold,
For which her virtue and her fame are sold,
And calmly calculates her trade of death,
Her groaning victims yield in pangs their breath;   190
Then save some portion of that suff'ring race
From ills the mind can scarce endure to trace!
Oh! whilst with mien august thy Leaders scan,
And guard with jealous zeal the rights of man,
Forget not that to all kind Nature gives   195
Those common rights, the claim of all that lives.—
But yet my filial heart its wish must breathe
That BRITAIN first may snatch this deathless wreath;
First to the earth this act divine proclaim,
And wear the freshest palm of virtuous fame;   200
May I, in foreign realms, her glories hear,
Catch the lov'd sounds, and pour th' exulting tear!
       And when, the destin'd hour of exile past,
My willing feet shall reach their home at last;
When, with the trembling hope Affection proves,   205
My eager heart shall search for those it loves,
May no sharp pang that cherish'd hope destroy,
And from my bosom tear the promis'd joy;

Shroud every object, every scene in gloom,
And lead my bleeding soul to Friendship's tomb!   210
But may that moment to my eyes restore
The friends whose love endears my native shore!
Ah! long may Friendship, like the western ray,
Chear the sad evening of a stormy day;
And gild my shadowy path with ling'ring light,   215
The last dear beam that slowly sinks in night.

FINIS.

Appendix C: Critical Reviews of Letters Written in France

[Contemporary reviews of the 1790 *Letters Written in France* appear in most of the major periodicals of late eighteenth-century London. The seven reviews reprinted here are largely positive about the style and content of *Letters*; the conservative *Gentleman's Magazine* is the most resistant to Williams's politics. Several of the reviews focus on Williams's status as a woman writer, some in order to dismiss the seriousness of her sympathy for the French Revolution. Many of these reviews also include substantial excerpts from the *Letters*, which are omitted below.]

1. From *The Analytical Review*, (December 1790): 431

Women have been allowed to possess, by a kind of prescription, the knack of epistolary writing; the talent of chatting on paper in that easy immethodical manner, which render letters dear to friends, and amusing to strangers. Who that has read Madame Sevigne's and Pope's letters, with an unprejudiced eye, can avoid giving the preference to the artless elegance of the former; interested by the eloquence of her heart, and the unstudied sallies of her imagination; whilst the florid periods of the latter appear, like state robes, grand and cumbersome, and his tenderness vapid vanity.

The interesting unaffected letters which this pleasing writer has now presented to the public, revived these reflections, and gave new force to them, at the same time that they confirmed the very favourable opinion we have entertained of the goodness of the writer's heart.

Her reflections on the French Revolution are truly feminine, and such an air of sincerity runs through the descriptive part of her letters, as leads us to hope that they may tend to remove from some polite circles, a *few* of the childish prejudices that have the *insignia* of raw-head and bloody-bones to sink them deeper in the vacant mind....

2. From *The General Magazine, and Impartial Review*, (December 1790): 541-43

With this lively and agreeable companion we have lately enjoyed some pleasing excursions in the fairy fields of fiction and romance. She now calls us from the regions of imagination to exhibitions of real life: and the scenes to which she has lately been a witness in a land so long celebrated for gaiety and taste, were well calculated for raising all her sensibilities. We agree with her in all she says and feels about the inestimable blessing of liberty, and heartily believe her sincere in all the encomiums she pronounces on that best privilege of the species; but we do not think it altogether worthy of her good sense to express such raptures with every thing French. This looks more like the childish admiration of a confined mind than the prudent and philosophical opinion of a writer, who certainly aims at instructing, as well as entertaining, the public. We however make allowance for the natural, and perhaps unavoidable effusion of a young and fervid imagination, situated among a people convulsed by all the extravagance of political freedom. They would not have deserved the wonderful escape they have made from the horrors of unqualified despotism, had they been less sensible of the change, or less relished their miraculous emancipation. And who can resist the contagion of so divine a sensation as joy, when universal? The best philosophy however consists in the moderation of the passions: and we will venture to assure our amiable authoress that she will never reach those excellencies in composition to which her genius aims, and of which she is capable, without holding the reigns of fancy with a tighter hand. There is much vivacity in these letters, and they will probably please the majority of her readers: but whoever would write well must write to the few, and must even be able to reject whatever is likely to charm the multitude. The familiarity so proper and becoming in epistolary composition, is not a mere flippancy: it is a simplicity which supposes both taste and correctness. In a young writer, and especially a female one, the little saucy pronoun *I* seldom makes its appearance with a good grace.

The story which concludes these letters is held up to the public as a matter of fact: this silences every surmise or demur which criticism might otherwise have put in to the probability of such a fiction. We conceive the piece, from its simple outlines, to be sufficiently dreadful; but many scenes in it, we do think, must owe much to the colouring of an artist whose sublimity is generally tinged with melancholy and horror.

We should not have indulged ourselves in these remarks, but that they may be of use to this writer, unless, like many of her inferiors, she is already too wise to learn. This is no unusual consequence of female literature; but Miss Williams's goodness of heart, and soundness of understanding, incline us to hope better things of her. We could wish to see her elegant talents employed in such a manner as would acquire her new celebrity from their utility: let her endeavour to reform the female world by exposing the present worthless system of boarding-school education: here a tyranny, infinitely more ferocious to human welfare than all the despotism that ever lorded it over political society, extends, establishes, and perpetuates a domination over the feelings and lives of men. What is there in the conduct of women, ridiculous, improper, or wicked, which does not originate in this polluted and polluting source! Miss Williams knows well to what practices we allude, and is better calculated than any writer within our recollection for exposing and probably cleansing this Augean stable. With her powers, her sentiments, her interest in the purity and dignity of the feminine character, we should imagine such a subject familiar to her mind: she possesses a fluency that will always do justice to her conceptions; and her delicacy will readily assist her in pointing out the most infallible mode of securing and improving the happiness of the sex. A revolution in the female world has been most devoutly desired by all the lovers of propriety and morality: and we recommend the attempt to this young lady as highly worthy of her ambition, and shall very sincerely accompany with our plaudits every reform she may adopt. The effort would be honourable; and no disgrace could attach itself to a failure, where so few have succeeded.

3. From *The Monthly Review,* (December 1790): 429–30

Miss Williams has been a successful candidate, both in verse and prose, for the public favour; and we are persuaded that she will continue to merit applause, while just thinking, and easy, though correct, expression, shall be deemed commendable qualities in a writer.

In these letters, she relates whatever she thought worthy of observation in her late tour in France. She arrived at Paris on the day preceding the ever memorable federation; the splendid ceremonial of which she relates with that rapturous feeling which so powerfully struck every spectator, from this country, with whom we have conversed, since that great event took place: she styles it "the most sublime spectacle which, perhaps, was ever represented on the theatre of this earth!"—The triumph of human kind!—It was, she adds, "Man asserting the noblest privileges of his nature; and it required but the common feelings of humanity to become in that moment a citizen of the world. For myself, I acknowlege that my heart caught with Enthusiasm the general sympathy; my eyes were filled with tears; and I shall never forget the sensations of that day, 'while memory holds her seat in my bosom.'"

On every occasion, this amiable letter-writer warmly expresses her abhorrence of despotism, and nobly exults in the triumph of liberty over this horrible scourge of mankind. She frequently takes notice of the rancorous (shall we call it? or envious,) disposition which, since this most extraordinary event, many of our countrymen have manifested toward the people of France, as if *they* possessed not the same right to the blessing of a free and equitable government, which other nations claim, and which we happily enjoy....

To give variety to her letters, Miss Williams has introduced the affecting story of Mons. Du F——, and his family, with whom she was personally acquainted. If any thing were wanting to increase our detestation of tyrannical government, that purpose would have been effectually answered by this little history of the private distress, and unnatural cruelty, which these virtuous and innocent victims endured;—and to the horrors of which they never could have been exposed in a FREE COUNTRY.

4. From *The Universal Magazine of Knowledge and Pleasure,* (December 1790): 289

Among the many recent publications relative to the great Revolution in France, we must not forget to notice a sprightly and entertaining one, by Miss Helen Maria Williams, with whose literary abilities our readers are already well acquainted. It is entitled "Letters written in France, in the Summer 1790, to a Friend in England; containing various Anecdotes relating to the French Revolution, and Memoirs of Mons. and Madame du F——."

The three first letters contain a very interesting relation of the procession and ceremonies on the day of the grand federation of the French Nation in the Champ de Mars, on the 14th of July 1790; of which an elegant copper-plate, in our last number, is a very pleasing illustration.—The fourth letter contains an equally interesting account of a visit to the ruins of the late formidable Bastille....

5. From *The Critical Review,* (January 1791): 117-18

Eh bien mademoiselle! Vous etes donc devenue democrate, & ne dites rien que l'assemblée nationale—Cela ce peut; mais pour les femmes etre folles de *liberté*—Ma foi, mademoiselle, vous ne vous marierez jamais. [So, Mademoiselle, you've become a democrat, and you talk about nothing but the National Assembly. Be that as it may, for women to be crazy about liberty—My goodness, Mademoiselle, you will never be married!]—But, in plain English, and in *sober sadness,* for we do not mean to condemn our author to the gloomy solitude of celibacy, miss H.M. Williams seems to be a little too fond of revolutions, though if, in her charming little nouvelle, M. du F. had owed his deliverance to a decree of the national assembly, we should have thought this charitable act might have covered a multitude of sins. It might have happened, however, as well under any administration.

Our author gives a pleasing picture of the solemnity of the federation; and her description of different parts of France is picturesque and animated. Her account of the national assembly, of Pere Gerard, of madame de Sillery, once madame de Genlis, and now sunk down to plain madam Brulart, no longer a marchioness, and of the present duc de Chartres, are highly pleasing: and we have not for a long time met with a little work from which we have received more entertainment. As to the political question, nous sommes parfaitement d'accord avec mademoiselle [we agree completely with mademoiselle]—"we had better leave it to the decision of posterity." ...

We are sorry, however, to find our young lady so idle as to have left the translation of the French quotations to some incompetent assistant. If she had attended to it herself she would undoubtedly have explained "Mons. Rabeau vaut deux de Mi—rabeau," even by printing it in the manner we have done, for *mi* is an abbreviation of *demi.* In p. 111, too, she would not have weakened the force of the people's reply to the curé. Vous etes une assemblé d'anes, exclaimed he—Oui, Mons. le Curé, disoient ils, et vous en etes le pasteur— "You are a parcel of asses." Yes, sir, they replied, and you are the shepherd. In this way, with no great violence, the equivoque might have been preserved; but, by translating pasteur, "preacher," as in the page before us, it is wholly lost. These, by the way, are not the only instances of inadvertency.

6. From *The Gentleman's Magazine,* (January 1791): 92-93

That an English lady should be fond of, or intoxicated with, liberty, is no phænomenon in these times; or even that an English lady should be eager to see the parade and deception of the French Confederation. Such was Helen Maria Williams. She "saw it, and was glad," and perhaps rejoices that she has made a profitable book of it. We will allow her to indulge all the enthusiasm of a sprightly writer, and to tell her *own* story with *naiveté*; but she must allow us to suspend our assent to every story she may have heard, or seen in private letters from French story-tellers or letter-writers, for whom many grains of allowance must be made. We, who have bestowed some little attention to the calm reasonings of Burke and Calonne, must be permitted to entertain very different notions of the French revolution, and indeed of the value of liberty, and the means of attaining and enjoying such an inestimable blessing, from those who look no further than the "solemnities perfectly calculated to awaken the general sympathy," and applied by "the leaders of the French revolution, men well acquainted with the human heart, to interest in their cause the most powerful passions of human nature." p. 62. We must be allowed to fear that "the French have gone too far;" not "because they have gone farther than ourselves," but because they have gone beyond every principle and axiom of practical government. We have seen the issue of the Flemish revolution. By the natural effect of such violent commotions, things have returned into their antient channel; and perhaps the present Sovereign, more exorable than the last, may lay aside his resentments, like a great and gracious prince. The Brabanters will certainly have reason to prefer a settled to an unsettled government. The springs of the machine have been so completely relaxed in France, that they must be tightened afresh, or the machine cannot go on. "They are, to use their own phrase, *devenus fous des Anglois* (become madly fond of the English), and fondly imagine that the applause they have received from a society of philosophers in our country is the general voice of the nation." p. 69.—Every trait that Miss W. relates bespeaks the levity, fickleness, and fantasticalness of the French. The whole is pantomime. Reflection is laid aside. The present moment is their only care. Miss W. has caught the contagion, and calls the good regent Duke of Bedford and William the Conqueror tyrants alike; and she cannot even bear to see any memorial of them. She persuades herself "the most determined democrats of the nation, whatever other privileges they may choose to exercise, will always suffer the privilege of *being rude* to lie dormant." p. 197. This is good *lady-like* reasoning. The pathetic tale of Monsieur and Madame de [*sic*] F——, which takes up 70 of 220 pages, is a very seasonable episode in a declamation against tyranny. The writer herself fears it has the air of a romance (p. 193); and we should perfectly agree with her, as she is used to such writing, that every incident is made perfectly to tally, did we not know, from undoubted authority, that the tale was true. With this good lady there is no country, no language in the world, equal to that of France. She has worn the scarf of Liberty, "that noble scarf," which no English woman that wore the English bandeau of 1789 should exult in. The French will no more comprehend the happiness of our Government than the genius of our Shakespeare. Miss W. when she returned to England, found the general sense of the French revolution so different from her own, that she is glad to close her narrative with probabilities, hopes, and wishes, instead of "*shivering lances* in every society she enters in the cause of the National Assembly."

7. From *The English Review; or, an Abstract of English and Foreign Literature*, (January 1791), 21-23

Miss Williams is already known in the literary world by some poems, published a few years ago under the patronage of Dr. Kippis, and which afforded no bad specimen of her talents. She now appears here in another character; and though these letters give us little new, or very interesting information, they will, we are confident, be read with pleasure, as they are, in general, well written. The style of them is neat, lively, and correct; often animated, and in many places elegant. They contain a description of the grand federation which took place at Paris; observations on the ruins of the Bastille; several particulars respecting the French revolution; and anecdotes of some of the leading members of the National Assembly, together with the singular history of Mons. and Madame du

F——, who were subjected to severities which no innocent persons, but those living under a government where the principles of feudal tyranny exist in their utmost vigour, can ever experience....

The part of these letters which claimed our chief attention was, the history of Mons. and Madame [du] F——, some circumstances of which give it so much the air of a romance, that we should believe it to be one, had we not too much confidence in the veracity of Miss Williams to suppose that she would substitute fiction for truth; or, instead of relating real incidents, amuse her readers with a false tale of woe. It, however, ends well; and we were amply repaid for the pain excited in our breasts on perusing the former part of it, by the *denouement* and conclusion, which are as happy and agreeable as we could wish. The sum of the whole is, that, after various sufferings, enough to melt even a heart of stone, constancy and conjugal fidelity at length meet with a just reward.

Appendix D: Other Contemporary Responses to Letters Written in France

1. Edward Jerningham, "On Reading 'Letters Written from France in the Summer 1790, to a Friend in England, by Helen Maria Williams.'"

[*The European Magazine* published excerpts of the *Letters* in its December 1790 issue. In the same issue, on p. 472, it also published a poem about Williams's *Letters* by "E.J.," identified by Gary Kelly as Edward Jerningham (c.1737-1812), a poet and dramatist.]

While Burke, equip'd for daring fight,
Steps forth a literary Knight,
In folds of ancient armour drest,
And boldly rears his feudal crest;
Waves high in air his brandish'd lance,   5
And his huge gauntlet throws at France;
Near the stern Chief, a lovely Maid
Comes in simplicity array'd:
The flowing robe in which she moves
Wove by the Graces and the Loves;   10
She tries no formal refutation
Of his elab'rate speculation,
Nor raves of Governments and Laws,
For she to Nature trusts her cause;
Makes to the heart her strong appeal,   15
Which all who have a heart must feel;
Bids the quick tear of pity roll,
And seizes on the vanquish'd soul.

2. Hester Thrale Piozzi, from *Thraliana*

[Hester Lynch Thrale Piozzi (1740-1821) is well known for her epistolary correspondence with literary figures, especially Samuel Johnson, and for her diaries, memoirs, and travel writing. She befriended Williams in the 1780s, but their friendship seems to have cooled because of Williams's revolutionary ideals. The following excerpt from her diary presents her conflicting feelings about Williams and is reprinted from *Thraliana: The Diary of Mrs. Hester Lynch Thrale* (Later Mrs. Piozzi), 1776-1809, Vol. II. Ed. Katherine C. Balderston (Oxford: Clarendon, 1951) 894-95.]

20 Sept. 1794: ... I have heard from Helen Williams again, tis just two Years since She wrote last, & beg'd an Ans^r but I was then fretting about Cecilia Thrale's Health & thought little of any other Concern but that. I had however discretion enough not to correspond with a profess'd Jacobine resident at Paris, tho' She requested a Letter very sweetly indeed, & with much appearance of true Regard for *me*: my refusal to answer such a Request from such a Writer put me in mind of the brutal Housekeeper in Clarissa; who to some Question asked with Intent to detect Fraud & Falsehood—replies "Indeed Miss one knoes not what Cumpiny you may have kipt sin you lefted home, and with Regard to that Tomlinson I says nothing, because thare may bee harme a brewin toward Master by *won Tomlinson*; soe I will have nothin on him."

This was exactly the reason why I did not write to her then, but now She is escaped from Paris poor Soul! I think I may congratulate her on her having had Power & Will to leave the Wretches:—but I fear *Reputation* has been left behind somehow—I *fear* so; tho' perhaps no real harm has been done. one could not write *then*, because there was no way of conveying a Letter but thro' some French Man She directed me to in London—& *he* as the Old Housekeeper says of *won Tomlinson*, might for ought I knew be sent from these Devils to *brew harm toward our Master*;—but now one may send a Letter by the Post, I think I will send a Letter.

Helena Williams is a very fine Genius.

3. Two Letters by Anna Seward

[Anna Seward (1742-1809) was a poet and close friend of Williams when *Letters Written in France* was published. Their friendship appears to have faded a few years later in light of Williams's continued support of revolutionary principles despite the Revolution's growing violence. Included here are two letters—one to Williams herself—expressing Seward's reactions to the *Letters*. They are reprinted from *Letters of Anna Seward: Written Between the Years 1784 and 1807. In Six Volumes* (Edinburgh: George Ramsay & Co., 1811) I, 44–46; III, 75–76.]

LETTER TO MISS WILLIAMS, COLTON, DEC. 12, 1790.

There is much for which I am to thank you, a kind letter of last spring unanswered, because your journey to the continent was so soon to succeed; and, since your return, a charming pamphlet, that shews me the sunny-side of the French Revolution. Right glad am I to see it. "Darkness, clouds, and shadows" have rested upon its surface—assiduously thrown by national envy, and deepened into a chaotic night by the able pen of Mr. Burke—as I am told, for I have not yet read that celebrated pamphlet, except newspaper extracts.

France is certainly in a perilous situation. Devoutly do I wish that she may escape those evils of anarchy which ill-omened eloquence would persuade us are inevitable.

This publication of Mr. Burke's, by what I can learn of it, seems the twin-brother of Johnson's "Taxation no Tyranny;"—the same apparent strength of reasoning, the same splendour of style. I hope time will prove the predictions of this statesman groundless, as it has already proved that of the literary and moral despot. Heaven forbid it should produce equal mischief. His boasted code of pure morality will never, by all the good it has done, or may yet produce, balance to his country the evils to which he was accessary, by vindicating the absurd and ruinous attempt to conquer America. Fatal was his eloquence, which "could make the worse appear the better reason."

Believe me, dear Helen, I take the most lively interest in every sentence of your charming little book. My heart is in unison with its generous and eloquent apostrophes to the, I hope, rising state; but great must be its difficulties, imminent its dangers.

What misfortunes, what woes have been the lot of your friends! We can hardly conceive that the parental heart was capable of such infernal induration. The present felicity of the injured pair must, from recollection of their past sufferings, acquire a degree of sweetness and poignance which cannot be connected with ordinary happiness, and with the former experience of common calamities.

Your last summer's sun was brightened by the cheering influence of that blessing upon surrounding multitudes, which, the song says, can alone give it fresh beauty. To me its most gilded days were sicklied over by the shades of grief and disease. Each are, in some degree, pervaded, but the latter are not passed away. Adieu.

FROM LETTER TO MRS. KNOWLES, MAY 19, 1791.

You inquire after my opinions on the momentous event, which draws to itself the anxious eyes of all Europe. Mine did not coldly behold a great nation emancipating itself from a tyrannous government—but I soon began to apprehend that its deliverers were pushing the levelling principle into extremes more fatal to civilized liberty than even an arbitrary monarchy, with all its train of evils. I read H. Williams's interesting letters from France. They do not attempt to reason, they only paint, and shew the illumined side of the prospect. My own enthusiasm, which apprehension had damped, rekindled beneath the glow of her feelings and imagination—but not into a firm dependence that France possessed a band of leaders, sufficiently exempted from selfish ambition, to promote the success and felicity of a new and hazardous experiment; in which all the links were broken in that great chain of subordination which binds to each other the various orders of existence.

Mr. Burke's book then came before me—and though I read, with contempt, his nonsensical Quixotism about the Queen of France—though I saw, with indignation, the apostate whig labouring to overturn the principles which produced the Revolution, and to prove a king of England's right to reign in despite of the wills of his subjects, yet I saw also a system of order and polity, elucidated and rendered interesting by every appeal to the affections of the human bosom; and it appeared to me more consonant to human nature, as it *is*, and less injurious to the public safety, than the levelling extreme into which France has rushed. Depending that the persuasive orator would not dare to misrepresent facts, I thought there was every thing to fear for France, and much to detest in her coercive circulation of the assignats, and in the wantonly tyrannous restraints she laid upon her monarch....

4. Society of Friends of the Constitution at Rouen

[In July 1791, Williams's mother and sister presented a copy of the *Letters* (almost certainly the French translation) to the Society of Friends of the Constitution at Rouen, during a public meeting at which it was read aloud. The Society sent Williams a copy of the minutes of this meeting along with a congratulatory letter. Our translation of this letter and Williams's response are based on the French text cited in Lionel D. Woodward, *Une Anglaise, amie de la révolution française, Helene-Maria Williams, et ses amis* (Paris: Honoré Champion, 1930) 43-46.]

Mademoiselle,

The French Revolution may well offer a sublime picture, but its portrayal required a painter capable of depicting it for all the peoples on earth. It fell to you, Mademoiselle, with your pure and sensitive heart, your strong soul and love of liberty, to do justice to the noble transports of a great people at the moment when it is becoming free. You have done this, Mademoiselle, in a way that mere glory-seekers have not come close to achieving. If your first letters stirred tears of admiration, the last ones made them flow even more abundantly. How distressing is the portrayal of despotism torturing innocent victims! M. Thomas du Fossé, his worthy wife, and Mlle. Thomas, their young and lovable daughter, will stand for all generations as an example of the crimes of arbitrary power. Our descendants will know that under the reign of tyranny the most respectable family—a model of virtue and holy union, now receiving the blessings of all who know them—was for fifteen years persecuted, imprisoned, and tormented almost to death. For it is through what we held most sacred that despotism exercised its wrath. It required unblemished victims.

The twofold portrait of the charms of liberty and the wrongs of slavery, which you were able to paint with the features specific to each, was received with the greatest gratitude by the Society of the Friends of the Constitution. We held a public reading of it, and every citizen present applauded. Imagine, Mademoiselle, the degree of attention everyone gave to it. We had the good fortune of having Madame your mother, Mademoiselle your sister, and the entire family of M. Thomas with us. You alone were missing. May the Society of the Friends of the Constitution one day be able to welcome you in our midst. We will regard that happy moment as a harbinger of the perfect union in which our two peoples, meant to love and respect one another, will one day dwell.

Meanwhile, Mademoiselle, please accept this tribute of the Society's affection and gratitude.

Society of the Friends of the Constitution at Rouen
Signed: Hardy
By the members of the Correspondence Department
Signed: Laumonier, LeContour, Blanche, Thiesse

Du Fossé, 13 September 1791

Gentlemen:

I could not be more cognizant of the honor you confer upon my work. The French Revolution is an event capable of providing the human spirit with the most sublime ideas, but the results it has already produced make it a topic not only for the mind but still more for the heart. One does not need a philosopher's wisdom to recognize the general happiness; it is enough to have a woman's sensibility. Born in a free country, how could I watch without compassion as the benefits of liberty spread to a great people who had enjoyed all the gifts of nature but were unhappily condemned to moan in the bosom of abundance, to envy the inhabitants of uncivilized lands where liberty is the only good? It was impossible for me to be an unfeeling witness to the majestic solemnity I have tried to portray. I will always remember with enthusiasm the joy of attending the first celebration of July 14, that beautiful day about which human nature must feel triumphant and which future ages will celebrate with cheers of gratitude. May France's budding liberty endure forever! May virtue no longer be oppressed by such misfortunes as it cost me so many tears to recount! May the new Legislature firmly uphold the principles of this Constitution and earn for the first National Assembly of France the eternal admiration of posterity. Gentlemen, let my hopes join with yours that France and Europe may follow the example of the most enlightened peoples, so that the French Revolution may be the epoch when the human species learns that it was created not for slavery, hatred and misery but for liberty, fraternity and happiness.

Signed: Helen Maria Williams

5. Laetitia Matilda Hawkins, from *Letters on the Female Mind*

[Laetitia Matilda Hawkins (1760-1835) was a writer and novelist who in 1793 produced *Letters on the Female Mind, Its Powers and Pursuits, Addressed to Miss H.M. Williams, With particular reference to her Letters from France*, a two-volume response to the 1790 and 1792 volumes of Williams's *Letters*. Hawkins and Williams were apparently literary acquaintances, but Hawkins published her response anonymously, ostensibly so "that if [Williams does] yield, it will be to argument, not to personal authority." Directly addressing Williams's letter about her visit to the National Assembly, the following excerpt touches upon all of Hawkins's major disagreements with Williams, including her disdain of "mob" mentality, sentiment, and women's involvement in politics. We reprint here pp. 185-92 of Hawkins's text.]

LETTER XII

You visited the National Assembly, my dear madam, and were pleased with the facility of your admission to a seat, a circumstance you have improved to the purpose of glancing obliquely at the want of *politesse* in an English court of judicature. I can readily forgive this resentment; but I am astonished that your ingenuity could so far aid your Gallic prejudice as to form not only an excuse for, but a justification of the tumult you found within the building. You describe the debate as what I do not doubt it is, a scene of confusion; but that the importance of the objects the Assembly deliberates on, should be a reason for vociferous clamour, is, according to my ideas, reasoning backwards: it is admitted in morals, that extremes center in one point; it is incontrovertible, that a deficiency of ideas and a redundancy of them will produce silence. Not to feel, and to feel excessively, will appear perfect apathy; but I never can grant that the importance of a *deliberation* is an incentive to do that which suspends the contemplative power of our intellects. To think is to generate ideas; to speak is to diffuse them. A mob will be clamorous when their interests are affected, because it is from the impulse of the moment that their clamour springs; but deep rumination and a silence which no one seems willing to break, are the characteristics of a senate anxious for the averting some great evil, or framing a system of public benefit.

In your predilection for these polite lawgivers, you say, "of how little consequence is this impetuosity in debate if their decrees are wise and beneficial!" &c. It is of *no* consequence, if decrees so made can be wise or beneficial; but that is the proposition I wish proved; for I protest it seems to me impossible, that decrees so made should be even common sense. 'If you talk to me, I cannot write,' is what we every day say to loquacious companions intruding on us; but the question is still stronger—if all talk, who shall think? You would have found a better excuse for your friends, my dear madam, in the volatility of their national character, which nothing can repress. "And this," repeated I with exultation to myself, "this is the National Assembly of France!!!"

It would be uncandid to judge of the *aspect* of public affairs, at the time when you visited France, by the *consequences* since. Perhaps the late events have moderated your opinion of the virtuous spirit you ascribe to all the opposers of monarchy: you may now doubt that principle of perfection on which wisdom seemed to you to be erecting a constitution. *I* should have doubted it: I *did* doubt it from the moment when the French proposed a new system of government rather than a correction of the former one, because without the slightest skill in politics, observation of the human heart alone proves that jealousy is greediness, and that it is not the power, but the hand in which that power is lodged, that rouses the inveteracy of mankind.

Those who have indulged in wandering through the aerial regions of fiction, are either disposed to judge of the inhabitants and occurrences of this nether sphere too favourably, or they are mortified at a disparity they find in comparing their own ideas with the reality. I have heard it objected to our fascinating poet Thomson, that he painted landscapes and figures not as they were, but as they *should* be; that he drew from fancy rather than from real life, and that consequently we derive from his poetry a pleasure which, though exquisite, has little foundation in truth.

There is a certain *routine* of sentiment which all this tribe of aerial travellers adopt; and it is found so congenial to a poetical imagination, that poetry loses many of its charms, and descends from all its superiority over prose, if it departs from it. Universal benevolence, universal peace, and every universality that soothes the mind, is depicted in poetry. Liberty and harmony are concords it cannot dispense with; but whoever should take a poet for his guide in the knowledge of the world, would soon find he had not only much to learn, but much to unlearn.

On the contrary, where opinions are formed only on authentic tradition or experience, our ideas are more correct though far less pleasing. We are taught by history, we are made to feel by the world, that whatever man in a state of nature might be, man in a state of civilization is a being whose conflicting passions are not greatly to be relied on for a virtuous principle or a virtuous victory. Those who will not bear the sword against him are yet forced to carry the shield; and however disposed they might be in the inexperience of youth to take up with pleasing fiction, the cooler season of reflection almost uniformly brings with it a conviction which gives common sense the preference over the most ingenious hypothesis.

You will not, I hope, be offended, my dear madam, if I rather class you with the former than the latter of these sects. Talents such as your's, pursuits such as your's, would, in my opinion, be degraded if they placed you otherwise. The error is, perhaps, more amiable here than the truth; and as neither you nor I can ever be called on to preside over any part of the properties of our fellow creatures but their affections, it is of no great consequence to them whether we please by amusing or instructing; but then, for consistency's sake, do not let us blend the characteristics of the two descriptions; do not let us imagine that the fairies and sprites of our fancy are terrestrial beings, that by our travels in the land of fiction we gain knowledge of the *human heart*, or that a world where every species of corruption has been increasing during ages, is to be now, by a sudden change of principles, regulated by pastoral simplicity. Till we see "the leopard lie down with the kid, and the calf and the young lion together," we are not to expect that "a young child shall lead them."

It was my intention in this cursory review of your benevolent work to have remarked to you how little faith is to be given to the raptures of a mob, and what slender security of the popular love their zeal in drawing the carriage of Mons. Barnave would probably turn out. I have so often heard of this species of pedestrian fanaticism, and so often seen it converted, like all violent love, into violent contempt, that I heartily despise it; but the Parisians have saved me the trouble of a comment on the fact.

6. William Wordsworth, from *The Prelude* (1805), Book IX

[William Wordsworth (1770-1850) was a passionate supporter of the French Revolution in the early 1790s. From 1791-92 he traveled throughout France. In Books IX and X of *The Prelude*, Wordsworth describes the often euphoric experiences of these travels. The passage excerpted below from Book IX relates the story of "Vaudracour" and "Julia," victims of paternal and state tyranny, whose persecution is modeled on Williams's narrative about the du Fossés in *Letters Written in France*. Wordsworth's version, however, has an unhappy ending, perhaps because it is also based on his own abruptly ended affair with the young French woman Annette Vallon, with whom he had an illegitimate child, and from whom he was separated when France declared war upon Great Britain in 1793, preventing travel between the countries. For Wordsworth's early admiration of Williams, see Appendix E. Our text is excerpted from *The Thirteen-Book Prelude by William Wordsworth*, ed. Mark L. Reed (Ithaca: Cornell UP, 1991) 246-66.]

Oh! happy time of youthful Lovers! thus
My Story may begin, Oh! balmy time
In which a Love-knot on a Lady's brow
Is fairer than the fairest Star in Heaven!
To such inheritance of blessedness   560
Young Vaudracour was brought by years that had
A little overstepp'd his stripling prime.
A Town of small repute in the heart of France
Was the Youth's Birth-place: there he vow'd his love
To Julia, a bright Maid, from Parents sprung   565
Not mean in their condition; but with rights
Unhonour'd of Nobility, and hence
The Father of the young Man, who had place
Among that order, spurn'd the very thought
Of such alliance. From their cradles up,   570
With but a step between their several homes
The Pair had thriven together year by year,
Friends, Playmates, Twins in pleasure; after strife
And petty quarrels had grown fond again,
Each other's advocate, each other's help   575
Nor ever happy if they were apart:
A basis this for deep and solid love,
And endless constancy, and placid truth.

[Eventually Julia becomes pregnant out of wedlock. Ashamed of her predicament, her parents remove her from the town to give birth. Julia and Vaudracour meet secretly and decide that he will return to his father's house, saving money so that they may live free from family interference, but his steadfast intention to marry Julia infuriates his father.]

Incensed at such obduracy and slight
Of exhortations and remonstrances   665
The Father threw out threats that by a mandate
Bearing the private signet of the State
He should be baffled in his mad intent,
And that should cure him. From this time the Youth
Conceived a terror, and by night or day   670
Stirr'd nowhere without Arms. Soon afterwards
His Parents to their Country Seat withdrew
Upon some feign'd occasion; and the Son
Was left with one Attendant in the house.
Retiring to his Chamber for the night,   675
While he was entering at the door, attempts
Were made to seize him by three armed Men,
The instruments of ruffian power; the Youth,
In the first impulse of his rage, laid one
Dead at his feet, and to the second gave   680
A perilous wound; which done, at sight
Of the dead Man he peacefully resign'd
His Person to the Law, was lodged in prison,
And wore the fetters of a Criminal.

[Through the help of an influential friend at court, Voudracour
recovers his freedom, but only at the price of renouncing Julia, a
pledge he does not intend to keep. Overwhelmed by remorse for
killing a man, he briefly reunites with Julia, only to be arrested
again at his father's instigation.]

                              ...The Father's mind,   725
Meanwhile, remain'd unchanged, and Vaudracour
Learn'd that a mandate had been newly issued
To arrest him on the spot. Oh! pain it was
To part! he could not—and he linger'd still
To the last moment of his time, and then,   730
At dead of night with snow upon the ground,
He left the City, and in villages
The most sequester'd of the neighbourhood
Lay hidden for the space of several days
Until the horseman bringing back report   735
That he was nowhere to be found, the search
Was ended. Back return'd the ill-fated Youth,

And from the House where Julia lodged (to which
He now found open ingress, having gain'd
The affection of the Family, who lov'd him   740
Both for his own, and for the Maiden's sake)
One night retiring, he was seized. But here
A portion of the Tale may well be left
In silence, though my memory could add
Much how the Youth, and in short space of time,   745
Was travers'd from without, much, too, of thoughts
By which he was employ'd in solitude
Under privation and restraint, and what
Through dark and shapeless fear of things to come,
And what through strong compunction for the past   750
He suffer'd, breaking down in heart and mind.
Such grace, if grace it were, had been vouchsafed
Or such effect had through the Father's want
Of power, or through his negligence, ensued
That Vaudracour was suffered to remain,   755
Though under guard and without liberty,
In the same City with the unhappy Maid
From whom he was divided. So they fared
Objects of general concern, till, moved
With pity for their wrongs, the Magistrate,   760
The same who had placed the Youth in custody,
By application to the Minister
Obtain'd his liberty upon condition
That to his Father's House he should return.

[Vaudracour and Julia are separated again, but he rejoins her just
before she gives birth. Because Vaudracour's father adamantly continues to object to the marriage, Julia's parents force her to give up
the child and enter a convent. After begging for assistance from his
father, Vaudracour decides to retire with his child and a female
domestic to a solitary retreat, where the child eventually dies "by
some mistake / Or indiscretion" of Vaudracour, who is devastated
by grief and never speaks another word.]

                    Thus liv'd the Youth
Cut off from all intelligence with man,
And shunning even the light of common day,   930
Nor could the voice of Freedom which through France

Soon afterwards resounded, public hope,
Or personal memory of his own deep wrongs
Rouze him; but in those solitary shades
His days he wasted, an imbecile mind.

Appendix E: Contemporary Responses to Williams

1. William Wordsworth

[William Wordsworth's first published poem, "Sonnet on Seeing Miss Helen Maria Williams Weep at a Tale of Distress," appeared in March 1787 in the *European Magazine* under the pseudonym, "Axiologus" (p. 202). Although Wordsworth and Williams did not meet until 1820, he deeply admired her poetic capabilities, particularly her capacity for sensibility, and had tried unsuccessfully to meet her earlier. We reprint the text of the "Sonnet" from the *European Magazine*.]

"Sonnet on Seeing Miss HELEN MARIA WILLIAMS Weep
at a Tale of Distress"

SHE wept.———Life's purple tide began to flow
In languid streams through every thrilling vein;
Dim were my swimming eyes—my pulse beat slow,
And my full heart was swell'd to dear delicious pain.
Life left my loaded heart, and closing eye;   5
A sigh recall'd the wanderer to my breast;
Dear was the pause of life, and dear the sigh
That call'd the wanderer home, and home to rest.
That tear proclaims———in thee each virtue dwells,
And bright will shine in misery's midnight hour;   10
As the soft star of dewy evening tells
What radiant fires were drown'd by day's malignant pow'r,
That only wait the darkness of the night
To chear the wand'ring wretch with hospitable light.

AXIOLOGUS

FROM *THE LETTERS OF WILLIAM AND DOROTHY WORDSWORTH*

[Despite differences in their ultimate views of the Revolution, Wordsworth continued to admire Williams's poetry, as late as 1830. Commenting on Williams and other renowned female poets in a letter to the publisher Alexander Dyce, Wordsworth asks Dyce to include them in his anthology *Specimens of British Poetesses*. The letter is here excerpted from *The Letters of William and Dorothy Wordsworth: The Later Years*. Ed. Ernest de Selincourt (Oxford: Clarendon, 1939) I, 478-79.]

Rydal Mount, Kendal, May 10th, [1830]

If a 2nd edition of your Specimens should be called for, you might add from H. M. Williams the Sonnet to the Moon, and that to Twilight; and a few more from Charlotte Smith, particularly "I love thee, mournful, sober-suited night." At the close of a sonnet of Miss Seward's are two fine verses—"Come, that I may not hear the winds of night, Nor count the heavy eave-drops as they fall."

2. James Boswell

[In 1791, James Boswell (1740-95) published his *Life of Samuel Johnson*, the biography of his friend and major eighteenth-century literary figure. In the second edition, published two years later, Boswell added the following footnote after describing Johnson and Williams's first meeting, excerpted here from *The Life of Samuel Johnson, LL.D.* 3 vols. 2d ed. (London: Charles Dilly, 1793) I, 543-44.]

In the first edition of my Work, the epithet *amiable* was given [in reference to Williams]. I was sorry to be obliged to strike it out; but I could not in justice suffer it to remain, after this young lady had not only written in favour of the savage Anarchy with which France has been visited, but had (as I have been informed by good authority,) walked, without horrour, over the ground at Thuillieries, when it was strewed with the naked bodies of the faithful Swiss Guards, who were barbarously massacred for having bravely defended, against a crew of ruffians, the Monarch whom they had taken an oath to defend. From Dr. Johnson she could now expect not endearment but repulsion.

3. The *Anti-Jacobin Review*

[Published anonymously in the September 1798 edition of the bitingly satirical and conservative *Anti-Jacobin Review and Magazine; or, Monthly Political and Literary Censor* is the following attack on Williams within a parody of medicinal remedies for revolutionary "factions."]

A MEDICINE FOR THE TIMES; OR, AN ANTIDOTE
AGAINST FACTION.

This is the title of a tract printed in 1641. As the same factious spirit which obtained at that period, unhappily, prevails, at this time, to a certain extent it may not be amiss to shew what remedy was *then* prescribed for this troublesome disease, with a view to ascertain whether, if properly administered, it would not prove more efficacious *now*. We shall extract the three first prescriptions ...

"2. *How to cure a woman so possessed [of a factious spirit].*
(Addressed to Mrs. B.—Mrs. S.—and *Citizenness* Helen Maria Williams.)

"A woman, being the weaker vessel, shall have the application of a weaker remedy; let her obey her husband when he hath taken his cure, and not disdain to conceive that (over his own family) *he is both a King and a Bishop*, one that is capable both of morall government and divine; this observation in her, will keep her from pulling off the sacred chain that is about the neck of *authority*, and free her from a strange madnesse she hath got in expounding scripture" ...

4. Mary Pilkington

[Mary Pilkington (1766-1839) was a prolific author of novels, short stories, and moralistic tales for children. Although her works stress Christian virtues and propriety, she provided an appreciative account of Williams's life and career in *Memoirs of Celebrated Female Characters Who Have Distinguished Themselves By Their Talents and Virtues* (1804). Our text is from the original Albion Press edition published in 1804, p. 341.]

As a female possessed of superior abilities, this lady is no less celebrated than admired, although it is evident that her political sentiments are rather of the republican kind. That revolution which she
had imagined would have been attended with such glorious consequences, she saw overwhelm its projectors in ruin and disgrace,
and she was ready to exclaim with the unfortunate Madame
Roland, "O liberty, how many crimes are committed in thy name!"
Amidst the various writings of this celebrated female, her Travels
through Switzerland have been the most generally admired; her
mode of narration gives a charm and interest to description, and
excites in the mind of the reader a mixture of pleasure and
applause: she enriches her performance with a redundancy of picturesque scenery, striking anecdotes of private life, biographical
sketches of distinguished individuals, and a detailed account of the
several governments of the different parts into which the commonwealth was divided, at the period when the entertaining
account was written. "Her powers of description (says one of the
reviewers), her sensibility, her patriotism, and her wit, are well
known to the public; and nothing in these volumes will detract in
any degree from a fame already so perfectly established. Her dic-
tion is lofty and animated, like the romantic and diversified country she traverses; she is often as bold and abrupt as the precipices
over which she travels; and her composition wears, in many places,
the aspect more of a masculine than a feminine compostion; she
says enough, with all her fondness for foreign parts, to satisfy young
women of the blessings they enjoy under a British government,
and to impress them with a due value of the many peculiar comforts they still enjoy in a degree much superior to the inhabitants
of any other country under heaven."

5. Henry Crabb Robinson

[Henry Crabb Robinson (1775-1867), best known for his diaries,
correspondence, and friendships with most of the major Romantic writers, met Williams for the first time in 1814 and introduced
Wordsworth to her in 1820. Robinson and Williams became
friends, and he assisted her in some later publishing efforts. The
following excerpts from his diaries and travel journals are
reprinted from *Henry Crabb Robinson on Books and Their Writers*.

Ed. Edith J. Morley. 3 volumes (London: J.M. Dent, 1938) I, 147, 148, 232.]

[*Travel Journal: Paris.*] Sept. 4th [1814].

... I accompanied them [the Clarksons] to see Helen Maria Williams, whose works I read with pleasure many years ago. She was a preacher of liberty at the beginning of the Revolution: I had suspected her of having been since an apologist of French tyranny, and was prepared to be by no means pleased with her.... However, the visit was an agreeable one, and I shall renew my calls.

Miss Williams is an old maid; Mrs. Clarkson thinks she must have been handsome—I see no traces of former beauty. Her features are strongly marked: her chin is very long, and an almost perpetual smile does not bring it within ordinary bounds. She reminds me a little of both Mrs. Barbauld and Mrs. Opie. She talks freely and on political subjects to us without restraint. With all her sentiments I was perfectly satisfied and they were always English.... He [Mr. Hurford Stone] was, however, afterwards arrested as well as Miss Williams and saved only by having friends among the Republican party. Buonaparte was their enemy also, said Stone, in consequence of Miss Williams refusing to write in his favour.... We conversed a little on literary subjects. Mrs. Clarkson and I repeated some sonnets, etc., by Wordsworth, of whom Miss Williams has never heard before....

Diary, Sept. 4th [1814, *Paris.*]

I was introduced by Mrs. Clarkson to *Helen Maria Williams*, a person who has been the subject of reproaches which have been stimulated by party spirit. Her faults have been exaggerated. She was introduced to the world as a poet when young by Dr. Kippis, and at the beginning of the Revolution went to France, from whence she wrote letters altogether in favour of the French cause.... In spite of the defamatory reports so maliciously, and perhaps unwarrantably, circulated, Mrs. Barbauld told me that if Miss Williams came to England she should invite her to stay in her house. Mrs. Clarkson and the Wordsworths and numerous ladies visited her all her life....

Diary, June 13th [1819].

During the spring of this year Helen Maria Williams applied to me to procure the publication of a volume of *Letters on the State of Politics in France*. She had written formerly *Letters* giving an account of the first French Revolution, a popular work in its day. Alas! the times had changed, and she, too. After much trouble and application to several publishers, I with difficulty persuaded my new acquaintance ... Robert Baldwin to publish the volume, but she got no money by it, and the house, I fear, lost a great deal. I had much to do in correcting the gallicisms of the style. Poor lady! She has been long dead in poverty.... Her connection with Stone, the traitor, whether justly or not, had injured her character....

6. Williams's Obituary in the *Gentleman's Magazine*

[The following obituary for Williams, who died on 15 December 1827, appeared in the *Gentleman's Magazine* for April 1828, p. 373.]

HELEN MARIA WILLIAMS.

At Paris, aged 65, Miss Helen Maria Williams, pre-eminent among the violent female devotees of the French revolution.

She was a native of London; but was resident at Berwick at the time of her composing "Edwin and Elfrida," a legendary tale in verse, upon publishing which in 4to [quarto], 1782, under the patronage of Dr. Kippis, she returned to the metropolis. This first production was so far successful as to induce her to pursue her literary career in a variety of ways. In 1783 she produced an "Ode on the Peace" (see vol. liii, p. 245); in 1784, "Peru, a poem;" in 1786, in two volumes, "A Collection of Miscellaneous Poems;" and in 1788, "Poems on the Slave-trade." Some of these, being published by subscription, were productive of considerable profit. About the last-mentioned year she visited France, and having formed there various literary and political connections, about two years after fixed her residence in Paris. In 1790 she published, in two volumes, a novel entitled "Julia;" also "Letters written from France, in the summer of 1790," to which work a second and third volume were added in 1792, the previous year, 1791, having produced "A Farewell for two years to England." The effects of these works were to render the

French revolution popular in this country (in which she was happily but little successful, see vol. lxi, p. 63),[1] and to recommend their author to the Brissotines at Paris. In the succeeding clash of factions, she was in great danger, and actually confined in the Temple, but was released at the fall of Robespierre. The first fruits of her pen, subsequently to her liberation, were, "A Sketch of the Politics of France, from May 31, 1793, to July 28, 1794; and of the scenes which have passed in the Prisons of Paris; in letters;" and extending to four volumes (reviewed in vol. lxv. 673, 1030). Her next publication was a "Translation of Paul and Virginia," the exquisite simplicity of which she destroyed, by interlarding the original with some of her own sonnets. In 1798 she produced a "Tour in Switzerland, with comparative Sketches of the present state of Paris;" in 1800, "Sketches of the State of manners and opinions in the French Republic;" and in 1803, a translation of the "Political and confidential Correspondence of Louis XVI, with Observations," in 3 vols. 8vo [octavo]. She for some years wrote that portion of the New Annual Register which relates to the affairs of France.

During the "hollow armed truce of Amiens," Miss Williams is understood to have had some intercourse with the English government; and, upon the subsequent war, she became an object of suspicion to the French police, by whom her papers were seized and examined. In 1814 she translated the first volume of "The Personal Travels of M. de Humboldt," which she completed in 1821. Her latest performances are, "A Narrative of Events in France," in 1815;— "On the Persecution of the Protestants in the South of France," in 1816;— "Letters on the Events which have passed in France since the Restoration of 1815," in 1819; and, subsequently, a slight sketch, entitled, "The Leper of the City of Aoste, from the French."

In her later political writings, Miss Williams appeared only as a friend of the Bourbons and an enemy of the revolution. She thus showed that her democratic consistency equalled the republican morality she had previously exhibited by living "under the protection" (as the phrase is) of the quondam Rev. Mr. Stone,—one of those singularly black sheep, which even the liberal politics of modern ecclesiastical government cannot tolerate [see note p. 242]. He

---

1 In the same volume, p. 299, is a letter from Paris, containing a deprecation of the reviewer's remarks, and very possibly written by Miss Williams herself. [Note by *Gentleman's Magazine*.]

was deprived of a living in Essex by Bishop Porteus in 1808, and died some years since. Yet had this talented female a large circle of acquaintance; perhaps it may be said, of admirers. A recent portrait of her has been lately published in a folio size in lithography.

Note: The next (May 1828) issue of *The Gentleman's Magazine* carries the following correction (p. 386):

A LOVER OF ACCURACY remarks, that with regard to Miss Helen Maria Williams (p. 373), in one particular our account is incorrect; it stated that she lived "under the protection (as the phrase is) of the quondam Rev. Mr. Stone," &c. &c. Our correspondent takes on him to assert, that the gentleman with whom Miss Williams is said to have lived, was never a clergyman, or a minister of any denomination. He was a man of letters, but a layman; and while he lived in England a hearer of the late Dr. Price at Hackney. In the early part of the French Revolution he and his lady removed to Paris, where he formed an intimacy with Miss Williams. His lady, from whom he was separated, lived in a state of seclusion, and, it is remarkable, died in London since the decease of her rival. The name of this gentleman was *John* Stone. The clergyman, in Essex, who was deprived of his living, was the Rev. Francis Stone, totally unconnected with the other.

Appendix F: The French Revolution: Selected Primary Documents

1. Declaration of the Rights of Man and Citizen

[No document of the French Revolution, and almost no document in European history, has been as significant as the Declaration of the Rights of Man and Citizen. At once the culmination of a century of Enlightenment thought and a radical departure from European political practice, the Declaration was approved by the National Assembly only a few weeks after the taking of the Bastille. Its principles became the blueprint for representative government in Revolutionary France and ultimately around the globe.]

DECLARATION OF THE RIGHTS OF MAN
AND CITIZEN
(Adopted 26 August 1789)
PREAMBLE

The representatives of the French people, constituted as a National Assembly, considering that ignorance, neglect, or contempt for the rights of man are the sole causes of public misfortunes and of the corruption of governments, have resolved to set forth, in a solemn declaration, the natural, inalienable and sacred rights of man, in order that this declaration, constantly present to all members of the social body, will ceaselessly remind them of their rights and their duties; so that the acts of the legislative and the executive powers, able to be compared at any moment with the aim of all political institutions, will be better respected; so that the claims of citizens, based henceforth on simple and incontestable principles, will always contribute to maintaining the Constitution and the happiness of all.

Therefore, the National Assembly recognizes and declares, in the presence and under the auspices of the Supreme Being, the following rights of man and citizen.

FIRST ARTICLE

Men are born and remain free and equal in rights. Social distinctions may be based only on common usefulness.

II.

The purpose of any political association is to preserve the natural and inalienable rights of man. These rights are liberty, property, security, and resistance to oppression.

III.

The principle of all sovereignty resides essentially in the nation. No body or individual may exercise authority that does not emanate expressly therefrom.

IV.

Liberty consists in being able to do anything that does not harm another; thus, the exercise of each man's natural rights has no limits except those that guarantee other members of the society the enjoyment of the same rights. These limits can be determined only by law.

V.

The law has the right to prohibit only those actions that are harmful to society. What is not prohibited by law cannot be forbidden, and no one may be forced to do what the law does not require.

VI.

The law is the expression of the general will. All citizens have the right to participate, as individuals or through their representatives, in its formation. It must be the same for all, whether it protects or punishes. All citizens, being equal in its eyes, are equally admissible to all public honors, offices, and employments, according to their abilities and without other distinctions than those of their virtues and talents.

VII.

No man can be charged, arrested, or detained except under circumstances determined by law, and according to the forms the law prescribes. Those who solicit, draw up, execute or cause to be executed arbitrary orders must be punished; but any citizen summoned or seized according to the law must obey promptly; he makes himself culpable by resisting.

VIII.

The law must establish only those punishments that are absolutely and obviously necessary, and no one can be punished except according to a law that is established and promulgated before the offense takes place, and is legally applied.

IX.

Every man being presumed innocent until he has been declared guilty, if it is deemed crucial to arrest him, every rigor that is not necessary to secure his person must be severely repressed by the law.

X.

No one may be bothered on account of his opinions, even religious ones, so long as their manifestation does not disturb the public order established by law.

XI.

The free communication of thoughts and opinions is one of the most precious rights of man; every citizen may therefore freely speak, write, and print, subject to responsibility for abuses that are determined by the law.

XII.

Safeguarding the rights of man and citizen requires a public force; this force is therefore instituted for the advantage of everyone and not for the particular benefit of those to whom it is entrusted.

XIII.

For maintaining a public force, and for the expenses of administration, a common tax is indispensable: it must be shared equally among all citizens according to their means.

XIV.

All citizens have the right to verify, on their own or through their representatives, the need for public taxation, to consent to it freely, to oversee its use, and to determine its rate, basis, collection, and duration.

XV.

Society has the right to require from every public agent an accounting of his administration.

XVI.

Any society in which the guarantee of rights is not assured, nor the separation of powers determined, has no constitution.

XVII.

Property being an inviolable and sacred right, no one may be deprived of it, unless this becomes a public necessity, legally determined and clearly required, and on the condition of a just compensation in advance.

2. Olympe de Gouges, "Declaration of the Rights of Woman and Female Citizen"

[By exposing the inconsistencies of laws and prohibitions that treated citizens differentially on the basis of their sex, race, class, or religion, the Declaration of the Rights of Man paved the way for further challenges. Some reforms, such as the extension of rights to Protestants, were enacted quickly; others met with more resistance. In 1790 both Nicolas de Condorcet and Etta Palm d'Aelders called on the National Assembly to extend civil rights to women. In 1791, the self-educated butcher's daughter Marie Gouze (1748-93), who published plays and pamphlets as Olympe de Gouges, drew up a Declaration of the Rights of Woman that parallels point for point the Declaration of the Rights of Man. Associated with the Girondins in the Convention, Gouges went to the guillotine under a system that held women politically responsible without giving them political rights.]

DECLARATION OF THE RIGHTS OF WOMAN
AND FEMALE CITIZEN

For the National Assembly to decree in its final sessions or in those of the next legislature:

PREAMBLE

Mothers, daughters, sisters, representatives of the nation, all demand to be formed into a national assembly. Considering that ignorance, neglect, or contempt for the rights of WOMAN are the sole causes of public misfortunes and of the corruption of governments, [they] have resolved to set forth in a solemn declaration the natural, inalienable, and sacred rights of woman, in order that this declaration, constantly present to all the members of the social body, will ceaselessly remind them of their rights and their duties, so that the acts of power by women and those of power by men, able to be compared at every moment with the aim of all political institutions, will be better respected, so that the claims of female citizens, based henceforth on simple and incontestable principles, will always contribute to maintaining the Constitution, good morals and the happiness of all.

Therefore, the sex that is as superior in beauty, as in courage during the sufferings of maternity, recognizes and declares, in the presence and under the auspices of the Supreme Being, the following rights of woman and female citizen:

FIRST ARTICLE.
Woman is born and remains equal to man in rights. Social distinctions can be based only on common usefulness.

II.
The purpose of any political association is to preserve the natural and inalienable rights of woman and man. These rights are liberty, property, security and, above all, resistance to oppression.

III.
The principle of all sovereignty resides essentially in the nation, which is nothing more than the reuniting of man and woman: no body or individual may exercise authority that does not emanate expressly therefrom.

IV.
Liberty and justice consist in restoring all that belongs to another; thus the exercise of the natural rights of woman has no other limits than those imposed by the perpetual tyranny of men; these limits must be reformed by the laws of nature and reason.

V.
The laws of nature and reason prohibit all actions that are harmful to society; what is not prohibited by these wise and divine laws cannot be forbidden, and no one may be forced to do what the law does not require.

VI.

The law must be the expression of the general will; all male and female citizens must participate personally, or through their representatives, in its formation; it must be the same for all, male and female citizens, and all citizens, being equal in its eyes, must be equally admissible to all public honors, offices, and employments, according to their abilities and without other distinctions than those of their virtues and talents.

VII.

No woman is exempted; she is charged, arrested, and detained under circumstances determined by law. Women, like men, obey this rigorous law.

VIII.

The law must establish only those punishments that are absolutely and obviously necessary, and no one can be punished except according to a law that is established and promulgated before the offense takes place, and that is legally applied to women.

IX.

If any woman is found guilty, complete rigor is to be exercised by the law.

X.

No one may be bothered on account of her opinions, even fundamental ones. Woman has the right to mount the scaffold; she must equally have the right to mount the rostrum; so long as her demonstrations do not disturb the public order established by law.

XI.

The free expression of thoughts and opinions is one of the most precious rights of woman, since this liberty assures the legitimation of children by their fathers. Every female citizen can then say freely, I am the mother of a child who belongs to you, without a barbaric prejudice forcing her to hide the truth, subject to responsibility for abuses of this liberty that are determined by the law.

XII.

Safeguarding the rights of woman and the female citizen implies a major benefit; this safeguard must be instituted for the advantage of all, and not for the particular benefit of those to whom it is entrusted.

XIII.

For maintaining a public force, and for the expenses of administration, the contributions of man and woman are equal; she shares all the duties and the burdens; she must then have the same role in the distribution of positions, employment, offices, honors, and tasks.

XIV.

Male and female citizens have the right to verify, on their own or through their representatives, the need for public taxation. This applies to female citizens only if they are granted an equal share, not simply in wealth, but in public administration, and in the rate, basis, collection, and duration of the tax.

XV.

The mass of women, conjoined for purposes of taxation to the mass of men, have the right to demand from every public agent an accounting of his administration.

XVI.

Any society in which the guarantee of rights is not assured, nor the separation of powers determined, has no constitution. The constitution is null and void if it has not been created by a majority of individuals comprising the nation.

XVII.

Property belongs to both sexes whether together or separately; it has for every person an inviolable and sacred right; no one may be deprived of it as a true natural heritage, unless public necessity, legally determined, obviously demands it, and then under the condition of a just and prior indemnity.

3. From *Address to the National Assembly Supporting Abolition of the Slave Trade* By the **Society of Friends of Black People, Paris Chapter**

[In 1788 a group of influential political thinkers founded the Société des Amis des Noirs (Society of Friends of Black People). Taking its impetus from the abolition movement already flourishing in Britain, and spurred by the obvious incompatibility of slavery with the Declaration of the Rights of Man, the Society began early in the Revolution to petition the legislature for an end to the slave trade and later pressed for the complete eradication of slavery. Opposition from colonial planters and commercial interests slowed the process, but on 4 February 1794, France became the first country in Europe to emancipate all people held in slavery. Ensuing rebellions in the largest and most profitable French colony, spurred by such leaders as Toussaint l'Ouverture, culminated in the independence of Saint-Domingue, renamed Haiti, in 1804. The *Address to the National Assembly* excerpted below, delivered on 5 February 1790 and widely published, typifies the cautious posture of the abolitionists at this stage of the Revolution but makes the ultimate necessity of emancipation uncompromisingly clear. (Our text is translated from the February 1790 edition, printed by L. Potier de Lille, pp. 2, 4, 11-12, 16, 18-21.)]

... [T]his august Assembly ... has engraved on a lasting monument that all men are born and remain free and equal in rights. You have restored to the French people those rights of which despotism had so long stripped them; you have just restored them to those good islanders, the Corsicans, cast into slavery under the veil of charity; you have broken the feudal bonds that still degraded a good number of our fellow citizens; you have forecast the destruction of all the corrupting distinctions that religious and political prejudice have introduced into the great family of the human race.

The men whose cause we defend have no other expectations than this: that as citizens of the same Empire and men like ourselves, they should have the same rights as we. We do not ask that you restore to French Blacks those political rights that would, however, alone testify to and uphold the dignity of man; we do not even ask for their liberty....

It is thus not yet time to demand this liberty; we ask only for an end to the butchering of thousands of Blacks each year in order to take hundreds of captives; we ask for an end henceforth to prostituting and profaning the French name in order to authorize these abductions, these atrocious murders; we demand, in a word, the abolition of the Slave Trade....

We will demonstrate that the abolition of the Slave Trade will benefit the Colonists because its first effect will be to bring about a situation that forces masters to treat and nourish their slaves well, to promote their reproduction, to help them to work with animals and tools that will increase their labors while making them easier, because these Negroes, once better equipped, being more fertile, will produce more and better in the same span of time, and consequently will yield more; because the black population growing by itself in the Islands, more labor, more clearing of land, and less mortality will result, since it has been proved that Island-born Negroes are harder working, more peaceful, better acclimatized and consequently less subject to illnesses than the African Negroes....

They will surely tell you that it would suffice to temper the Slave Trade instead of abolishing it; that one could diminish its horrors.... Useless palliatives! The English Parliament has tried these, and the Law has been fruitless. The Shippers have themselves declared that these easements were incompatible with the Trade....

Have no doubt, the moment when this commerce will be abolished, even in England, is not far off. It is already condemned there in public opinion, in the opinion even of the ministers. Parliament would not have consented to the solemnity of these great proceedings, would not have taken charge of it in such great detail, if it had not foreseen that all that remained was to spur on its destruction. If there seems to be a slowdown, that is because the administration—and there are proofs of this fact—is quietly occupied with presenting, at the very instant when abolition of the Trade will be announced, a replacement that will immediately offer English commerce, accustomed to expeditions to Africa, an occupation that provides proper recompense....

Finally they will tell you, in order to divert you from this pressing matter, that abolishing the Trade, or even making a resolution to consider it, will fuel revolt among the Blacks....

If, however, some motive could lead to insurrection, wouldn't it be the National Assembly's indifference to their fate? Wouldn't it be the continued weighing them down with chains even while sanctioning everywhere the eternal axiom that all men are born free and equal in rights. Well, then, would there be for the Blacks only shackles and gallows, while happiness shines for whites alone? Have no doubt, our fortunate revolution will surely galvanize the Blacks, whom vengeance and resentment have galvanized for so long; and torture is not the way to suppress the effects of this upheaval. From one insurrection badly put down, twenty others will arise, a single one of which could ruin the Colonists forever. There is but one means for preventing them: to abolish the Slave Trade or at least for this Assembly to resolve to occupy itself with this issue without delay. The news of an Edict, even one in preparation, will produce two good effects at once: it will calm the agitation of the Blacks, it will force the Planters, who will no longer be able to expect African recruits, to treat their Blacks better. Thus you will stop, with a single word, the flow of blood on the coasts of Africa and the barbaric treatment in our Islands, and you will inaugurate lasting prosperity in our Colonies based on a different order of things.

Ah! don't let yourselves be intimidated by the fear of arousing the resentment of towns engaged in the Slave Trade and leading them to oppose the revolution. It insults them to attribute to them such vengeance, as it insults you to fear it. Woe to those towns that, to avenge a just decree, would have recourse to so criminal an opposition! They would not be worthy of being free. Woe to the Legislators who would pay attention to these fears! they would be unworthy of their title.

So if you are greatly concerned about your own honor, about large principles, and about the preservation of the colonies, hasten, not to abolish the Slave Trade—we are not trying to rush this decision, however we may be convinced of its justice and its benefits—but hasten to take under immediate consideration our request for this abolition, and if the great matters that now take your attention do not permit you to listen to us and to examine all the facts and calculations we can offer you, hasten at least to declare your principles on this issue, to declare to the universe that you are not trying to discard them when another Nation's interests are at stake. The honor of the French name demands it. Free peoples of former times dishonored liberty by establishing slavery for their own profit. It is worthy of the first free Assembly of France, to establish the principle of philanthropy that makes the human species a single family, to declare its loathing for this annual carnage inflicted on the coasts of Africa, which it intends to abolish one day, to alleviate the slavery that results from it, and to search for and prepare the means for doing so, from this point forth.

We beseech you—in the name of the Colonies themselves, which such a declaration alone can reassure—in the name of your honor, in the name of justice, in the name of humanity, which pays with streams of blood for one month, one day of delay. We beseech you finally in the name of Heaven, which surely looks down with joy upon the revolution that you have brought about, and which will bless and even more strongly protect it when it sees you using your power to dry the tears of those wretches against whom European cupidity has for so long conspired.

4. The Fête de la Fédération as described by the *London Times*

[The following newspaper account provides an example of what the British people would have known about the Fête de la Fédération [Festival of Federation] before Williams's *Letters Written in France* was published.]

From July 20, 1790

GRAND FRENCH CONFEDERACY.

ON

THURSDAY, the 14th of July 1790

In conformity to what we promised, so we shall perform. Our recital of this Grand Spectacle of Freedom shall be accurate, and sanctioned by the first authority in Paris; and though we may recapitulate somewhat of that which appeared in our paper of yesterday, yet we think the repetition necessary, in order to make the present account more perfect.

Such a magnificent association of FREE MEN, emancipated from the shackles of despotism within so short a space of time, is hitherto unparalleled in the annals of History. It is a Phænomenon on which surrounding empires look with Admiration—it is a subject that deserves the most minute attention; and with no small degree of satisfaction, we feel ourselves happy in being the FIRST that announced with authenticity, the conclusion of the day, without any of those horrid consequences which were apprehended by many, and wished for by some.

Excepting the bursting of a cannon, and the fall of a tree by which one man lost his life, we have not heard of any other accident. The idea of freedom was general, and as the ultimate end was happiness, common sense and proper prudence directed every man to keep the peace, and rejoice in the event.

On the 11th Inst. the following proclamation was issued:

"The King having been informed of the measures taken, as well by the Mayor of Paris, as by the Committee of the Municipality and Fœderative Assembly of the said city, to regulate the preparation for the ceremony which is to take place on the 14th, and willing to prevent all difficulties which might give rise to any troubles or interruptions, has thought proper to manifest by the present proclamation, the order which seemeth best to be observed, as well for the placing the Members of the Confederation, as for their march to the place of the ceremony. So that no obstacle may arise to trouble the order of the day, or to derogate from its majesty,

"The general rendezvous of the different corps which might compose the confederation, is appointed to be at the Boulevards du Temple at six in the morning.

"They are to march and enter the Champs de Mars in the order pointed out in the table annexed to this Proclamation, which has been approved of by his MAJESTY.

"No troops but those on guard are to be armed with guns. No carriages can be suffered to follow those of his MAJESTY, the ROYAL FAMILY and their train. If any Deputy of the Confederation, or any person invited there, should be in a state to be unable to go on foot to the Champs de Mars, they shall receive from the Mayor of Paris, a ticket permitting them the use of a carriage, and a Chevalier d'Ordonnance to escort them to the military school.

"M. de la FAYETTE, Commander General of the Parisian National Guard, already charged by a decree of the National Assembly, and sanctioned by his Majesty with the care of the public tranquillity, shall fulfill, under the King's orders the functions of Major General of the Confederation; and in that quality the orders he shall give shall be observed as the orders of his MAJESTY himself.

"The KING has, in like manner, nominated M. GOUVION, Major General of the Parisian Guard, Lieutenant General of the Confederation for the day of ceremony.

"When all persons are placed, the blessing the flags and colours shall be proceeded to, and the celebration of mass.

"The KING empowers the said M. de la FAYETTE to pronounce the Confederation Oath in the name of all the deputies of the National Guards, and those of the Troops and Marines, according to the forms decreed by the National Assembly, and accepted by his MAJESTY; and all the Deputies of the Confederation shall hold up their hands.

"Then the President of the National Assembly shall pronounce the Civic Oath for the Members of the National Assembly; and the King shall in like manner pronounce the Oath, the form of which was decreed by the National Assembly, and accepted by his MAJESTY.

"The Te Deum shall be then sung, and conclude the ceremony; after which the procession shall return from the Champs de Mars in the same order it came. Done at Paris the 11th of July 1790."

(Signed)   LOUIS.

(And lower down)

PAR LE ROI, GUIGNARD.

According to the notice which had been issued, by the Marquis de la FAYETTE, the whole body of National Confederation met on the *Boulevards* between the gates *of St. Martin* and *St. Antoine*, at six o'clock in the morning, in order to form a procession from thence to the *Champs de Mars*.

At nine o'clock the procession being formed, it marched along the *Boulevards*, down the *Rue St. Denis*, and through the streets *Feronnerie, St. Honore, Royale*, the *Place* of *Louis Quinze*, the *Cour de la Reine* and the *Quai* as far as the bridge of boats, and being there met by other bodies, the whole procession then entered the field in the following order:

A Troop of Horse, with a Standard, and Six Trumpets.
One Division of the Music, consisting of several hundred Instruments.
A Company of Grenadiers.
The Electors of the City of Paris.
A Company of Volunteers.
The Assembly of the Representatives of the Commons.
The Military Committee.
A Company of Chasseurs.
A Band of Drums.
The Presidents of the Districts.
The Deputies of the Commons appointed to take for them the Federal Oath.
The Sixty Administrators of the Municipality,
with the City Guards.
Second Division of Music.
A Battalion of Children carrying a Standard, with the words,—
"The Hopes of the Nation."

A Detachment of the Colours of the National Guard of Paris.
A Battalion of Veterans.
The Deputies of the *Forty-two* chief Departments of the Nation
in alphabetical order.
The ORIFLAMME; or GRAND STANDARD
of FRANCE, borne by the
Marischalls of France.
General Officers.
Officers of the Staff.
Subaltern Officers.
Commissioners of War.
Invalids.
Lieutenants of the Marischalls of France.
Deputies of Infantry.
Deputies of Cavalry.
Deputies of Hussars, Dragoons, and Chasseurs.
General Officers and Deputies of the Marine,
according to rank.
The Deputies of the *forty-one* last Departments in alphabetical
order.
A Company of Volunteer Chasseurs.
A Company of Cavalry, with a Standard and
two Trumpets.

Each different department was preceded by a banner carried by the oldest officer of each department, on which were written these words; on one side. "THE NATIONAL CONFEDERATION *of Paris on the 14th July 1790*," and on the other side, "THE CONSTITUTION."

Being arrived on the *Place de Louis XV*, the Standard bearers moved to the right and left, in order to receive the National Assembly between two lines. It was then eleven o'clock.

The whole procession was not closed until midday, when there was a grand salute of 100 cannon.

The Field of *Mars* represented an immense circle, round which were placed very large Amphitheatres, containing about 400,000 spectators.

The procession entered the field under a triumphal arch, opposite to the bridge of boats, on which were painted the different Insignia of War. The following inscriptions were conspicuously engraved near the entrance.... [We omit the French, but include the translation by the *Times* below:]

"The POWER of a KING consists in the FREEDOM of his people.

Cherish the Liberty you have now obtained, and by preserving its purity, make yourselves worthy its continuance."

"The RIGHTS of MAN have been enveloped by darkness for ages past—but humanity at last found out the recesses of misery, opened the door, and let in the light of Justice. We are now no longer in dread of that subaltern tyranny, which has so long oppressed us under its many hundred forms—WE ARE FREE."

On the side of the bridge of boats, these other Inscriptions were very conspicuously written [We omit the French, but include the translation by the *Times* below:]

"Under our present defender, the poor shall no longer tremble for the safety of his inheritance. The strength of the Great—the power of the wealthy shall not tear it from him."

"Sacred to the great work of the Constitution, we now lay the finishing stone. Each circumstance is propitious to our happiness; everything flatters our wishes. May the gentle breath of peace dissipate the storm of adversity, and may the mind glow with the ineffable delight of acknowledged Freedom.

"Our country now, and its law are the sole authority that can call us to arms; and we will die in its defence, for we only live to preserve it."

In the middle of the *Field of Mars* was erected the grand ALTAR of LIBERTY, where the civic oath was administered. The approach to it was up a lofty flight of steps, composed of four different staircases. The steps were formed from the stones of the BASTILLE, and supported by large pillars.

On the altar were placed the RECORDS of the CONSTITUTION, the ROYAL SCEPTRE, the HAND of JUSTICE, with a spear, bearing the CAP of LIBERTY.

About the altar were painted several allegorical designs on the subject of the day. Four grand paintings were hung—one on each front of it. The first, represented the GENIUS of FRANCE, pointing to the word CONSTITUTION, with a picture of PLENTY, holding two cornucopias.

The second painting described some of the glorious descendants of France, blowing the trumpet of Fame, and bearing this inscription: ... [The French omitted, but translation by the *Times* below:]

"Hold in your remembrance these three sacred words, which are the guarantee of your decrees;—the NATION, the LAW, and the KING. The Nation is yourselves—the Law is your own, for it is your will—and the King is the Guardian of the law."

The third painting represented the National Deputies taking the civic oath, and the 4th described the arts and sciences, with the following verses underneath: ... [The French omitted, but translation by the *Times* below:]

"Men are equal.—It is their virtue, and not their birth which distinguishes them.—The law ought to form the basis of every state, in its presence all men are equal."

Myrrh and frankincense were burnt in large urns about the altar: the form of it was round, the cieling [sic] painted of sky blue, and was ornamented with large chandeliers. At the end of it was placed the sword of justice.

At the bottom of the *Field of Mars*, opposite to the triumphal arch, was an amphitheatre allotted for his Majesty, the Royal Family, the foreign Ministers, the National Assembly, the Municipality of Paris, and other persons of distinction.

While the procession was advancing, the National Parisian guard, antecedent to its arrival, performed different evolutions, in order to divert the attention of the spectators, and to bear up their spirits against the heavy and incessant rains. Dances were likewise performed.

At half past twelve the late Marquis DE LA FAYETTE, who had been nominated Major General of the Confederation, entered the field under a general discharge of all the artillery, accompanied by the beating of drums and other martial music.

The company had no sooner taken their seats, than the King entered under a very large escort of the National Guard. On his entrance he was met by the Major General, and conducted to his *Throne*. The President of the National Assembly sat on his right hand. His Majesty was very magnificently dressed in a suit of gold and silver Tissue. The QUEEN, M. de PROVENCE, and the DAUPHIN were seated near him.

The Procession did not finally close till half past three o'clock.

The KING being seated, there was another general discharge of artillery, and beating of the drums. The grand mass did not begin till towards four o'clock. The Bishop of METZ officiated as High Almoner, and was assisted by 60 other Priests, nominated by the 60 districts of Paris.

Previous to the commencement of this sacred ceremony, the Grand Standard of France, (*Poriflamme*) [sic] and the banners belonging to each district were carried to the altar, and there received a benediction. This was followed by another general discharge of artillery, and the sound of martial music.

The mass being over, the 60 banners belonging to the districts of Paris, were placed so as to form a line between the altar and the amphitheatre where the King was seated.

A long delay took place in the expectation that the KING would advance to the Altar and there take the Civic Oath. But his Majesty remained on the throne. M. DE LA FAYETTE then gave the signal for the National Representatives to come forward and take the oath. He was the first person who ascended the Altar, and on the sound of the trumpet,—he took the CIVIC OATH in the name of himself and all the National Guards. The oath is longer than that formerly taken, and is as follows:

"We swear to be faithful to the NATION—the LAW and the KING;—to maintain with all our power, the Constitution decreed by the Assembly and accepted by the King; to protect the individual and preserve his property according to law:—To see that there be a free circulation of grain throughout the kingdom, to enforce with all our power the collection of the public revenues; and to remain united to every Frenchman by the bands of brotherly love."

The President of the National Assembly, in the name of the Municipal Bodies, afterwards pronounced the same form of oath as above.

The King then took the oath, prescribed for his acceptance, from the throne. (It is the same as was given in our Paper of yesterday.)

At the same moment, all the spectators, with uplifted hands, repeated—I SWEAR IT—and immediately there was one general shout of—*Vive la Nation, la Loi, et le Roi.*

This acclamation being subsided—the signal that the ceremony was over—was made by the waving of one of the banners, and at half past five o'clock, the company began to retire.

The principal company were invited to a feast at the Castle of *la Muettre* [*sic*], whose tables were spread under the trees in those gardens. At night there was a general illumination.

FROM *THE TIMES*, JULY 21, 1790

The full and authentic statement in our Paper of yesterday of the Procession in Paris, on the day of the Grand Confederation, is the only official account that has yet appeared of that event. It was published by authority of the late Marquis de la FAYETTE, in order to be sent to the different Courts of Europe. As such, it must be highly acceptable to the Public. I[t] contained the whole detail of every circumstance that passed, and as very few copies are yet in London, those who did not read it in the TIMES *of yesterday, must wait till this day to see it copied into the other morning papers.*

It was a promise we made to our readers that the news of this grand festival should first appear in this Paper; and we trust they have not been disappointed. The general result of the day was made known through this Paper alone, 48 hours after the close of it, an instance of dispatch that can scarcely be equalled.

5. Beneficial Effects of the French Revolution

[One of the Revolution's most important activities was the publication of its own accomplishments. Just as the Festival of Federation commemorated the successes of the Revolution's first year, journals, pamphlets and broadsides honored the achievements of the National Assembly and the broad benefits of the new laws and practices. The following enumerative table of the benefits of the Revolution, published in November 1790, details not only large changes such as those proclaimed in the *Declaration of the Rights of Man*, but smaller and often very specific economic, legal, and social improvements affecting ordinary French citizens.]

Enumerative Table: Beneficial Effects of the French Revolution

The destruction of the Bastille.

Abolition of *lettres-de-cachet.*

The diminution of the power and arrogance of the Ministers.

Royalty established on the basis of equity & reason; and executive power restricted to fair limits.

The pride of the High worn down by the suppression of their titles of Nobility & of their finery.

The annihilation of feudal Rights, & of all odious titles of Servitude.

The establishment of the great principle of the equality of the Rights of Man.

The suppression of the Intendents and Subdelegates who were the true Tyrants in the Provinces; and the establishment of Departments.

The formation of the brave and patriotic National Guard throughout the Kingdom.

The denunciation of the *Livre-Rouge*, & the extinction of pensions
encroaching upon the Royal Treasury.

Eradication of the Parlements, & their replacement by Judges
appointed by the Nation.

Wise and well-merited correction given at the Chatelet.

The establishment of a Cassation Chamber; this next to a high
National Court for judging crimes against the Nation.

The great reform, that long ago became indispensable, in civil and
criminal Laws, & and a considerable decrease in legal expenses.

A pay increase for Troops on land and sea.

A more equitable proportion henceforth in fortunes, as a means of
compensating those who are acknowledged to have real merit
and recognized talents.

The imminent reform of the depraved principles in public and
private Education; and hope justified for studious young people
to reach honorable stations; similar hope for parents who under-
take to give their children a good education.

Liberty to speak and write granted to the people.

The inevitable diminution of the advancement of luxury, which
was at its height.

The certain re-establishment of the finances of the State, whose
ruin, which was imminent and inevitable, would have caused a
hideous upheaval throughout the Kingdom.

The elimination of the *gabelle* and its atrocities.

The opening of barriers to the borders.

The imminent and ardently desired dissolution of the *Fermiers-
généraux*.

The not-far-off prospect of a drop in interest rates, which will
stimulate Agriculture, Manufacture, and general Commerce as
well as the Arts.

The conditions of Farmer & Storekeeper will henceforth enjoy
the just consideration that is their due.

The destruction of Privileges, and especially of tax exemptions for
the very individuals who were most able to pay.

Liberty restored to clerics.

Already less frivolity in the character of our attractive members of
one and even the other sex.

The profession of patriotic faith by the new minister of war, who
will serve as a model for all the others.

The admiration of the Citizen-patriots of the entire world for our courage in regaining our liberty, as well as for the unflagging steadfastness of our good Representatives in working on the constitution.

P.S. The nomination of M. Duport de Tertre as Keeper of the Seals.

Executed at the Observatory this 22 November 1790.

Appendix G: The French Revolution: Selected Early British Responses

[This Appendix provides excerpts from some of the most important contributions to the debate about the French Revolution that raged through Great Britain in the early 1790s. For more about this debate, see the Introduction, pp. 29-40.]

1. Richard Price

From *A Discourse on the Love of Our Country, Delivered on Nov. 4, 1789, at the Meeting-House in the Old Jewry, to the Society for Commemorating the Revolution in Great Britain* (1789)

[Richard Price (1723-91) was a leading Dissenting preacher as well as an intellectual and political thinker. Price delivered this sermon precisely one year after the centennial anniversary of the Glorious Revolution of 1688 in order to bring home the significance of the French Revolution in terms of Great Britain's own political history. His controversial work, first published at the end of 1789 by T. Cadell and then widely reprinted, spawned a debate and a series of political rejoinders, most famously including Edmund Burke's *Reflections on the Revolution in France.* These excerpts are taken from a 1790 edition of the *Discourse* published by Cadell, pages 2-6, 28-42, 49-51.]

The love of our country has in all times been a subject of warm commendations; and it is certainly a noble passion; but, like all other passions, it requires regulation and direction. There are mistakes and prejudices by which, in this instance, we are in particular danger of being misled.—I will briefly mention some of these to you, and observe,

First, That by our country is meant, in this case, not the soil or the spot of earth on which we happen to have been born; not the forests and fields, but that community of which we are members; or that body of companions and friends and kindred who are associated with us under the same constitution of government, protected by the same laws, and bound together by the same civil polity.

Secondly, It is proper to observe, that even in this sense of our country, that love of it which is our duty, does not imply any conviction of the superior value of it to other countries, or any particular preference of its laws and constitution of government.... All our attachments should be accompanied, as far as possible, with right opinions.—We are too apt to confine wisdom and virtue within the circle of our own acquaintance and party. Our friends, our country, and in short every thing related to us, we are disposed to overvalue. A wise man will guard himself against this delusion. He will study to think of all things as they are, and not suffer any partial affections to blind his understanding....

Thirdly, It is proper I should desire you particularly to distinguish between the love of our country and that spirit of rivalship and ambition which has been common among nations.— What has the love of their country hitherto been among mankind? What has it been but a love of domination; a desire of conquest, and a thirst for grandeur and glory, by extending territory, and enslaving surrounding countries? What has it been but a blind and narrow principle, producing in every country a contempt of other countries, and forming men into combinations and factions against their common rights and liberties? ... As most of the evils which have taken place in private life, and among individuals, have been occasioned by the desire of private interest overcoming the public affections; so most of the evils which have taken place among bodies of men have been occasioned by the desire of their own interest overcoming the principle of universal benevolence: and leading them to attack one another's territories, to encroach on one another's rights, and to endeavour to build their own advancement on the degradation of all within the reach of their power ...

... I have just observed, that there is a submission due to the executive officers of government, which is our duty; but you must not forget what I have also observed, that it must not be a blind and slavish submission. ... the tendency of every government is to despotism; and in this the best constituted governments must end, if the people are not vigilant, ready to take alarms, and determined to resist abuses as soon as they begin.... This vigilance, therefore, it is our duty to maintain. Whenever it is withdrawn, and a people cease to reason about their rights and to be awake to encroachments, they are in danger of being enslaved, and their *servants* will soon become their *masters*.

... We have, therefore, on this occasion, peculiar reasons for thanksgiving—But let us remember that we ought not to satisfy ourselves with thanksgivings.... Let us, in particular, take care not to forget the principles of the Revolution....

First; The right to liberty of conscience in religious matters.

Secondly; The right to resist power when abused. And,

Thirdly; The right to chuse our own governors; to cashier them for misconduct; and to frame a government for ourselves....

I would farther direct you to remember, that though the Revolution was a great work, it was by no means a perfect work; and that all was not then gained which was necessary to put the kingdom in the secure and complete possession of the blessings of liberty....

But the most important instance of the imperfect state in which the Revolution left our constitution, is the INEQUALITY OF OUR REPRESENTATION.... When the representation is partial, a kingdom possesses liberty only partially ... but if not only extremely partial, but corruptly chosen, and under corrupt influence after being chosen, it becomes a *nuisance*, and produces the worst of all forms of government—a government by corruption ... We are, at present, I hope, at a great distance from it. But it cannot be pretended that there are no advances towards it, or that there is no reason for apprehension and alarm.

The inadequateness of our representation has long been a subject of complaint. But all attention to it seems now lost, and the probability is, that this inattention will continue, and that nothing will be done towards gaining for us this essential blessing, till some great calamity again alarms our fears, or till some great abuse of power again provokes our resentment; or, perhaps, till the acquisition of a pure and equal representation by other countries ... kindles our shame....

What an eventful period is this! I am thankful that I have lived to it [*sic*] ... I have lived to see a diffusion of knowledge, which has undermined superstition and error—I have lived to see the rights of men better understood than ever; and nations panting for liberty, which seemed to have lost the idea of it.—I have lived to see THIRTY MILLIONS of people, indignant and resolute, spurning at slavery, and demanding liberty with an irresistible voice; their king led in triumph, and an arbitrary monarch surrendering himself to his subjects.—After sharing in the benefits of one Revolution, I have been spared to be a witness to two other Revolutions, both glorious.—And now, methinks, I see the ardour for liberty catching and spreading; a general amendment beginning in human affairs; the dominion of kings changed for the dominion of laws, and the dominion of priests giving way to the dominion of reason and conscience.

Be encouraged, all ye friends of freedom, and writers in its defence!... Behold kingdoms, admonished by you, starting from sleep, breaking their fetters, and claiming justice from their oppressors! Behold, the light you have struck out, after setting AMERICA free, reflected to FRANCE, and there kindled into a blaze that lays despotism in ashes, and warms and illuminates EUROPE!

Tremble all ye oppressors of the world! Take warning all ye supporters of slavish governments, and slavish hierarchies! Call no more (absurdly and wickedly) REFORMATION, innovation. You cannot now hold the world in darkness. Struggle no longer against increasing light and liberality. Restore to mankind their rights; and consent to the correction of abuses, before they and you are destroyed together.

2. Edmund Burke

From *Reflections on the Revolution in France* (1790)

[Edmund Burke (1729-97) was one of the leading English politicians and writers of the later eighteenth century. In the *Reflections*, he offers a critique of revolutionary events in France during the years 1789 and 1790. The text is formulated as a letter in response to C.-J.-F. DePont, a young French politician who sought advice from Burke. More importantly, however, the work is a reply to Richard Price's sermon, *A Discourse on the Love of Our Country* (excerpted above). The *Reflections* ultimately functions not only as a critique of contemporary political events in France, but as a warning to England to guard itself from similar political corruption. It has been recognized as a founding treatise of political conservatism. See Appendix A for the argument in Series I, Volume 4, of *Letters from France* that "in all probability, [Burke's] predictions, and those of the writers who followed him on the same side in France, were in a great measure the causes of the evils they foretold" (pp. 166-67). Our text is taken from the first edition, published by J. Dodsley in 1790, pages 7-12, 47-57, 95-120, 275-83, with cuts.]

I flatter myself that I love a manly, moral, regulated liberty as well as any gentleman of that society [The Revolution Society, to whom Price spoke], be he who he will; and perhaps I have given as good proofs of my attachment to that cause, in the whole course of my public conduct. I think I envy liberty as little as they do, to any other nation. But I cannot stand forward, and give praise or blame to any thing which relates to human actions, and human concerns, on a simple view of the object, as it stands stripped of every relation, in all the nakedness and solitude of metaphysical abstraction. Circumstances (which with some gentlemen pass for nothing) give in reality to every political principle its distinguishing colour, and discriminating effect. The circumstances are what render every civil and political scheme beneficial or noxious to mankind. Abstractedly speaking, government, as well as liberty, is good; yet could I, in common sense, ten years ago, have felicitated France on her enjoyment of a government (for she then had a government) without enquiry what the nature of that government was, or how it was administered? Can I now congratulate the same nation upon its freedom? Is it because liberty in the abstract may be classed amongst the blessings of mankind, that I am seriously to felicitate a madman, who has escaped from the protecting restraint and wholesome darkness of his cell, on his restoration to the enjoyment of light and liberty? Am I to congratulate an highwayman and murderer, who has broke prison, upon the recovery of his natural rights?...

Solicitous chiefly for the peace of my own country, but by no means unconcerned for your's, I wish to communicate more largely, what was at first intended only for your private satisfaction. I shall still keep your affairs in my eye, and continue to address myself to you. Indulging myself in the freedom of epistolary intercourse, I beg leave to throw out my thoughts, and express my feelings, just as they arise in my mind, with very little attention to formal method. I set out with the proceedings of the Revolution Society; but I shall not confine myself to them. Is it possible I should? It looks to me as if I were in a great crisis, not of the affairs of France alone, but of all Europe, perhaps of more than Europe. All circumstances taken together, the French revolution is the most astonishing that has hitherto happened in the world....

It cannot however be denied, that to some this strange scene appeared in quite another point of view. Into them it inspired no other sentiments than those of exultation and rapture. They saw nothing in what has been done in France, but a firm and temperate exertion of freedom; so consistent, on the whole, with morals and with piety, as to make it deserving not only of the secular applause of dashing Machiavelian politicians, but to render it a fit theme for all the devout effusions of sacred eloquence....

You will observe, that from Magna Charta to the Declaration of Rights, it has been the uniform policy of our constitution to claim and assert our liberties, as an *entailed inheritance* derived to us from our forefathers, and to be transmitted to our posterity ...

... Our political system is placed in a just correspondence and symmetry with the order of the world, and with the mode of existence decreed to a permanent body composed of transitory parts ... Thus, by preserving the method of nature in the conduct of the state, in what we improve we are never wholly new; in what we retain we are never wholly obsolete ... In this choice of inheritance we have given to our frame of polity the image of a relation in blood; binding up the constitution of our country with our dearest domestic ties; adopting our fundamental laws into the bosom of our family affections; keeping inseparable, and cherishing with the warmth of all their combined and mutually reflected charities; our state, our hearths, our sepulchres, and our altars.

Through the same plan of a conformity to nature in our artificial institutions, and by calling in the aid of her unerring and powerful instincts, to fortify the fallible and feeble contrivances of our reason, we have derived several other, and those no small benefits, from considering our liberties in the light of an inheritance. Always acting as if in the presence of canonized forefathers, the spirit of freedom, leading in itself to misrule and excess, is tempered with an awful gravity ... It has a pedigree, and illustrating ancestors. It has its bearings, and its ensigns armorial. It has its gallery of portraits; its monumental inscriptions; its records, evidences, and titles....

You [France] might, if you pleased, have profited of our example, and have given to your recovered freedom a correspondent dignity. Your privileges, though discontinued, were not lost to memory. Your constitution, it is true, whilst you were out of possession, suffered waste and dilapidation; but you possessed in some parts the walls, and in all the foundations of a noble and venerable castle. You might have repaired those walls; you might have built on those old foundations. Your constitution was suspended before it was perfected; but you had the elements of a constitution very nearly as good as could be wished....

Compute your gains: see what is got by those extravagant and presumptuous speculations which have taught your leaders to despise all their predecessors, and all their contemporaries, and even to despise themselves, until the moment in which they became truly despicable. By following those false lights, France has bought undisguised calamities at a higher price than any nation has purchased the most unequivocal blessings! France has bought poverty by crime! France has not sacrificed her virtue to her interest; but she has abandoned her interest, that she might prostitute her virtue....

This was unnatural. The rest is in order. They [the French people] have found their punishment in their success. Laws overturned; tribunals subverted; industry without vigour; commerce expiring; the revenue unpaid, yet the people impoverished; a church pillaged, and a state not relieved; civil and military anarchy made the constitution of the kingdom; every thing human and divine sacrificed to the idol of public credit, and national bankruptcy the consequence; and to crown all, the paper securities of new, precarious, tottering power, the discredited paper securities of impoverished fraud, and beggared rapine, held out as a currency for the support of an empire, in lieu of the two great recognized species that represent the lasting conventional credit of mankind, which disappeared and hid themselves in the earth from whence they came, when the principle of property, whose creatures and representatives they are, was systematically subverted.

Were all these dreadful things necessary? were they the inevitable results of the desperate struggle of determined patriots, compelled to wade through blood and tumult, to the quiet shore of a tranquil and prosperous liberty? No! nothing like it. The fresh ruins of France, which shock our feelings wherever we can turn our eyes, are not the devastation of civil war; they are the sad but instructive monuments of rash and ignorant counsel in time of profound peace....

In France you are now in the crisis of a revolution, and in the transit from one form of government to another—you cannot see that character of men exactly in the same situation in which we see it in this country.... The worst of these [France's] politics of revolution is this; they temper and harden the breast, in order to prepare it for the desperate strokes which are sometimes used in extreme occasions. But as these occasions may never arrive, the mind receives a gratuitous taint; and the moral sentiments suffer not a little, when no political purpose is served by the depravation. This sort of people are so taken up with their theories about the rights of man, that they have totally forgot his nature. Without opening one new avenue to the understanding, they have succeeded in stopping up those that lead to the heart. They have perverted in themselves, and in those that attend to them, all the well-placed sympathies of the human breast.

This famous sermon of the Old Jewry [by Richard Price] breathes nothing but this spirit through all the political part. Plots, massacres, assassinations, seem to some people a trivial price for obtaining a revolution. A cheap, bloodless reformation, a guiltless liberty, appear flat and vapid to their taste. There must be a great change of scene; there must be a magnificent stage effect; there must be a grand spectacle to rouze the imagination, grown torpid with the lazy enjoyment of sixty years security, and the still unanimating repose of public prosperity....

... There they sit [the National Assembly], after a gang of assassins had driven away all the men of moderate minds and moderating authority amongst them, and left them as a sort of dregs and refuse, under the apparent lead of those in whom they do not so much as pretend to have any confidence. There they sit, in mockery of legislation, repeating in resolutions the words of those whom they detest and despise. Captive themselves, they compel a captive king to issue as royal edicts, at third hand, the polluted nonsense of their most licentious and giddy coffeehouses. It is notorious, that all their measures are decided before they are debated. It is beyond doubt, that under the terror of the bayonet, and the lamp-post, and the torch to their houses, they are obliged to adopt all the crude and desperate measures suggested by clubs composed of a monstrous medley of all conditions, tongues, and nations....

Who is it that admires, and from the heart is attached to national representative assemblies, but must turn with horror and disgust from such a profane burlesque, and abominable perversion of that sacred institute? Lovers of monarchy, lovers of republicks, must alike abhor it. The members of your Assembly must themselves groan under the tyranny of which they have all the shame, none of the direction, and little of the profit. I am sure many of the members who compose even the majority of that body, must feel as I do.... Miserable king! miserable Assembly! How must that assembly be silently scandalized with those of their members, who would call a day [6 October 1789] which seemed to blot the sun out of Heaven, "un beau jour!" ... What must they have felt, when they were besieged by complaints of disorders which shook their country to its foundations, at being compelled coolly to tell the complainants, that they were under the protection of the law, and that they would address the king (the captive king) to cause the laws to be enforced for their protection; when the enslaved ministers of that captive king had formally notified to them, that there were neither law, nor authority, nor power left to protect?...

[The following is Burke's famous (and inaccurate) version of the events of the 6th of October and the treatment of the royal family.]

... The king of France will probably endeavour to forget these events ... But history, who keeps a durable record of all our acts, and exercises her awful censure over the proceedings of all sorts of sovereigns, will not forget, either those events, or the æra of this liberal refinement in the intercourse of mankind. History will record, that on the morning of the 6th of October 1789, the king and queen of France, after a day of confusion, alarm, dismay, and slaughter, lay down, under the pledged security of public faith, to indulge nature in a few hours of respite, and troubled melancholy repose. From this sleep the queen was first startled by the voice of the centinel at her door, who cried out to her, to save herself by flight—that this was the last proof of fidelity he could give—that they were upon him, and he was dead. Instantly he was cut down. A band of cruel ruffians and assassins, reeking with his blood, rushed into the chamber of the queen, and pierced with an hundred strokes of bayonets and poniards the bed, from whence this persecuted woman had but just time to fly almost naked, and through ways unknown to the murderers had escaped to seek refuge at the feet of a king and husband, not secure of his own life for a moment.

This king, to say no more of him, and this queen, and their infant children (who once would have been the pride and hope of a great and generous people) were then forced to abandon the sanctuary of the most splendid palace in the world, which they left swimming in blood, polluted by massacre, and strewed with scattered limbs and mutilated carcases. Thence they were conducted into the capital of their kingdom.... After they had been made to taste, drop by drop, more than the bitterness of death, in the slow torture of a journey of twelve miles, protracted to six hours, they were, under a guard, composed of those very soldiers who had thus conducted them through this famous triumph, lodged in one of the old palaces of Paris, now converted into a Bastile for kings.

Is this a triumph to be consecrated at altars? to be commemorated with grateful thanksgiving? to be offered to the divine humanity with the fervent prayer and enthusiastick ejaculation?...

[Burke describes what he characterizes as France's shameless and abominable treatment of Marie Antoinette, depicting her as an innocent victim of revolutionary terror.]

I hear, and I rejoice to hear, that the great lady ... bears the imprisonment of her husband, and her own captivity, and the exile of her friends, and the insulting adulation of addresses, and the whole weight of her accumulated wrongs, with a serene patience, in a manner suited to her rank and race, and becoming the offspring of a sovereign distinguished for her piety and her courage; that like her she has lofty sentiments; that she feels with the dignity of a Roman matron; that in the last extremity she will save herself from the last disgrace, and that if she must fall, she will fall by no ignoble hand.

It is now sixteen or seventeen years since I saw the queen of France, then the dauphiness, at Versailles; and surely she never lighted on this orb, which she hardly seemed to touch, a more delightful vision. I saw her just above the horizon, decorating and cheering the elevated sphere she just began to move in,—glittering like the morning-star, full of life, and splendor, and joy. Oh! what a revolution! and what an heart must I have, to contemplate without emotion that elevation and that fall! Little did I dream that, when she added titles of veneration to those of enthusiastic, distant, respectful love, that she should ever be obliged to carry the sharp antidote against disgrace concealed in that bosom; little did I dream I should have lived to see such disasters fallen upon her in a nation of gallant men, in a nation of men of honour and of cavaliers. I thought ten thousand swords must have leaped from their scabbards to avenge even a look that threatened her with insult.—But the age of chivalry is gone....

But now all is to be changed. All the pleasing illusions, which made power gentle, and obedience liberal, which harmonized the different shades of life, and which, by a bland assimilation, incorporated into politics the sentiments which beautify and soften private society, are to be dissolved by this new conquering empire of light and reason. All the decent drapery of life is to be rudely torn off....

Why do I feel so differently from the Reverend Dr. Price, and those of his lay flock, who will choose to adopt the sentiments of his discourse?—For this plain reason—because it is *natural* I should ... because when kings are hurl'd from their thrones by the Supreme Director of this great drama, and become the objects of insult to the base, and of pity to the good, we behold such disasters in the moral, as we should behold a miracle in the physical order of things. We are alarmed into reflexion; our minds ... are purified by terror and pity; our weak unthinking pride is humbled, under the dispensations of a mysterious wisdom.—Some tears might be drawn from me, if such a spectacle were exhibited on the stage. I should be truly ashamed of finding in myself that superficial, theatric sense of painted distress, whilst I could exult over it in real life. With such a perverted mind, I could never venture to shew my face at a tragedy. People would think the tears that Garrick formerly, or that Siddons not long since, have extorted from me, were the tears of hypocrisy; I should know them to be the tears of folly....

Finding no sort of principle of coherence with each other in the nature and constitution of the several new republics of France, I considered what cement the legislators had provided for them from any extraneous materials. Their confederations, their *spectacles*, their civic feasts, and their enthusiasm, I take no notice of; They are nothing but mere tricks ...

All these considerations leave no doubt on my mind, that if this monster of a constitution can continue, France will be wholly governed by the agitators in corporations, by societies in the towns formed of directors of assignats, and trustees for the sale of church lands, attornies, agents, money-jobbers, speculators, and adventurers, composing an ignoble oligarchy founded on the destruction of the crown, the church, the nobility, and the people. Here end all the deceitful dreams and visions of the equality and rights of men....

3. Mary Wollstonecraft

From *A Vindication of the Rights of Men, in a Letter to the Right Honourable Edmund Burke; occasioned by his Reflections on the Revolution in France* (1790)

[An intellectual and a passionate supporter of the Revolution, Mary Wollstonecraft (1759-97) produced the first extended critical reply to Burke's *Reflections on the Revolution in France*. In the *Vindication*, Wollstonecraft argues for reason and justice, condemning oppression by and privilege for those of rank or title. She believes in the rights of all persons and in the power of the Revolution to secure those rights. She later published *A Vindication of the Rights of Woman* (1792) in which she defends the right of equality for women. Our text is excerpted from the second edition, published by J. Johnson in 1790, pages 7-9, 27, 97-100, 118-19, 151-56, with cuts.]

...The birthright of man, to give you, Sir, a short definition of this disputed right, is such a degree of liberty, civil and religious, as is compatible with the liberty of every other individual with whom he is united in a social compact....

I glow with indignation when I attempt, methodically, to unravel your slavish paradoxes, in which I can find no fixed first principle to refute; ...

I perceive, from the whole tenor of your Reflections, that you have a mortal antipathy to reason; ...

... Misery, to reach your heart, I perceive, must have its cap and bells; your tears are reserved, very *naturally* considering your character, for the declamation of the theatre, or for the downfall of queens, whose rank alters the nature of folly, and throws a graceful veil over vices that degrade humanity; whilst the distress of many industrious mothers, whose *helpmates* have been torn from them, and the hungry cry of helpless babes, were vulgar sorrows that could not move your commiseration, though they might extort an alms....

[Wollstonecraft then compares Richard Price's sermon with Burke's *Reflections*.]

Time only will shew whether the general censure, which you afterwards qualify, if not contradict, and the unmerited contempt that you have ostentatiously displayed of the National Assembly, be founded on reason, the offspring of conviction, or the spawn of envy. Time may shew, that this obscure throng knew more of the human heart and of legislation than the profligates of rank, emasculated by hereditary effeminacy....

But, in settling a constitution that involved the happiness of millions, that stretch beyond the computation of science, it was, perhaps, necessary for the Assembly to have a higher model in view than the *imagined* virtues of their forefathers; and wise to deduce their respect for themselves from the only legitimate source, respect for justice. Why was it a duty to repair an ancient castle, built in barbarous ages, of Gothic materials? Why were the legislators obliged to rake amongst heterogeneous ruins; to rebuild old walls, whose foundations could scarcely be explored, when a simple structure might be raised on the foundation of experience, the only valuable inheritance our forefathers could bequeath?...

In order that liberty should have a firm foundation, an acquaintance with the world would naturally lead cool men to conclude that it must be laid, knowing the weakness of the human heart, and the "deceitfulness of riches," either by *poor* men, or philosophers, if a sufficient number of men, disinterested from principle, or truly wise, could be found. Was it natural to expect that sensual prejudices should give way to reason, or present feelings to enlarged views?—No; I am afraid that human nature is still in such a weak state, that the abolition of titles, the corner-stone of despotism, could only have been the work of men who had no titles to sacrifice. The National Assembly, it is true, contains some honourable exceptions; but the majority had not such powerful feelings to struggle with, when reason led them to respect the naked dignity of virtue....

Surveying civilized life, and seeing, with undazzled eye, the polished vices of the rich, their insincerity, want of natural affections, with all the specious train that luxury introduces, I have turned impatiently to the poor, to look for man undebauched by riches or power—but, alas! what did I see? a being scarcely above the brutes, over which he tyrannized; a broken spirit, worn-out body, and all those gross vices which the example of the rich, rudely copied, could produce. Envy built a wall of separation, that made the poor hate, whilst they bent to their superiors; who, on their part, stepped aside to avoid the loathsome sight of human misery.

What were the outrages of a day [6 October] to these continual miseries? Let those sorrows hide their diminished head before the tremendous mountain of woe that thus defaces our globe! Man preys on man; and you mourn for the idle tapestry that decorated a gothic pile, and the dronish bell that summoned the fat priest to prayer. You mourn for the empty pageant of a name, when slavery flaps her wing, and the sick heart retires to die in lonely wilds, far from the abodes of men.... Why is our fancy to be appalled by terrific perspectives of a hell beyond the grave?—Hell stalks abroad;—the lash resounds on the slave's naked sides; and the sick wretch, who can no longer earn the sour bread of unremitting labour, steals to a ditch to bid the world a long good night—or, neglected in some ostentatious hospital, breathes his last amidst the laugh of mercenary attendants.

Such misery demands more than tears—I pause to recollect myself; and smother the contempt I feel rising for your rhetorical flourishes and infantine sensibility....

I have before animadverted on our method of electing representatives, convinced that it debauches both the morals of the people and the candidates, without rendering the member really responsible, or attached to his constituents; but, amongst your other contradictions, you blame the National Assembly for expecting any exertions from the servile principle of responsibility, and afterwards insult them for not rendering themselves responsible. Whether the one the French have adopted will answer the purpose better, and be more than a shadow of representation, time only can shew. In theory it appears more promising.

4. Thomas Paine

From *The Rights of Man* (Part 1, February 1791; Part II, February 1792)

[Thomas Paine (1737-1809) wrote *The Rights of Man* in two parts, as a direct response to Burke's *Reflections on the Revolution in France*. Contrary to Burke, Paine argues in support of the actions French revolutionaries have taken to obtain liberty. This work was extraordinarily popular and influential at the time of its publication. In 1792, because of the politically controversial arguments of *The Rights of Man*, Paine was indicted in England for treason. He fled to France, where he was elected to the National Assembly and where he was imprisoned during the Terror. Our text is excerpted from *The Works of Thomas Paine, ESQ.*, published by D. Jordan in 1792: I, 1-26, 43-45, 106; II, 28-29, 129-30.]

There is scarcely an epithet of abuse to be found in the English language, with which Mr. Burke has not loaded the French Nation and the National Assembly. Every thing which rancour, prejudice, ignorance, or knowledge, could suggest, are poured forth in the copious fury of near four hundred pages. In the strain, and on the plan Mr. Burke was writing, he might have written on to as many thousands. When the tongue or the pen is let loose in a frenzy of passion, it is the man, and not the subject, that becomes exhausted....

As Mr. Burke occasionally applies the poison drawn from his horrid principles, not only to the English nation, but to the French Revolution and the National Assembly, and charges that august, illuminated and illuminating body of men with the epithet of *usurpers*, I shall, *sans ceremonie*, place another system of principles in opposition to his.

The English Parliament of 1688 did a certain thing, which, for themselves and their constituents, they had a right to do, and which it appeared right should be done: But, in addition to this right, which they possessed by delegation, *they set up another right by assumption*, that of binding and controuling posterity to the end of time. The case, therefore, divides itself into two parts; the right which they possessed by delegation, and the right which they set up by assumption. The first is admitted; but, with respect to the second, I reply—

There never did, there never will, and there never can exist a parliament, or any description of men, or any generation of men, in any country, possessed of the right or the power of binding and controuling posterity to the "*end of time*," or of commanding for ever how the world shall be governed, or who shall govern it; and therefore, all such clauses, acts, or declarations, by which the makers of them attempt to do what they have neither the right nor the power to do, nor the power to execute, are in themselves null and void.—Every age and generation must be as free to act for itself, *in all cases*, as the ages and generations which preceded it. The vanity and presumption of governing beyond the grave, is the most ridiculous and insolent of all tyrannies.... It is the living, and not the dead, that are to be accommodated. When man ceases to be, his power and his wants cease with him; and having no longer any participation in the concerns of this world, he has no longer any authority in directing who shall be its governors, or how its government shall be organized, or how administered....

While I am writing this, there are accidentally before me some proposals for a declaration of rights by the Marquis de la Fayette (I ask his pardon for using his former address, and do it only for distinction's sake) to the National Assembly, on the 11th of July 1789, three days before the taking of the Bastile; and I cannot but remark with astonishment how opposite the sources are from which that Gentleman and Mr. Burke draw their principles. Instead of referring to musty records and mouldy parchments to prove that the rights of the living are lost, "renounced and abdicated forever," by those who are now no more, as Mr. Burke has done, M. de la

Fayette applies to the living world, and emphatically says, "Call to mind the sentiments which Nature has engraved in the heart of every citizen, and which take a new force when they are solemnly recognized by all:—For a nation to love liberty, it is sufficient that she knows it; and to be free, it is sufficient that she wills it." ...

It was not against Louis the XVIth, but against the despotic principles of the government, that the nation revolted. These principles had not their origin in him, but in the original establishment, many centuries back ... Perhaps no man, bred up in the stile of an absolute King, ever possessed a heart so little disposed to the exercise of that species of power as the present King of France. But the principles of the government itself still remained the same. The Monarch and the Monarchy were distinct and separate things; and it was against the established despotism of the latter, and not against the person or principles of the former, that the revolt commenced, and the revolution has been carried.

... When despotism has established itself for ages in a country, as in France, it is not in the person of the King only that it resides. It has the appearance of being so in show, and in nominal authority; but it is not so in practice, and in fact. It has its standard every-where. Every office and department has its despotism, founded upon custom and usage. Every place has its Bastile, and every Bastile its despot. The original hereditary despotism, resident in the person of the King, divides and subdivides itself into a thousand shapes and forms, till at last the whole of it is acted by deputation. This was the case in France; and against this species of despotism, proceeding on through an endless labyrinth of office, till the source of it is scarcely perceptible, there is no mode of redress. It strengthens itself by assuming the appearance of duty, and tyrannises under the pretense of obeying....

As to the tragic paintings, by which Mr. Burke has outraged his own imagination, and seeks to work upon that of his readers, they are very well calculated for theatrical representation, where facts are manufactured for the sake of show, and accommodated to produce, through the weakness of sympathy, a weeping effect. But Mr. Burke should recollect that he is writing History, and not *Plays*; and that his readers will expect truth, and not the spouting rant of high-toned exclamation....

[Here Paine remarks on Burke's disregard of the Bastille in his *Reflections*.]

Not once [*sic* for "one"] glance of compassion, not one commiserating reflection, that I can find throughout his whole book, has he bestowed on those who lingered out the most wretched of lives, a life without hope, in the most miserable of prisons.... His [Burke's] hero or his heroine must be a tragedy-victim expiring in show, and not the real prisoner of misery, sliding into death in the silence of a dungeon.

As Mr. Burke has passed over the whole transaction of the Bastile (and his silence is nothing in his favour), and has entertained his readers with reflections on supposed facts distorted into real falsehoods, I will give, since he has not, some account of the circumstances which preceded that transaction. They will serve to show, that less mischief could scarcely have accompanied such an event, when considered with the treacherous and hostile aggravations of the enemies of the Revolution....

The mind can hardly picture to itself a more tremendous scene than what the city of Paris exhibited at the time of taking the Bastile, and for two days before and after, nor conceive the possibility of its quieting so soon. At a distance, this transaction has appeared only as an act of heroism, standing on itself; and the close political connection it had with the Revolution is lost in the brilliancy of the atchievement. But we are to consider it as the strength of the parties, brought man to man, and contending for the issue. The Bastile was to be either the prize or the prison of the assailants. The downfal of it included the idea of the downfal of Despotism....

That the Bastile was attacked with an enthusiasm of heroism, such only as the highest animation of liberty could inspire, and carried in the space of a few hours, is an event which the world is fully possessed of. I am not undertaking a detail of the attack; but bringing into view the conspiracy against the nation which provoked it, and which fell with the Bastile. The prison to which the new ministry were dooming the National Assembly, in addition to its being the high altar and castle of despotism, became the proper object to begin with. This enterprise broke up the new ministry, who began now to fly from the ruin they had prepared for others....

[Paine notes the historical inaccuracies and theatrical qualities of Burke's version of the October Days. He offers a quite different account.]

During the latter part of the time in which this confusion was acting, the King and Queen were in public at the balcony, and neither of them concealed for safety's sake, as Mr. Burke insinuates. Matters being thus appeased, and tranquillity restored, a general acclamation broke forth, of *Le Roi à Paris—Le Roi à Paris*—The King to Paris. It was the shout of peace, and immediately accepted on the part of the King. By this measure, the King and his family reached Paris in the evening, and were congratulated on their arrival by Mr. Bailley the Mayor of Paris, in the name of the citizens....

[Paine commends the National Assembly and their project of creating a constitution. He comments on various pieces of the document.]

The French constitution says, *There shall be no titles;* and, of consequence, all that class of equivocal generation, which in some countries is called "*aristocracy*," and in others "*nobility*," is done away, and the *peer* is exalted into MAN....

It is, properly, from the elevated mind of France that the folly of titles has fallen. It has outgrown the baby-cloaths of *Count* and *Duke*, and breeched itself in manhood. France has not levelled; it has exalted. It has put down the dwarf, to set up the man. The punyism of a senseless word like *Duke*, or *Count*, or *Earl*, has ceased to please. Even those who possessed them have disowned the gibberish; and, as they outgrew the rickets, have despised the rattle. The genuine mind of man, thirsting for its native home, society, contemns the gewgaws that separate him from it. Titles are like circles drawn by the magician's wand, to contract the sphere of man's felicity. He lived immured within the Bastile of a word, and surveys at a distance the envied life of man....

The patriots of France have discovered, in good time, that rank and dignity in society must take a new ground. The old one has fallen through.—It must now take the substantial ground of character, instead of the chimerical ground of titles; and they have brought their titles to the altar, and made of them a burnt-offering to Reason.

If no mischief had annexed itself to the folly of titles, they would not have been worth a serious and formal destruction, such as the National Assembly have decreed them; and this makes it necessary to enquire farther into the nature and character of aristocracy.

That, then, which is called aristocracy in some countries, and nobility in others, arose out of the governments founded upon conquest. It was originally a military order ... to keep up a succession of this order, for the purpose for which it was established, all the younger branches of those families were disinherited, and the law of *primogenitureship* set up.

The nature and character of aristocracy shews itself to us in this law. It is a law against every law of nature, and Nature herself calls for its destruction....

With what kind of parental reflections can the father or mother contemplate their younger offspring? By nature they are children, and by marriage they are heirs; but by aristocracy they are bastards and orphans.... To restore, therefore, parents to their children, and children to their parents—relations to each other, and man to society—and to exterminate the monster Aristocracy, root and branch—the French constitution has destroyed the law of PRIMOGENITURESHIP. Here then lies the monster; and Mr. Burke, if he pleases, may write its epitaph....

...All the old governments have received a shock from those that already appear, and which were once more improbable, and are a greater subject of wonder, than a general revolution in Europe would be now.

When we survey the wretched condition of man under the monarchical and hereditary systems of Government, dragged from his home by one power, or driven by another, and impoverished by taxes more than by enemies, it becomes evident that those systems are bad, and that a general revolution in the principles and construction of Governments is necessary....

Nothing can appear more contradictory, than the principle on which the old governments began, and the condition to which society, civilization, and commerce, are capable of carrying mankind. Government, on the old system, is an assumption of power, for the aggrandisement of itself; on the new, a delegation of power, for the common benefit of society. The former supports itself by keeping up a system of war; the latter promotes a system of peace, as the true means of enriching a nation. The one encourages national prejudices; the other promotes universal society, as the means of universal commerce. The one measures its prosperity, by the quantity of revenue it extorts; the other proves its excellence, by the small quantity of taxes it requires....

Never did so great an opportunity offer itself to England, and to all Europe, as is produced by the two Revolutions of America and France. By the former, freedom has a national champion in the Western world; and by the latter, in Europe. When another nation shall join France, despotism and bad government will scarcely dare to appear. To use a trite expression, the iron is becoming hot all over Europe. The insulted German and the enslaved Spaniard, the Russ and the Pole, are beginning to think. The present age will hereafter merit to be called the Age of Reason, and the present generation will appear to the future as the Adam of a new world.

5. Hannah More

From *Village Politics. Addressed to all the mechanics, journeymen, and day labourers, in Great Britain. By Will Chip, a country carpenter* (1792)

[Hannah More (1745-1833) was an ardent advocate for the poor and oppressed, dedicating much of her literary work to educating the lower classes in England. For all of their other political differences, More, like Williams, was a passionate abolitionist whose works include "Slavery, a Poem" (1788) in heroic couplets. In the 1790s, she published numerous popular and widely distributed stories, tracts, and songs that the common person could afford and understand. She believed that the lives of the poor could be improved only if they adopted Christian habits and practices and looked for assistance to their social superiors. *Village Politics*, the first of her tracts for the poor, was written at the behest of the Bishop of London, Beilby Porteus. With great success it translated Burkean philosophy into working class prose and used common men as characters to argue against *The Rights of Man*. Our text is excerpted from a pamphlet, published in Durham in 1793, through the Subscription for the Publication of Constitutional Pamphlets, pages 8-16.]

A DIALOGUE, Between Jack Anvil, the *Blacksmith, And* Tom Hod, *the Mason.*

... *Tom.* But I say all men are equal. Why should one be above another?

Jack. If that's thy talk, Tom, thou dost quarrel with Providence, and not with government. For the woman is below her husband, and the children are below the mother, and the servant is below his master.

Tom. But the subject is not below the king; all kings are "crowned ruffians:" and all governments are wicked. For my part, I'm resolved I'll pay no more taxes to any of them.... I say we shall never be happy, till we do as the French have done.

Jack. The French and we contending for liberty, Tom, is just as if thou and I were pretending to run a race; thou to set out from the starting post, when I am in already; why we've got in, man; we've no race to run—we're there already. Our constitution is no more like what the French one was, than a mug of *Newcastle* beer is like a platter of their soup-maigre.

Tom. I know we shall be undone if we do not get a new constitution,—that's all.

Jack. And I know we shall be undone if we *do*. I do not know much about politics, but I can see by a little, what a great deal means....

Tom. Well, still as the old saying is—I should like to do as they do in France.

Jack. What! should'st like to be murdered with as little ceremony as Hackabout the butcher knocks down a calf? Then for every little bit of tiff, a man gets rid of his wife? And as to liberty of *conscience*, which they brag so much about, why they have driven away their parsons, (aye and murdered many of 'em) because they would not sware as they would have them. And then they talk of liberty of the press; why, Tom, only t'other day they hanged a man for printing a book against this pretty government of theirs.

Tom. But you said yourself it was sad times in France before they pulled down the old government.

Jack. Well, and suppose the French were as much in the right as I know them to be in the wrong; what does that argue for *us*? Because neighbour Furrow t'other day pulled down a crazy old barn, is that a reason why I must set fire to my tight cottage?

Tom. I don't see why one man is to ride in his coach and six, while another mends the highway for him.

Jack. I don't see why the man in the coach is to *drive over* the man on foot, or hurt a hair of his head. And as to our great folks, that you levellers have such a spite against; I don't pretend to say they are a bit better than they should be; but that's no affair of mine; let them look to that; they'll answer for that in another place....

I have got the use of my limbs, of my liberty, of the laws, and of my Bible ... My cottage is my castle; I sit down in it at night in peace and thankfulness, and "no man maketh me afraid." Instead of indulging discontent, because another is richer than I in this world (for envy is at the bottom of your equality works,) I read my bible, go to church, and think of a treasure in heaven.

Tom. Aye; but the French have got it in *this* world.

Jack. 'Tis all a lye, Tom. Sir John's butler says his master gets letters which *say* 'tis all a lye. 'Tis all murder, and nakedness, and hunger; many of the poor soldiers fight without victuals, and march without clothes. These are your *democrats*! Tom.

Tom. What then, dost think all the men on our side wicked?

Jack. No—not so neither—they've made fools of the most of you, as I believe. I judge no man, Tom; I hate no man. Even republicans and levellers, I hope will always enjoy the protection of our Laws; though I hope they will never be our law-*makers.*... These poor French fellows used to be the merriest dogs in the world; but since equality came in, I don't believe a Frenchman has ever laughed.

Tom. What then dost thou take French *liberty* to be?

Jack. To murder more men in one night, than ever their poor king did in his whole life.

Tom. And what dost thou take a *Democrat* to be?

Jack. One who likes to be governed by a thousand tyrants, and yet can't bear a king.

Tom: What is *Equality*?

Jack. For every man to pull down every one that is above him, till they're all as low as the lowest.

Tom. What is *the new Rights of Man*?

Jack. Battle, murder, and sudden death.

Tom. What is it to be an *enlightened people*?

Jack. To put out the light of the gospel, confound right and wrong, and grope about in pitch darkness.

Tom. What is *Philosophy*, that Tim Standish talks so much about?

Jack. To believe that there's neither God, nor devil, nor heaven, nor hell.—To dig up a wicked old fellow's rotten bones [Voltaire], whose books, Sir John says, have been the ruin of thousands; and to set his figure up in a church and worship him.

Tom. And what mean the other hard words that Tim talks about— *organization* and *function*, and *civism*, and *incivism*, and *equalization*, and *inviolability*, and *imperscriptible*?

Jack: Nonsense, gibberish, downright hocus-pocus. I know 'tis not

English; Sir John says 'tis not Latin; and his valet de sham says 'tis not French neither.

Tom. And yet Tim says he shall never be happy till all these fine things are brought over to England.

Jack. What into this Christian country, Tom? Why dost know they have no *sabbath*? Their mob parliament meets on a Sunday to do their wicked work, as naturally as we do to go to church. They have renounced God's word and God's day, and they don't even date in the year of our Lord....

Tom. And dost thou think our Rights of Man will lead to all this wickedness?

Jack. As sure as eggs are eggs.

Tom. I begin to think we're better off as we are.

Jack. I'm sure on't. This is only a scheme to make us go back in every thing. 'Tis making ourselves poor when we are getting rich.

Tom. I begin to think I'm not so very unhappy as I had got to fancy.

Jack. Tom, I don't care for drink myself, but thou dost, and I'll argue with thee in thy own way; when there's all equality there will be no *superfluity*; when there's no wages there'll be no drink; and levelling will rob thee of thy ale more than the malt-tax does.

Tom. But Standish says if we had a good government there'd be no want of any thing.

Jack. He is like many others, who take the king's money and betray him. Tho' I'm no scholar, I know that a good government is a good thing. But don't go to make me believe that *any* government can make a bad man good, or a discontented man happy.—What art musing upon, man?

Tom. Let me sum up the evidence, as they say at 'sizes—Hem! To cut every man's throat who does not think as I do, or hang him up at a lamp-post!—Pretend liberty of conscience, and then banish the parsons only for being conscientious!—Cry out liberty of the press, and hang up the first man who writes his mind!—Lose our poor laws!... Jack, I never knew thee tell a lie in my life.

Jack. Nor wou'd I now, not even against the French.

Tom. And thou art very sure we are not ruined.

Jack. I'll tell thee how we are ruined. We have a king so loving, that he would not hurt the people if he cou'd: and so kept in, that he cou'd not hurt the people if he wou'd. We have as much liberty as can make us happy, and more trade and riches than allows us to be good. We have the best laws in the world, if they were more strictly enforced; and the best religion in the world, if it was but better followed. While Old England is safe, I'll glory in her and pray for her, and when she is in danger, I'll fight for her and die for her.

Tom. And so will I too, Jack, that's what I will. *(Sings)* "O the roast beef of Old England!"

Jack. Thou art an honest fellow, Tom....

6. Anna Barbauld

"To a Great Nation" (first published 1793)

[A poet and educator of the period, Anna Barbauld (1743-1825) was also an important literary and social critic. She wrote political pieces that advocated democracy and education, and she also condemned the slave trade. Barbauld was very influential and corresponded with leading literary figures about these critical issues. "To a Great Nation" clearly depicts her views on the Revolution around the time of the establishment of the Republic. The poem later appeared under the title "On the Expected General Rising of the French Nation in 1792" in the posthumously published *The Works of Anna Lætitia Barbauld, with a Memoir by Lucy Aikin* (1825). Our text is from the original publication in *The Cambridge Intelligencer* for 2 November 1793.]

"TO A GREAT NATION"
Written by a Lady

RISE mighty nation! in thy strength,
And deal thy dreadful vengeance round;
Let thy great spirit rous'd at length,
Strike hordes of Despots to the ground.

Devoted land! thy mangled breast,   5
Eager the r———l [royal] vultures tear:
By friends betray'd, by foes oppress'd,
And virtue struggles with despair.

The tocsin sounds! arise, arise,
Stern o'er each breast let country reign;   10

Nor virgin[']s plighted hand, nor sighs
Must now the ardent youth restrain.

Nor must the hind who tills thy soil,
The ripen'd vintage stay to press,
'Till rapture crowns the flowing bowl,   15
And Freedom boasts of full success.

Briareus[1] like, extend thy hands,
That every hand may crush a foe;
In millions pour thy generous bands,
And end a warfare by a blow.   20

Then wash with sad repentant tears,
Each deed that stains thy glory's page;
Each phrensied start impell'd by fears,
Each transient burst of headlong rage.

Then fold in thy relenting arms,   25
The wretched outcasts where they roam;
From pining want and war's alarms,
O call the child of Misery home.

Then build the tomb—O not alone,
On him who bled in freedom's cause;   30
With equal eye the martyr own,
Of faith revered and antient laws.

Then be thy tide of glory stay'd,
Then be thy conquering banners furl'd,
Obey the laws thyself hast made,   35
And rise—the model of the world!

---

[1] Briareus was a giant of ancient fable, represented with a hundred hands,
and fifty heads. [Barbauld's note]

7. Mary Alcock

"Instructions, Supposed to be Written in Paris, for the Mob in England" (c.1792, published 1799)

[Daughter of a Bishop and wife of an Archdeacon, Mary Alcock (c. 1742-98) seems to have published during her lifetime only two works: *The Confined Debtor. A Fragment from a Prison* (1775), which was undertaken for charity, and "The Air Balloon; or, The Flying Mortal" (1784). A volume of her collected poems, *Poems, &c. &c. by the late Mrs. Mary Alcock*, was published in 1799, one year after her death, by her niece Joanna Hughes. Alcock's aversion to the principles of the French Revolution is powerfully stated below. Our text is from the 1799 *Poems*, published by C. Dilly, Poultry, pp. 48-49.]

"Instructions, Supposed to be Written in Paris, for the Mob in England"

OF Liberty, Reform, and Rights I sing,
Freedom I mean, without or Church or King;
Freedom to seize and keep whate'er I can,
And boldly claim my right—The Rights of Man:
Such is the blessed liberty in vogue,   5
The envied liberty to be a rogue;
The right to pay no taxes, tithes, or dues;
The liberty to do whate'er I chuse;
The right to take by violence and strife
My neighbour's goods, and, if I please, his life;   10
The liberty to raise a mob or riot,
For spoil and plunder ne'er were got by quiet;
The right to level and reform the great;
The liberty to overturn the state;
The right to break through all the nation's laws,   15
And boldly dare to take rebellion's cause:
Let all be equal, every man my brother;
Why one have property, and not another?
Why suffer titles to give awe and fear?
There shall not long remain one British peer;   20
Nor shall the criminal appalled stand
Before the mighty judges of the land;

Nor judge, nor jury shall there longer be,
Nor any jail, but every pris'ner free;
All law abolish'd, and with sword in hand   25
We'll seize the property of all the land.
Then hail to Liberty, Reform, and Riot!
Adieu Contentment, Safety, Peace, and Quiet!

Selected Bibliography

Works by Helen Maria Williams

Edwin and Eltruda. A Legendary Tale. London: T. Cadell, 1782.
An Ode on the Peace. London: T. Cadell, 1783.
Peru, a Poem. In Six Cantos. London: T. Cadell, 1784.
Poems. 2 vols. London: T. Cadell, 1786.
A Poem on the Bill Lately Passed for Regulating the Slave Trade.
    London: T. Cadell, 1788.
Julia, a Novel; Interspersed with Some Poetical Pieces. London:
    T. Cadell, 1790.
*Letters Written in France, in the Summer 1790, to a Friend in
    England; Containing Various Anecdotes Relative to the French
    Revolution; and Memoirs of Mons. and Madame du F———*.
    London: T. Cadell, 1790.
A Farewell, for Two Years, to England. A Poem. London: T. Cadell,
    1791.
Poems. 2 vols. 2nd ed. London: T. Cadell, 1791.
*Letters from France: Containing Many New Anecdotes Relative to
    the French Revolution, and the Present State of French Manners*.
    London: G.G. and J. Robinson, 1792.
*Letters from France: Containing a Great Variety of Interesting and
    Original Information Concerning the Most Important Events that
    have Lately Occurred in that Country, and Particularly Respecting
    the Campaign of 1792*. 2 vols. London: G.G. and J. Robinson,
    1793.
Paul and Virginia. Translated from the French of Jacques-Henri
    Bernadin de Saint-Pierre. London: G.G. and J. Robinson, 1795.
*Letters Containing a Sketch of the Politics of France, from the Thirty-
    first of May 1793, till the Twenty-eighth of July 1794, and of the
    Scenes which have Passed in the Prisons of Paris*. 2 vols. London:
    G.G. and J. Robinson, 1795.
*Letters Containing a Sketch of the Scenes which Passed in Various
    Departments of France during the Tyranny of Robespierre, and of the
    Events which Took Place in Paris on the 28th of July 1794*. Lon-
    don: G.G. and J. Robinson, 1795.
*Letters Containing a Sketch of the Politics of France, from the Twenty-
    eighth of July 1794, to the Establishment of the Constitution in
    1795, and of the Scenes which have Passed in the Prisons of Paris*.
    London: G.G. and J. Robinson, 1796.

A Tour in Switzerland; or a View of the Present State of the Governments and Manners of those Cantons: with Comparative Sketches of the Present State of Paris. London: G.G. and J. Robinson, 1798.

The History of Perourou; or, The Bellows-Mender. Dublin: N. Kelly, 1801.

Sketches of the State of Manners and Opinions in the French Republic, Towards the Close of the Eighteenth Century, in a Series of Letters. 2 vols. London: G.G. and J. Robinson, 1801.

The Political and Confidential Correspondence of Lewis the Sixteenth; with Observations on Each Letter. Translation. 3 vols. London: G.G. and J. Robinson, 1803.

Researches, Concerning the Institutions and Monuments of the Ancient Inhabitants of America: with Descriptions and Views of Some of the Most Striking Scenes in the Cordilleras! Translated from the French of Alexander von Humboldt. London: Longman, Hurst, Rees, Orme & Brown, J. Murray & H. Colburn, 1814.

Personal Narrative of Travels to the Equinoctial Regions of the New Continent, During the Years 1799-1804. Translated from the French of Alexander von Humboldt and Aimé-Bonpland. 5 vols. London: Longman, Hurst, Rees, Orme, Brown & Green, 1814-21.

A Narrative of the Events which have Taken Place in France, from the Landing of Napoleon Bonaparte on the 1st of March, 1815, till the Restoration of Louis XVIII, with an Account of the Present State of Society and Public Opinion. London: John Murray, 1815.

On the Late Persecution of the Protestants in the South of France. London: T. and G. Underwood, 1816.

The Leper of the City of Aoste: A Narrative. Translated from the French of Xavier de Maistre. London: G. Cowie & Co., 1817.

Letters on the Events which have Passed in France since the Restoration in 1815. London: Baldwin, Cradock, & Joy, 1819.

Poems on Various Subjects; with Introductory Remarks on the Present State of Science and Literature in France. London: G. & W.B. Whittaker, 1823.

Souvenirs de la Révolution française. Paris, 1827.

Modern Editions

Fruchtman, Jack, ed. *An Eye-Witness Account of the French Revolution by Helen Maria Williams: Letters Containing a Sketch of the Politics of France.* New York: Peter Lang, 1997.

Facsimile Reprints

Letters from France. 2 vols. [includes entire series] Introduction by
Janet Todd. Delmar, NY: Scholar's Facsimiles and Reprints, 1975.
Letters Written in France 1790. Introduction by Jonathan
Wordsworth. Oxford: Woodstock Books, 1989.
Poems, 1786. Introduction by Jonathan Wordsworth. Oxford and
New York: Woodstock Books, 1994.

Select Secondary Works

Adams, M. Ray. "Helen Maria Williams and the French Revolution." *Wordsworth and Coleridge: Studies in Honor of George
McLean Harper*. Ed. Earle Leslie Griggs. Princeton: Princeton UP, 1939. 87-117.

Adickes, Sandra. *The Social Quest: The Expanded Vision of Four
Women Travelers in the Era of the French Revolution*. New York:
Peter Lang, 1991.

Blakemore, Steven. *Crisis in Representation: Thomas Paine, Mary
Wollstonecraft, Helen Maria Williams, and the Rewriting of the
French Revolution*. Madison: Fairleigh Dickinson UP, 1997.

———. "Revolution and the French Disease: Laetitia Matilda
Hawkins's *Letters to Helen Maria Williams*." *Studies in English
Literature* 36.3 (1996): 673-91.

Bohls, Elizabeth A. *Women Travel Writers and the Language of Aesthetics, 1716-1818*. Cambridge: Cambridge UP, 1995.

Bray, Matthew. "Helen Maria Williams and Edmund Burke:
Radical Critique and Complicity." *Eighteenth-Century Life* 16.2
(1992): 1-24.

———. "Sensibility and Social Change: Charlotte Smith, Helen
Maria Williams, and the Limits of Romanticism." Ph.D. Diss.,
University of Maryland, 1994.

Ellison, Julie. "Redoubled Feeling: Politics, Sentiment, and the
Sublime in Williams and Wollstonecraft." *Studies in Eighteenth-
Century Culture* 20 (1990): 197-215.

Favret, Mary A. *Romantic Correspondence: Women, Politics, and the
Ficton of Letters*. Cambridge: Cambridge UP, 1993.

———. "Spectatrice as Spectacle: Helen Maria Williams at Home in
the Revolution." *Studies in Romanticism* 32.2 (1993): 273-95.

Fruchtman, Jack, Jr. "Public Loathing, Private Thoughts: Historical Representation in Helen Maria Williams' *Letters from
France*." *Prose Studies* 18 (1995): 223-43.

Jones, Chris. *Radical Sensibility: Literature and Ideas in the 1790s.* London and New York: Routledge, 1993.

——. "Helen Maria Williams and Radical Sensibility." *Prose Studies: History, Theory, and Criticism* 12.1 (1989): 3-24.

Jones, Vivien. Femininity, Nationalism and Romanticism: The Politics of Gender in the Revolution Controversy." *History of European Ideas* 16.1-3 (1993): 299-305.

——. "Women Writing Revolution: Narratives of History and Sexuality in Wollestonecraft and Williams." *Beyond Romanticism: New Approaches to Texts and Contexts, 1780-1832.* Ed. Stephen Copley and John Whale. Syracuse: Syracuse UP, 1991. 178-99.

Keane, Angela. "Helen Maria Williams's *Letters from France: A National Romance.*" *Prose Studies* 15 (1992): 271-94.

Kelly, Gary. *Women, Writing, and Revolution, 1790-1827.* Oxford: Clarendon Press, 1993.

Kennedy, Deborah. *Helen Maria Williams and the Age of Revolution.* Lewisburg, PA: Bucknell UP, forthcoming.

——. "Revolutionary Tales: Helen Maria Williams's *Letters from France* and William Wordsworth's "Vaudracour and Julia." *Wordsworth Circle* 21.3 (1990): 109-14.

——. "Spectacle of the Guillotine: Helen Maria Williams and the Reign of Terror." *Philological Quarterly* 73.1 (1994): 95-113.

——. "'Storms of Sorrow': The Poetry of Helen Maria Williams." *Lumen* 10 (1991): 77-91.

LeBlanc, Jacqueline. "Politics and Commercial Sensibility in Helen Maria Williams's *Letters from France.*" *Eighteenth-Century Life* 21.1 (1997): 26-44.

Ledden, Mark. "Perishable Goods: Feminine Virtue, Selfhood and History in the Early Writings of Helen Maria Williams." *Michigan Feminist Studies* 9 (1994-95): 37-65.

——. "Revolutionary Plots: Helen Maria Williams' *Letters from France.*" *Prism(s): Essays in Romanticism* 3 (1995): 1-13.

Michael-Johnston, Georgina D. "Helen Maria Williams: Liberty, Sensibility, and Education." Ph.D. Diss. University of Alberta, 1999.

Sha, Richard. "Expanding the Limits of Feminine Writing: The Prose Sketches of Sydney Owenson (Lady Morgan) and Helen Maria Williams." *Romantic Women Writers: Voices and Countervoices.* Ed. Paula Feldman and Theresa Kelley. Hanover, NH: UP of New England, 1995. 194-206.

Scheffler, Judith. "Romantic Women Writing on Imprisonment and Prison Reform." *Wordsworth Circle* 19.2 (1988): 99-103.

Ty, Eleanor. *Unsex'd Revolutionaries: Five Women Novelists of the 1790's.* Toronto: U of Toronto P, 1993.

Watson, Nicola J. "Novel Eloisas: Revolutionary and Counter-Revolutionary Narratives in Helen Maria Williams, Wordsworth and Byron." *Wordsworth Circle* 23.1 (1992): 18-23.

Woodward, Lionel D. *Une Anglaise, amie de la révolution française: Hélène-Maria Williams et ses amis.* Paris: Librairie Ancienne Honoré Champion, 1930.